Microsoft® SQL Server

What Database Administrators Need to Know

Jeffry L. Byrne

To join a Prentice Hall Internet mailing list,
point to http://www.prenhall.com/register.

Prentice Hall PTR, Upper Saddle River, New Jersey 07458

Editorial/Production Supervision: *Joe Czerwinski*
Acquisitions Editor: *Mark Taub*
Editorial Assistant: *Kate Hargett*
Manufacturing Manager: *Alexis R. Heydt*
Cover Design Director: *Jerry Votta*
Cover Design: *Design Source*

©1997 by Prentice Hall PTR
Prentice-Hall, Inc.
A Division of Simon and Schuster
Upper Saddle River, NJ 07458

ISBN: 0-13-495409-2

Prentice-Hall International (UK) Limited, *London*
Prentice-Hall of Australia Pty. Limited, *Sydney*
Prentice-Hall of Canada Inc., *Toronto*
Prentice-Hall Hispanoamericana, S.A., *Mexico*
Prentice-Hall of India Pte. Ltd., *New Delhi*
Prentice-Hall of Japan, Inc., *Tokyo*
Simon & Schuster Asia Pte. Ltd., *Singapore*
Editora Prentice-Hall do Brasil, Ltda., *Rio de Janeiro*

Acknowledgments

There have been many people involved in the creation of this book. Each and every one of them deserve my deepest thanks for all the help they have given, and the effort they have gone to.

In particular, I would like to thank Mark Taub of Prentice Hall for his help and dedication to this project, and to many other individuals at Prentice Hall who labored to bring this book to fruition.

I would also like to thank Joe Czerwinski for his tremendous efforts at ensuring that all my t's were crossed and i's were dotted.

Finally, I would like to thank Bill Vaughn of Microsoft for his work at ensuring the technical accuracy of this book. He had some great suggestions and helped keep the book focused.

Dedication

This book is dedicated to my wife, Marisa. Without her help, and especially putting up with the many long hours to meet deadlines, this book would remain unfiinshed today.

About the Author

Jeffry L. Byrne has been working with and teaching about computers, and particularly database applications for more than 15 years. He is the author of numerous computer software books in five languages, including books on Microsoft Access®, Corel's Quattro Pro™ and Borland's Paradox™ for Windows, Intuit's QuickBooks™ for Windows, and Computer Associates' CA-Simply Money™. He has worked on the beta test teams for most of these products and for several other accounting and database software packages. When not writing about and testing software, Jeff works as the product/purchasing manager for a Portland, Oregon-based network VAR and computer retailer.

Table of Contents

1 - An Overview of Microsoft SQL Server.............................. 1

Client/Server and Microsoft SQL Server 2

Why use SQL Applications? 4

    Ease of Use 4

    Simplify Systems.. 5

    Enforcement of Business Procedures 7

    Building Custom Applications.. 7

    Cost Factors 8

Multiprocessing versus Multithreaded 9

    Multiprocess Systems 9

    Multithreaded Systems 10

Networking.. 12

Summary 12

2 - What is SQL? 13

The Relational Database 14

    The Normalized Database.. 16

    Tables, Columns, and Rows 19

    What is a Relational Database?.. 19

    Device Independence... 21

SQL Commands.. 22

    Data Definition Language (DDL)... 22

    Data Manipulation Language (DML) 23

    Data Control Language (DCL) 23

Commonly Used Commands..23
  SELECT..24
    Using a SELECT Statement...24
    Joining Tables and Sorting Values With a SELECT Statement 27
    Creating an Alias 31
  INSERT 34
  UPDATE..37
  DELETE 38

Transactions and SQL...39

Summary 41

3 - Logical Structures 43

Devices 44
  Database Devices...44
  Backup Devices 50

Database Objects...51
  Tables...55
  Views 59
  Cursors...63
  Indexes...64
    Clustered Indexes...67
    Nonclustered Indexes..68
  Defaults...70
  Rules 72
  Triggers...74
  Stored Procedures 78
  Identifiers..80
    Rules 81
    As Object Names 82
    Quoted Identifiers 83

Database Sizing 84
  Pages..88
  Extents 88
  Allocation Units..89

System Catalog...89

Summary 90

4 - Microsoft SQL Server Structures 91

Server Architecture 92
    Database Devices 92
    Backup Devices 93

Processes 95

Files 98
    master Database 98
    model Database 99
    msdb Database 100
    pubs Database 101
    Transaction Log Files 101
    Web Files 104

Summary 114

5 - What Is Data Integrity? 115

Entity Integrity 116
    Primary Key Constraint 116
    UNIQUE Constraint 118

Domain Integrity 119
    Domain Rules 119
    Datatypes 120
    CHECK/NOCHECK Constraint 126

Referential Integrity 127
    What is Referential Integrity? 128
    Defining Primary/Foreign Keys 130
    Enforcing Referential Integrity 133

User-defined Integrity 134

Summary 138

6 - Data Consistency and Concurrency 139

Statements and Transactions 140

Using Locks for Consistency 141

Understanding a Lock 141

Shared Locks 142

Update Locks 142

Exclusive Locks 143

What Is Lock Granularity? 143

Row Locks 145

Page Locks 146

Table Locks 147

Deadlocks 147

Using Locks with SELECT 148

Setting Transaction Isolation Level 149

Summary 150

7 - Startup and Shutdown 151

Starting Microsoft SQL Server 152

Options for Startup 154

Shutting Down Microsoft SQL Server 156

Pausing the Server 156

Shutting Down the Server 157

Summary 159

8 - Managing Database Space 161

Planning Database Space Requirements 162

Sizing the Database 163

Sizing the Transaction Log 165

Expanding a Database 167

On the Same Database Device 168

On Other Database Devices 175

Shrinking a Database 175

Dropping Database Devices 179

Summary 181

9 - Optimizing Performance 183

Optimizing Memory Usage 184
  System Memory 184
  Allocating Memory 191
Optimizing Disk Performance 194
Using Segments 196
The Multithreaded Server 197
Optimizing Queries 199
  Cost-based Optimization 200
    Gathering Statistics 200
    Updating Statistics 204
  Clustered Indexes 207
  Using Nonclustered Indexes 208
  Creating Useful Indexes 208
Dropping Databases 212
Summary 214

10 - Security 215

Identification and Authentication 216
  Windows NT Security 218
  SQL Server Security 218
  Database Security 219
The Role of the System Administrator 219
  Selecting the Type of Security 220
    Integrated Security 220
    Standard Security 226
    Mixed Security 227
    Trusted Connections 227
    Setting Security Modes 228
  Creating Users 230
    Devising Usernames 230
    Guest User 233
    Building Groups 234
    An Owner 236
    Using Aliases 238
    Passwords 241

Granting and Revoking Permissions...242

    Permissions By Object...245

    Permissions By User...248

Using SQL Security Manager...249

Summary **254**

11 - Backups and Disaster Recovery.................................. 255

Types of Failures...**256**

    Client Application Failure...257

    Program Failure 258

    Disk or Media Failures...258

Backup and Recovery...**259**

    Forms of Backups 260

      Offline, or Static, Backups...261

      Online, or Dynamic, Backups...261

    Creating Your Backup Strategy 261

    Creating a Backup...263

Restoring a Database...**269**

    Reloading a Lost Database...270

      Dropping a Defective Database 270

      Restoring a Database Backup 274

    Using Transaction Logs...279

    Recovering the master Database...282

Rebuilding a Lost Device...**285**

Heavy Duty Protection—Mirrors and RAID **286**

    Mirroring a Device...287

    RAID Disk Arrays 290

Using Removable Media...**291**

Summary **292**

12 - Distributed Transactions, Replication, Publishing and Subscribing.................................. 293

Distributed Databases...**294**

    Setting Up Your Servers 296

      Creating the Distribution Server 296

      Setting Up Publishing and Subscribing Servers 299

    Replication...306

Distributing 316
    Synchronization Process 317
    Log Reader Process 317
    Distribution Server and Database 318
    Replication Cleanup 319

Two-phase Commit **322**
Definitions 323
How the Two-phase Commit Works 323
Configuring MS DTC 327
Problem Areas 331

Summary **333**

Index **335**

Chapter 1

An Overview of Microsoft SQL Server

IN THIS CHAPTER

- Client/Server and Microsoft SQL Server
- Why use SQL Applications?
- Multiprocessing versus Multithreaded
- Networking

If you have picked up this book you are interested in learning more about Microsoft® SQL Server™. Microsoft SQL Server is the best selling database server for the Windows NT market. Microsoft SQL Server is a *relational database-management system* (RDBM). It is one-half of the client/server equation, and is often referred to as the back-end program. Front-end, or client programs are often custom designed applications, or can be standalone database programs that you can buy off the shelf, such as Microsoft Access.

In this chapter, you will learn what Microsoft SQL Server is and how it fits into your client/server schema.

Client/Server and Microsoft SQL Server

Mainframe systems, while fast and powerful, are, and always have been, expensive. They also require a dedicated MIS staff to program and maintain them. This means that every request for information from another department must be written down and given to the MIS department. Then, they must determine if the information is available in the mainframe database, how to query that database, and then how to format the report for the departmental customer. Each of these steps takes time and costs the organization money, and if each department is billed for the additional expenses needed, they may decide to make critical business decisions based on incomplete information instead of paying for another potentially expensive report.

Conversely, the personal computer/local area network (PC/LAN) has been very attractive for many small businesses and departmental computing needs. Many departments in an organization have found that they can provide for their own information needs by building an application with a commercially available database or spreadsheet in a very short amount of time and for relatively little money. Remember, in most businesses the cost involved in creating an application for your department will be charged to your departmental budget by the MIS department. Using a PC/LAN may eliminate the need to transmit a request to the MIS department, and the necessary time for them to decide what you are asking for, how to get the information, build an application or query, and then transmit the resulting data set back to you—hopefully in a format that means something to you.

This laissez-faire form of construction the PC/LAN system is both its greatest asset and its greatest liability. While allowing individuals and departments access to needed information quickly, it has led to wide spread redundant and incompatible information. This may seem like a contradiction in terms, but is assuredly not. Large organizations—though this can also happen in small organizations—will find that the same basic information is being stored in many different departments. Each department's information is similar, but stored in different formats, different programs, and even different operating systems. Each of these problems can require much expensive programming and conversion time so that the departments can share each other's data. It is also a great waste of money and computer resources than can be better used in other ways.

Client/server systems bridge the gap between mainframe systems and PC/LAN-based systems. Instead of keeping all of the processing power on only the mainframe, or distributing all processing power to each individual user, client/server systems share the processing responsibilities. The server RDBM stores virtually all of the data and retains much of responsibility for the basic database structure. You can institute quite strict centralized control over data integrity, administration, and security. Storing data in a central server enables the database administrator to easily perform backups of data and periodic maintenance of both data and server. Each client provides its own application—the front-end—selected information to be forwarded from the server to the client. This sharing allows the server to concentrate on what it does best: storing data, ensuring its security, and providing requested data. The client can then handle such processor-intensive functions as complex user interfaces—for example, windows and graphical representations of forms and data.

The glue that binds the client and the server is the *Structured Query Language* (SQL). Unlike most file-sharing LAN database management systems (DBMS) which respond to a query by delivering large quantities of unnecessary data—usually the entire file—the client/server will deliver only the specific information requested in the query. This helps to make SQL a more efficient manager of your information system. Both the server database engine and the client applications use SQL to communicate with each other. The client application sends a SQL query to the server. The server then interprets the query. The server runs the query through a procedure called *optimization* in which it will decide the fastest method of obtaining the information requested. Finally, the data is forwarded to the requesting application. This format places a greater portion of the processing burden on the server where the data resides than in earlier file-share systems. The client workstation then can work with a smaller subset of the real data, resulting in less network traffic and less processing for the workstation CPU.

One of the most powerful features of Microsoft SQL Server is its ability to manage data integrity. By having the server manage the integrity of your data, you don't have to rely on the many different programmers of varying abilities who created the many applications used in each department. While you can use the integrity checking available within an application, you do not have to wholly rely on it. With Microsoft SQL Server, you can guarantee the integrity and consistency of the information in your database across the entire LAN.

Why use SQL Applications?

All office-automation computer programs can be considered an application of some type: word processor, spreadsheet, database, or desktop publishing. These programs are designed to automate specific tasks; for example, word processing. With a word processing application, you can easily create complex documents and then edit, reformat, and finally print them without having to draft them in long-hand, nor retype long sections of a document.

SQL applications are, by nature, information-oriented and may include accounts payable, payroll, sales, weather data, patient records, purchasing, customer and vendor data, and almost any other aspect related to the information needs of the business or institution collecting the data. Most SQL applications are designed to simplify the management of data collection and storage for a business, but there are several reasons for using a SQL client/server application.

Ease of Use

Most client/server applications are very easy to use. They provide an intuitive interface, often showing an on-screen representation of a commonly used paper form. Therefore, salespeople who may be used to filling out a sales order form will see a familiar form on their screen when they use their sales order application. The client application then automatically updates the server application, which contains the actual data, using the SQL language. In addition to an easy-to-use screen form, the salesperson often doesn't have to lookup information about a customer or items to be sold. The application will provide pop-up lists so that the salesperson only has to select a customer from a list, and then choose items for sale from another list. This helps to ensure consistency in the company database by eliminating duplicate information, or selling items for the wrong price. With a few simple keystrokes or clicks on a mouse the form can be completed, filed away in the server application, and then printed for the customer.

With the addition of user-friendly, on-screen forms in the front-end application, the productivity of a salesperson, buyer, or inventory clerk may increase dramatically—at the same time improving accuracy of the company's records and accounting information.

Simplify Systems

Many business systems do not follow the client/server model. While they may use some aspects of office automation in their business for certain jobs, the degree of integration that a front-end client application and Microsoft SQL Server as the back-end can provide does not exist. Look at a typical transaction chain for almost any business:

A customer calls in an order, which is received by a salesperson. This order is written down on an order pad. The salesperson may have to add up a total for the customer using a hand calculator. The completed handwritten order is then placed in an out basket for the order entry clerk. This person takes the orders and enters them into a computer. This computer then sends the order down to the warehouse, where a picking ticket is printed. The picking ticket is used by the warehouse worker to pull the order. Once the order has been pulled, the picking ticket is typed into a packing list and a copy forwarded to accounts receivable and inventory control. The accounts receivable clerk enters the quantities ordered and picked, along with the pricing information, to create an invoice, checks the customer's credit information, and enters this information into the customer's account file. At the same time, the inventory control clerk must adjust the inventory file to reflect the reduction for the items sold.

This typical system involves at least seven different transactions, and six different people. Errors can be made at any point along this chain, and the system requires the same data to be entered and re-entered at each transaction point. While the usage and format of the information may vary from transaction to transaction, each transaction consists of only a few distinct information pieces: customer, part, quantity, and sales price.

Looking at this chain from a client/server viewpoint, you can easily see that almost all of these redundant transactions can be eliminated or reduced. With a client/server application, the order is entered only once—the application then takes care of all of the remaining transactions automatically. The order entry clerk takes the customer's order and enters it using an on-screen form. This application automatically displays a list of customers, items to be sold, and displays a total for the customer. If there are hold flags due to credit problems on this customer, they can be flagged to the order takers attention at this point. The application then can update the customer file if there are any changes to address or phone numbers, update the inventory, prints the picking list at the warehouse, generates an invoice, adds the sale to the customers accounts receivable file, and inform the buyer if an item falls below a specified on-hand level.

Each transaction may be handled by a different front-end client application, but by a single back-end SQL server database. This consolidation of data with the SQL server helps to ensure both the integrity of the data and its security. Each application allows the user to work with their own representation of the same basic data, but the information needs only to be entered into a single application. Figure 1.1 shows how the information flows through these transactions from an original order to the completed shipment and billing cycle.

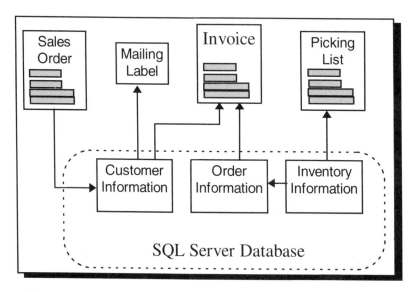

Figure 1.1: By using a server-based database you can easily reduce many redundant transactions within a business. Each of the different front-end applications meet needs of the various departments that are involved with this transaction.

Enforcement of Business Procedures

Business procedures can include many things, but with Microsoft SQL Server, business procedures, usually called *rules*, principally have to do with what data is allowed into a field—these types of procedures or rules help to ensure the accuracy and integrity of the data. By using an application with well designed integrity features, you can help enforce data input accuracy and enforce other types of rules.

For example, business often will want to be sure that goods or services have been received or performed before payment of a vendors invoice. Good accounting controls require that the person who orders goods and services—the purchaser—is not the same person who writes the checks that pay the vendors' invoices, and neither of these people should actually receipt for the goods and services. With a Microsoft SQL Server database you can easily provide these controls. The application will not allow a check to be cut for an invoice if a purchase order hasn't already been created and receipt of the goods isn't verified.

With a well-designed application you can eliminate many of the repetitive, low skill jobs that were required of skilled workers. A purchaser can spend more of their time on the important tasks of qualifying vendors and reviewing products, rather than laboriously typing purchase orders. An accounts payable clerk can quickly approve payments and print checks instead of checking a receiving file against each invoice and then writing out a check. At the same time, you can help to eliminate many of the potential inaccuracies that occur when there is too great a reliance is placed on unnecessary hand-checking of paperwork.

Building Custom Applications

Many front-end packages you can purchase are equipped with a generic group of business rules and procedures that may or may not fit your individual needs. Some applications make allowances for this, permitting you to make changes to these procedures, while others may require you to contract for expensive programming changes by the software publisher. While many of these off-the-shelf programs can work for you, they will often require you to make changes to the way that you do business, instead of the program fitting your own business requirements.

By using any one of a variety of front-end applications, you can build your own customized applications to meet your own specific business rules and needs. Front-end applications can be created using a high-end programming language such as Visual C++™, PowerBuilder™, and even Visual Basic™, or alternatively you can build an application with a database program such as Microsoft Access™. Each option has its own advantages and disadvantages. The ability to create powerful application products in less time not only reduces the development costs of a system, but enables the organization to open new markets, to enhance its customer service, and to strengthen its competitiveness.

Cost Factors

The final factor in the decision to create a client/server system is its cost. Many client/server systems are being created to replace legacy mainframe systems, which are expensive to maintain, or as an alternative to new mainframe systems of a similar type. The up-front costs of a mainframe are compounded by its high annual maintenance costs. Many companies that are considering "downsizing" or "rightsizing" are driven to the client/server model for the possible cost savings.

Many business are already investing in a corporate LAN or WAN system for many reasons, most often for some type of office automation: document sharing, telephony, group fax and modem sharing, and video conferencing. With a LAN/WAN already in place, adding a client/server system doesn't place a great deal of additional costs—in dollars or network traffic—on a business. This assumes that the existing system is not already so overloaded that it cannot support the additional load and traffic imposed by the new application.

WARNING

It is critical that you understand what a client/server system can do for your organization so that you can intelligently inform management and obtain realistic goals. Many database programmers have met the goals they believed were set by management, but failed in management's eyes because of a difference in expectations.

Multiprocessing versus Multithreaded

Client/server database architecture comes in two basic flavors: multiprocessing and multithreaded. Each has their proponents and detractors. Microsoft SQL Server uses a multithreaded basis for its architecture.

Multiprocessing systems are distinguished by having multiple executable programs running at the same time. Generally, when a new user logs into the system, an entire set of executable programs is launched—this is known as starting an *instance*. These types of systems typically may use more system resources than multithreaded engines.

The multithreaded engine, on the other hand, is a single-process system. Microsoft SQL Server is a multithreaded database engine. Instead of each user starting their own instance, a single process is started when Microsoft SQL Server is launched and each user has their own unique thread. This architecture requires dramatically fewer resources than a multiprocess system.

Multiprocess Systems

The multiprocess database engine uses a system of executable applications that perform the necessary client query work. As each user logs onto the database, they are actually starting their own separate instance of the programs. In order to coordinate all of the users working with the same data files, other global coordinator tasks are used to schedule resources for each instance that is open.

The most popular of the multiprocess SQL database engines is Oracle Corporation's® Oracle Server™. As a user logs onto the system a new Oracle instance is started. The queries that the user generates are passed to this instance from the front-end program they are using. The instance coordinates with other executable programs and returns the results to the user. These other common executable programs manage file and record locks, write log files and commit updated files to the disk files. As shown in figure 1.2, each time another user logs onto the database a new instance is started along with its associated executable programs, each requiring more system resources.

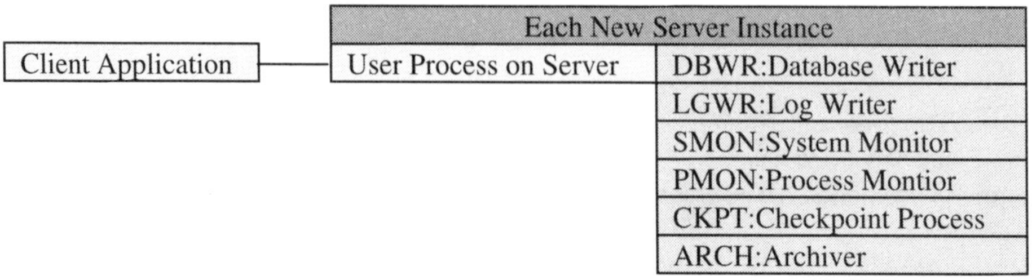

		Each New Server Instance
Client Application	User Process on Server	DBWR:Database Writer
		LGWR:Log Writer
		SMON:System Monitor
		PMON:Process Montior
		CKPT:Checkpoint Process
		ARCH:Archiver

Figure 1.2: Each instance started by a new user requires many systems resources to be duplicated for each user because of the way processes are allocated on a per user basis.

The multiprocess database engine has been used for many years, and was among the first of the multi-user databases. Both multiprocess and multithreaded servers can provide for scalability with the addition of more CPUs and memory to the physical machine. With an operating system that can use multiple CPU's, such as Windows NT, SQL Server really begins to shine. Threads can be assigned to use different processors, ensuring the best usage of the number of processor cycles available from all of the CPUs installed.

Multithreaded Systems

The multithreaded database takes responsibility for managing multiple users itself, instead of assuming that the operating system will handle user management. The multithreaded engine is more conservative with available system resources than the multiprocess system. When the multithreaded engine is started, only a single instance of the program is begun. As new users log onto the database, each is given a thread. This thread is the pipe through which all of the user queries and instructions are passed to the database engine and through to the operating system.

Microsoft SQL Server uses native Win32 operating threads, not simulated threads in the database kernel as do other multithreaded engines. These native threads run in their own protected memory space, and have preemptive scheduling by the Microsoft Windows NT Server operating system kernel. This type of multithreading ensures that a single corrupt thread can no longer crash an application; instead, this thread can be trapped and isolated.

Microsoft SQL Server has a maximum pool of 1024 worker threads, and a default setting of 255 worker threads. If the number of concurrent users does not exceed the number of worker threads in the pool, then each user is assigned to a thread. If the number of concurrent workers exceeds the number of worker threads, then pooling will occur. Pooling means that as a user completes a task, their thread is assigned to the next user who needs to have access to the database.

There are other pools in addition to the pool of worker threads. These additional pools are used to allocate other system resources, such as disk devices, backup stripes, and parallel table scanning.

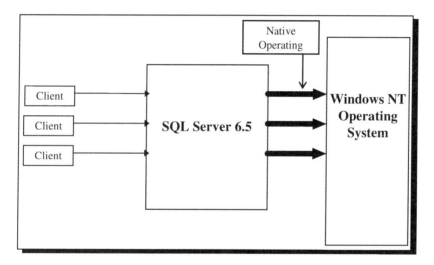

Figure 1.3: Microsoft SQL Server uses native Win32 threads from the Microsoft Windows NT Server operating system.

Microsoft SQL Server has different memory requirements depending upon what you intend to do with the particular system:

- Systems used primarily for the development of SQL Server applications can be run with 16MB of RAM, if replication features are not being used.

- Systems used in a production database environment can use as much RAM as you want, or can afford, to make available.

- Systems that will be used in replication must have a minimum of 32MB of RAM on the system, and a minimum of 16MB dedicated to SQL Server.

Networking

The client/server model assumes that the server application—in this case, Microsoft SQL Server—resides in a computer that is set up as a Microsoft Windows NT server. Client machines are physically connected to the server through network cabling, network cards, and the appropriate software. All clients must be able to communicate with the server so that SQL queries can be passed to the server and results passed back to the client.

With Microsoft SQL Server you can use the networking abilities of Microsoft Windows NT Server to communicate with a wide variety of clients: PCs, Macintoshes™, UNIX workstations, or NetWare™ clients. Since Microsoft SQL Server uses the native networking abilities of its host operating system, Microsoft Windows NT Server, any computer attached to the server can be granted access to the SQL database.

Summary

In this chapter, you have become familiar with some of the basics of what Microsoft SQL Server actually is, and how it fits into the client/server architecture. Specifically, this chapter covered:

- How Microsoft SQL Server fits into a client/server network system as the back-end piece.

- The reasons why you should use a client/server database program for storing information: ease of use, simplifying your database systems, ability to enforce business rules and procedures, and ease of incorporating custom applications as the front-end piece of client/server.

- The difference between multiprocessing and multithreaded systems, and the advantages that Microsoft SQL Server and Windows NT bring to a multithreaded scheme.

Chapter 2

What is SQL?

IN THIS CHAPTER

- The Relational Database
- SQL Commands
- Commonly Used Commands
- Transactions and SQL

13

In order for a client application and the server database engine to communicate with each other they must use a common language, that language is *Structured Query Language*, commonly called just *SQL*. Their are several different versions of SQL, and Microsoft SQL Server uses a version called Transact-SQL. Currently there are two SQL standards: *ANSI SQL-89* and *ANSI SQL-92*. These standards were published by the American National Standards Institute in 1989 and 1992. Transact-SQL meets all of the standards set forth in both ANSI SQL-89 and ANSI SQL-92, and provides extensions for additional programming needs.

In this chapter, you will see how a relational database is constructed, and how data is organized within it. By understanding the database's basic structure, you will more easily understand how Transact-SQL works with it.

The Relational Database

A *relational database management system*, or RDMS, is a system of information that is stored in tables. These tables are linked by a series of relationships. These links are composed of relationships between a set of data in one table and a corresponding set of data in another table.

As you begin to design your database, you must first understand the data that will be stored in it. Ask yourself and answer, these and as many other questions that you can think of about the information which you must deal with.

- What kind of information will you be storing?
- Is the data static and never changing, or is it dynamic and constantly being updated?
- How are records now kept, and how are they accessed?
- Does each record currently have a unique identifying characteristic which you can use?
- How can the information within each record be broken down into fields?

As you begin to answer these and many other questions, you will come to have an understanding about the information that you will be working with, and how that information is used by the people who must use it everyday. This process helps you to understand the logical design necessary for your database.

Once you are familiar with the data which you will be working with, you will start to see relationships between different pieces of the data. Some of the best database designers will use diagrams to illustrate the relationships between different pieces. As you become even more intimate with the data, you will be able to see how and why different pieces of related data will be placed into separate tables.

The logical design is not necessarily the best database design. The final physical database design, the one that you will use when actually building the tables and columns that your data will be stored in may be different that your initial logical design. Many database design shops feel that once the logical database design has been diagrammed on paper, it is set in stone. Do not become so wedded to a design that you can not change it when necessary.

The final physical database design should focus on three things:

- The integrity of the data contained in it.

- Creating a structure which allows your users easy access to the data.

- Performance, or speed.

The physical database design should help to facilitate the consistency and integrity of the data that is stored within its tables. While this is a requirement most often seen as the most important to the database designer or database administrator, users tend to look at things a little differently. To the end users, the most important things are usually speed and access. Often, the end user wants the ability to browse tables and access data in a free-form type of format. Finally, the success or failure of a particular database is often based on the speed of data updates and retrieval—if the database appears to be slow, you can bet that the user coalition will be back demanding speed increases, or a completely new system.

These criteria are what will be used to test your mettle as a database designer. These three criteria, consistency/integrity, performance/speed, and ease of access tend to be mutually exclusive. By meeting one set of criteria, you will have a tendency to take away from one or both of the others. How well you balance each will be your final test.

The Normalized Database

As a database is designed, you work towards a *normalized* relational database system. A normalized database must meet several conditions:

- All *entities* (tables), are made up of *attributes* (columns/fields) that define *properties* (datatypes) about each *row* (record) contained within the entity.

- Each row of a table defines a single event or item.

- Each row is uniquely identified through the use of the *primary key*.

- The primary key can made up of a single column or multiple columns.

- Primary key values can not be null.

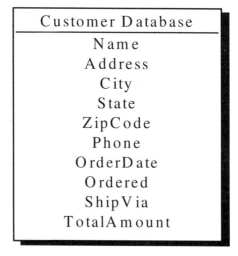

Figure 2.1: This unnormalized database will contain many duplicated rows, one for each item ordered, and it also has several columns that should be broken out into separate tables.

One of the characteristics of a normalized database is that it will contain many more numerous *narrow* tables. A table is considered narrow when it has few columns; conversely, a table is considered wide when it has many columns, most often containing data which is repeated throughout many rows. Figure 2.1 shows an unnormalized database.

This unnormalized Customer Database contains several flaws, common to databases designed by someone new to the concept.

- There is no single or multiple column primary key.

- The Name field should be divided into First and Last Name fields. This will enable you to search by a customer's last name only.

- Columns that force repeat grouping of information, such as the Ordered and ShipVia columns, exist. These columns should never be included in this table. They will force you to repeat all of the customer information in a new row, one new row for every item they order. Think how many thousands of additional rows can possibly be added to a table.

- The TotalAmount column is not a necessary column, it is a calculated value that can be derived from columns which already exist:

    ((((Quantity * Price) for each item ordered) + ShippingCharges for entire order.)

By working toward a normalized database, you will reap several benefits. You will reduce the duplicated data, and in so doing, the storage requirements of your database. The level of data integrity will increase severalfold by normalization. The reduction in the duplicated data will help to ensure that mistakes are not made through simple data entry errors.

By creating many tables with a narrow focus on the data entered in them, you can place more rows of data on each storage page in SQL Server. This can help to speed queries and table scans, improving the overall performance of your database.

A simplified, normalized version of this database would look something like figure 2.2.

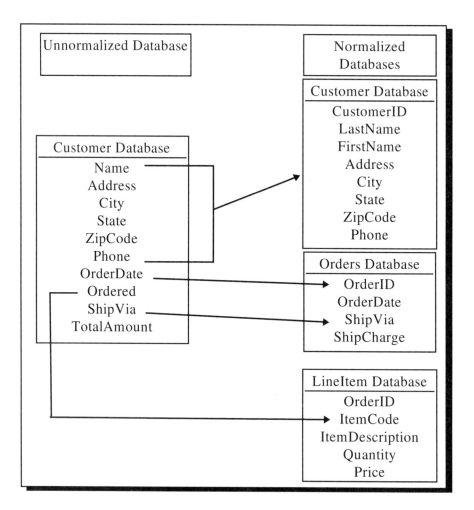

Figure 2.2: The old, unnormalized database is now broken down into three normalized databases.

There are some disadvantages to completely normalizing a database, and they primarily have to do with performance. In some cases, you may find that your database performance can be substantially increased by denormalizing some parts of your database. Denormalizing a database should be a planned step, and be done only for specific performance increases. Remember, denormalizing a database, and subsequently increasing redundancy in your information, may increase your database performance during queries which require many joins (more on that later, in Chapter 9), but you may suffer decreased performance during updates.

Tables, Columns, and Rows

At its simplest, a database is a collection of information. For a relational database, a table is used as a storage unit for related data of a particular type: vendors, customers, inventory items, accounts payable, accounts receivable, and so on. You would not have a single table that included information about customers, accounts payable, and inventory items, all jumbled together. This would be an inefficient waste of computer resources, but would also be very confusing—this could easily be likened to a filing system where every scrap of paper is placed in any drawer, with no thought of possibly having to retrieve a specific page later.

A table is divided into rows and columns, much like a spreadsheet or ledger. A row is often called a *record*, while columns are commonly called *fields*—more specifically, each intersection of a row and column is a single field. Each record contains all of the information available about a specific item, like a customer, a vendor, or a single inventory item. Each column contains a distinct part of a record, such as a customer's name or address, a product's name, cost, and quantity on hand. In most cases you will find that the database is easier to work with when the information contained in a record is broken down into the smallest logical parts, for example; first name, last name, street address, city, state, zip code. Dividing your data into the smallest entities to which they belong is the process of normalizing your database.

As you build your database, you must decide how to break your information into logical groups—these groups will become your tables. As you further divide these groups into their component fields, ask yourself if this piece of information really should go with this group or does it really belong to another table. For example, information about orders does not belong in a customer table, while information about products does not belong in a vendor file.

What is a Relational Database?

A relational database has already been described as a group of tables that are linked by relationships. A good relational database is a collection of data that is organized into tables. Each table uses a unique primary key column, whose value points to one and only one row. The data contained in separate tables is related to each other through the use of the primary keys of one table being related to the foreign key column of another table. This system of relationships is used to give you easy access to the information that it contains.

Relationships are created between tables fields that contain data common to both. Most relationships are created using special field constraints called *Primary* and *Foreign* key fields. By definition a primary key field is unique in a table and all of the data in the table can be automatically indexed, or sorted, by this field. You can't use a NULL value in a primary key field. A foreign key is a field whose values match those of the primary key in another table. A foreign key field can use a NULL value. By creating your database with tables that are linked together using the relationships created with primary and foreign key fields, you can easily divide information between tables in a logical manner.

By dividing your information into discrete tables, you will begin the creation process of a database that will be less prone to errors and duplication of information. A relational database can be a very efficient means of storing and retrieving data. Unlike a flat-file database, where you must search through the entire file for specific data, in a relational database you can use the SQL language to define what you are specifically looking for. SQL will then return a result set to you with the data that meets the criteria which you stated in the SQL query statement.

For example, figure 2.3 is a list of the fields in three tables. Because each table has a field in common with one of the other tables, SQL can create a result set across multiple tables through this common field.

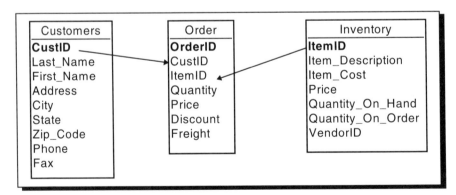

Figure 2.3: Here you can see how three tables are related through the use of common fields.

The Customers table uses the CustID field as its primary key. All customer records are indexed on this field and no records can have a NULL value in this field. The Order table uses the CustID field as a foreign key, so that the two tables can be linked together. The Inventory table uses the ItemID field as a primary key, and again, the Order table also uses this field as a foreign key so that it can be linked to the Inventory table.

Device Independence

Microsoft SQL Server shields you from knowing how information is physically stored on a disk. SQL only requires that you know the name of the table(s) in which the information you are looking for is located in and the specific columns that should be searched. SQL then decides how and where to find the data, returning a results set to you. This makes using SQL to manage a database much easier than using a programming language, such as C and C++, which are third-generation languages, while SQL is a fourth-generation, or 4GL, language. As a 4GL language, SQL is a step further removed from the hardware of the system than earlier languages. A 4GL language such as SQL Server is device independent because it takes care of all the I/O and storage requirements for you.

Classic programming languages are procedural languages and require you to set out, step-by-step, exactly what information you are looking for:

- Where it will be physically found on a disk

- The file name where the data is located

- Where within the file the data is located

- Check in the specified field of each record for the specified value

- When found display or print the selected records as a standard output

Conversely, with SQL you can issue a simple query statement using your front-end program, or with the ISQL/w program and display just the selected data, not necessarily the entire record.

SQL Commands

Microsoft SQL Server uses a version of the SQL language called Transact-SQL, or T-SQL for short. Standard ANSI-SQL provides you with devices to define and to modify or manipulate data. T-SQL extends ANSI-SQL by adding program flow-control devices, such as *if* and *while*, local variables, and other hooks that enable you to write very complex queries, stored procedures, triggers, and other objects that you can build using standard programming techniques.

SQL commands can be divided into three types: Data Definition Language (DDL), Data Manipulation Language (DML), and Data Control Language (DCL). You will use each of these different aspects of T-SQL to build, add data to, and to work with the data in your database. The differences between data definition, manipulation, and control commands are similar to the differences between organization, composition, and regulation.

By using this split between SQL command groups, it is much easier to create a client/server database structure. The system administrator uses DDL commands to create a structure of tables which will remain on the server. The end-user then uses a front-end program created with DML and/or programming code to manipulate the data within the database structure. The system administrator or database owner can use DCL commands to restrict the access to the database objects and the information contained within.

Data Definition Language (DDL)

Simply put, the *Data Definition Language (DDL)* concerns any aspects of T-SQL that are used to create, manage, and drop any data structure that you build within your database. In order to use these commands you must have permission to create or edit the object you wish to define or redefine—this includes both the object and any properties that it may have. Examples of DDL commands that you may use include:

        CREATE TABLE
        DROP TABLE
        CREATE VIEW
        DROP VIEW

Data Manipulation Language (DML)

Data Manipulation Language (DML) is the aspect of T-SQL that you will probably use the most often. This part of T-SQL concerns all commands that are used to manipulate objects in the database, and more commonly, the data contained in your database. Beginning with Microsoft SQL Server 6.0, there have been several significant enhancements to many of the DML commands available to you. To use these commands you must have permission from the database owner to make changes to the information contained in the tables. Examples of DML commands include:

    INSERT
    SELECT
    UPDATE
    DELETE
    EXECUTE

Data Control Language (DCL)

Data Control Language (DCL) concerns those commands that give access to a database object. Permission to use DCL commands starts with the system administrator, the *sa* login, who can grant permission to use them to the database owner, listed within Microsoft SQL Server as the *dbo*. The system administrator can use the highest level of the DCL, having authorization to use any of the database objects, while a database owner can use DCL commands to give access to only those objects that they own. Examples of DCL commands are:

    GRANT
    REVOKE

Commonly Used Commands

Almost all T-SQL statements will include at least one command. (A SQL command tells the server what action is to be performed by the statement.) Each of the T-SQL commands discussed in this chapter are DML commands. SQL commands are also known as *keywords*, and as such are reserved words that have special meaning to Microsoft SQL Server. In this section you will see how several commonly used commands work. The format used with these commands is similar with most versions of SQL since they concern basic data manipulation tasks of selecting, inserting, updating, and deleting data from a database.

When you are using a SQL program or other type of front-end application, T-SQL commands can be sent to the Microsoft SQL Server in batches. A batch is a group of SQL statements that are sent to the server at one time. Batches can be sent to the server in several ways, the most common being: from a front-end application over the network, using ISQL in command mode, or using ISQL/w, which is the graphical version of ISQL, or from the SQL Server Enterprise Manager.

SELECT

The SELECT command is the most often used of all SQL commands because it is used at any time you want to retrieve information from your database. By using the SELECT command, you can choose the specific rows of data you need. Microsoft SQL Server will interpret the batch of SQL statements that you send to the server and display the information that you request.

Using a SELECT Statement

Use the ISQL/w program to create a simple SELECT statement. This SELECT statement will query the server and display the first and last name, telephone number and show the state for all authors who live in the state of California. These records will be selected from the pubs database and from the authors table. Create this SQL statement by following these steps:

1.   Open the ISQL/w program by clicking its icon in the Microsoft SQL Server 6.5 (Common) program group. Before you can use ISQL/w you must connect to the server on which you have login rights using the Connect Server dialog box. Select the name of the server in the Server text box, and then choose the type of connection by clicking either: Use Trusted Connection, or Use Standard Security. If you are not sure which connection you need, check with the SQL Server system administrator. If you are using standard security, you must also provide a valid Login Id and Password in the appropriate text boxes. Finally click the Connect button.

If you are using a trusted connection, your ability to login to Windows NT provides you with your access to SQL Server, if you have been granted appropriate permission.

Figure 2.4: Before you can use ISQL/w, you must first connect to a server through the Connect Server dialog box.

2.   Be sure that the Query tab is selected, and that you have selected the pubs database from the **DB** list box. Now type the following SELECT statement into the query window.

        SELECT au_fname, au_lname, state, phone
        FROM authors
        WHERE state = 'ca'

The SELECT command tells Microsoft SQL Server what fields you want displayed in your results set. The next line specifies which tables to look in by using the qualification clause, FROM. The final clause is the WHERE condition. The records and fields selected must meet the conditions specified by the WHERE clause.

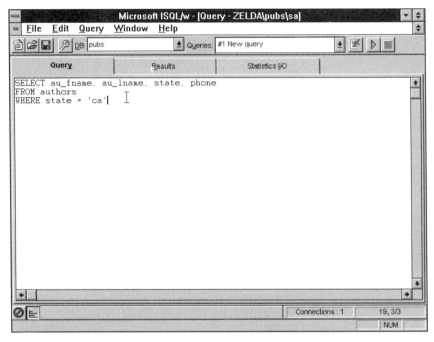

Figure 2.5: Here is the T-SQL SELECT statement in the ISQL/w query window.

NOTE

T-SQL is not case-sensitive when you build an SQL statement if you have selected the normal default settings when installing SQL Server. The keywords are capitalized only so that you can easily distinguish between commands and table, column, and variable names.

3.   Click the Execute Query button, or select **Q**uery, **Ex**ecute, or press Ctrl+E. Any of these actions will cause ISQL/w to send the SELECT statement batch to the server. The server will then return a results set and display it in the window labeled with the **R**esults tab.

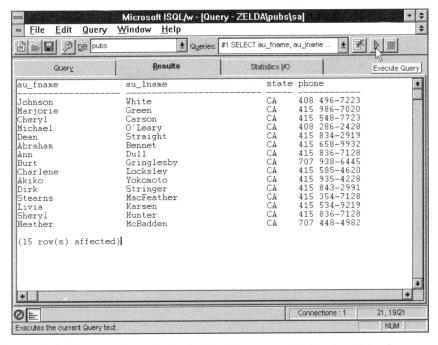

Figure 2.6: The results set selected by the server is displayed in the query results window.

NOTE

If you use ISQL instead of ISQL/w, you must end each SQL statement with the go command. This command tells ISQL that you have completed the statement batch and send it on to the server. The results set output will be displayed on your screen. The go command is also recognized in ISQL/w, allowing you to create more complex T-SQL statements as groups of smaller statements. This is much easier to debug than is one very long statement without any sort of break.

Joining Tables and Sorting Values With a SELECT Statement

You can also combine the information from several tables using the SELECT query by joining the tables through a common field. This is one of the most powerful features of a RDBMS. Whenever you are drawing data from several tables with a

SELECT statement to build a single results set, you are creating a join between the tables. Often the WHERE clause is used to narrow the results set to a specific group of records, by specifying multiple conditions within the clause. Follow these steps to see how this can be done:

1.   Click the Query tab in the ISQL/w window to return to the SELECT statement that you have already created. Select the old statement and delete it by pressing the Delete key, then type this new statement:

```
SELECT au_fname, au_lname, title
FROM authors, titleauthor, titles
WHERE authors.au_id = titleauthor.au_id
AND titleauthor.title_id = titles.title_id
```

This SELECT statement tells Microsoft SQL Server to display all authors and the titles that are associated with them. Notice that there are three tables listed; authors, titleauthor, and titles. This is because there is no direct link between authors and titles—the table titleauthor provides the link used to join the other two tables. The joins are specified by the fields listed in the WHERE clause: au_id joins both authors and titleauthor, while the field title_id joins titleauthor and titles together. Notice how the column names are qualified with both the table and column name, *authors.au_id*. Whenever you use a column which exists in more than one table, you must qualify the column name by identifying its table. Otherwise the query optimizer will not be able to compile the statement, and will return a set of error messages telling you that the references to the column names is ambiguous—in other words, the optimizer can not determine what you are asking for.

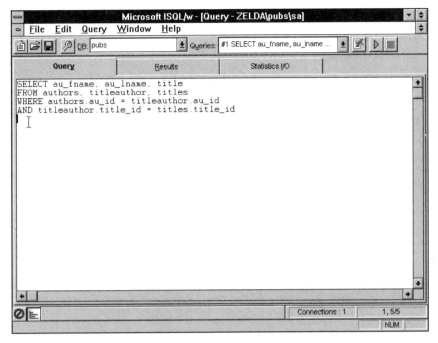

Figure 2.7: This SELECT query statement links three tables and displays information from two of them.

2.   Click the Execute Query button to view the resulting data set in the **R**esults window.

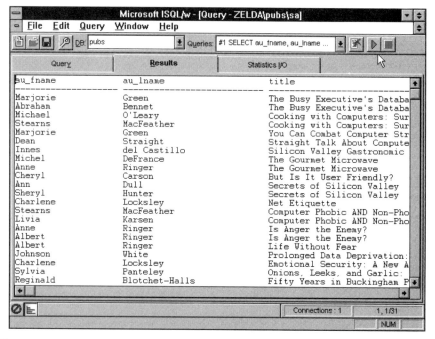

Figure 2.8: Only part of the resulting data set can be viewed in this window. Use the scroll bars to view all of the data.

3.   Notice how this results set does not appear to be displayed in any particular order. They are actually sorted in the order specified by the clustered index of the authors table, which is on the au_id column. You can change the sort order of the results set with the addition of another line in the SELECT statement. Click the Query tab again and type this line as the fifth line in the query statement, and then click the Execute Query button:

ORDER BY au_lname

This modified SQL command will cause Microsoft SQL Server to sort the results set by the listed column—au_lname (last name). Figure 2.9 shows the new results set.

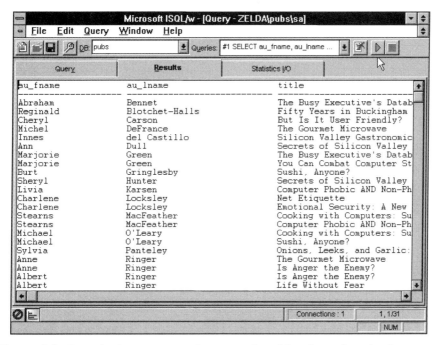

Figure 2.9: Here is the same results set ordered by the values in the column au_lname.

Creating an Alias

As you will already have noticed when displaying a results set, SQL uses the column names as headings for the displayed results set. At times, you will find that the column names are not the most easily understood headings for columns of data. Unless you were the programmer who created the pubs table it may take you a moment before you see that the column labeled au_lname means that this column comes from the authors table and contains the last name for each of the authors.

There is an easy way to alleviate this potential problem—by using an *alias*. An alias is used to rename a column in the results set—for example, you may want to rename the au_lname to something easily understood, such as "Last Name." Using an alias to rename a column is quite simple when you are building an SQL statement. In the next example you will learn how an alias can be used:

1.   Click the Query tab in the ISQL/w window and clear any existing SQL statements by clicking the Remove Current Query Set button. Type the following SQL statement into the window.

> SELECT au_lname 'Last Name', au_fname 'First Name', phone
> Phone
> FROM authors

Note

While you can use double quotation marks to indicate the label names, it is generally regarded as good practice to use single quotation marks for labels. Use double quotation marks when you are using T-SQL reserved words as labels, or in other cases when you do not want them to perform the actions that they would normally.

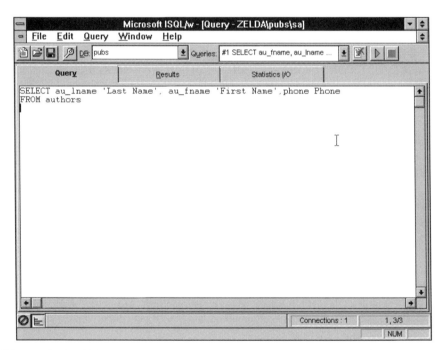

Figure 2.10: This query statement will display a results set with column labels with alias, or new, names.

You will have noticed that quotation marks were placed around the first two aliases but not the third. This is because T-SQL needs the quotations surrounding alias names of more than one word, otherwise it would assume that the first word was the alias while the second was another command.

2.   Click the Execute Query button to view the new results set.

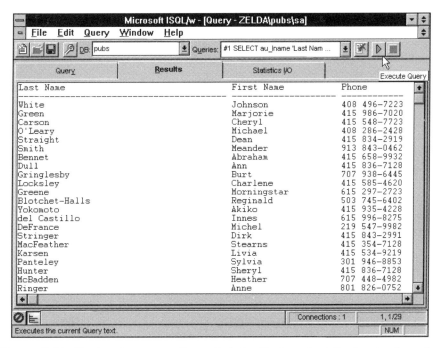

Figure 2.11: Notice the new column labels displayed at the beginning of the list.

As you begin your sojourn into SQL, you may forget the necessity of the comma when delineating the column select list. If you do not separate each and every column name with a comma the following problem will be displayed:

33

Query: SELECT au_lname au_fname FROM authors
            au_fname

            White
            Green
            Carson

            ...

The results set shows a list of names with a column label of au_fname—but is it correct and what happened to the au_lname column? If you look at the data contained in the authors table you will find that you have a list of last names, not first names. What has happened is that without the comma separating the two column names, SQL assumes that the second name is to be used as a column alias. Always be sure that you have inserted commas between each name in a select list, whether it be columns or tables.

INSERT

Once you know how to select records from a database you will want to do more. The simplest method to add new rows, or records, to a table is with the INSERT command. INSERT does not require that you fill all of the columns in a table, you can go back later and add additional data, or change existing data in any row by using the UPDATE command.

> **Note**
> There are other methods of adding large amounts of data into a table. The BCP utility (Bulk Copy Program) is a special utility which allows you to insert large blocks of new data into an existing table. This procedure is often used when you are converting from an older database system currently in use to a new SQL Server client/server system. You would then use the BCP utility to bulk load data from your old system to the new.

When adding new rows you are only required to complete those columns which are designated as key columns, or those which do not allow NULL values. SQL will return an error if a value is not stated for any column that does not allow NULL values, or has not been assigned a default value. You do not have to specify values for columns which use either the *identity* property or *timestamp* datatype. A column with the identity property will automatically be sequentially numbered, while a timestamp datatype will provide an increasing counter with a unique value within the database. A timestamp value will be automatically updated each time a new row is inserted or a value in any column of that row is updated.

INSERT is used with the following syntax:

1.   Be sure that the pubs database is selected in the **DB** list box, and then type the following INSERT statement in the ISQL/w Query window.

```
INSERT jobs
(job_desc, min_lvl, max_lvl)
VALUES
("Sales Rep Intl", 30, 125)
INSERT jobs
(job_desc, min_lvl, max_lvl)
VALUES
("Designer II", 75, 150)
```

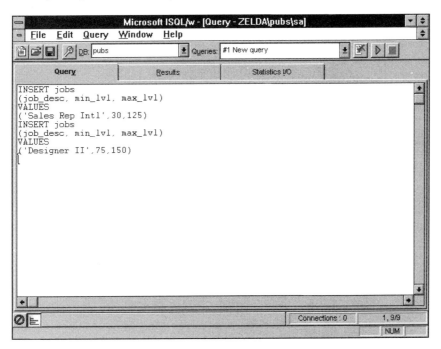

Figure 2.12: An INSERT SQL statement that adds two new records into the jobs table.

> **Note**
>
> The jobs table's first column is job_id. This field is not included in an INSERT statement because it uses an identity property. Microsoft SQL Server will automatically assign a value for this field. For each record that you insert into a table you must repeat the INSERT command, the column list, and the values list.

2.   Click the Execute Query button to insert your two new records into the jobs table. For each record successfully added, you will see the statement "(1 row(s) affected)."

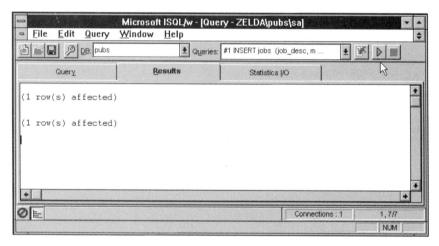

Figure 2.13: Notice how an INSERT query does not return a list of values as a SELECT query does. You are simply told that the query was successful. If it was not, an error message would be displayed.

You can omit the column list in an INSERT statement if you provide values for each column—except identity and timestamp columns—in the same order in which the columns occur in the table. If you do accidentally place values in an incorrect order, Microsoft SQL Server may trap the error and display an error message, but only if the statement tries to insert a value incompatible with the column data type—such as an alphanumeric value in a number column. Microsoft SQL Server will not automatically trap two alphanumeric values that are transposed, such as a city and state value. SQL will simply insert the state value into the city column and the city value into the state column. The value inserted into the state column will most likely be truncated to a two letter value.

Later in this book you will learn about referential integrity, rules and triggers which you can use and to help insure that errors of this type are caught and allow the user to make corrections before the INSERT is allowed to go through, or is summarily rejected.

UPDATE

The UPDATE statement is used to change values that already exist in a row. For example, if an author already listed in the authors table of the pubs database were to move, you would want to simply update his or her address, not insert a new record for the author.

Common uses for UPDATE statements are to change addresses, telephone numbers, prices, item descriptions, and other information contained in a column. In most cases you must identify a specific record to be updated, as without such an identification Microsoft SQL Server will update every row with the same information. For example, a simple UPDATE SQL statement could be constructed that said:

```
UPDATE authors
SET city = "San Francisco"
```

This SQL statement is an unqualified and would result in changing the city column of all rows to the value "San Francisco." This type of mass update is useful when you need to change the same information for many records. Many of you may have to do just this type of UPDATE each time the phone company adds a new area code.

Most often you will use an UPDATE SQL statement that is qualified by selecting a specific row to be updated using a WHERE clause. A poorly qualified statement can cause all of the rows, or the wrong rows, to be selected and updated with the new data. In the above statement, you would want to identify a specific author and so could qualify this statement by adding:

```
WHERE au_id = '274-80-9391'
```

With the addition of this WHERE clause SQL knows exactly which individual row is to be updated with the new information. In the case of a change of city, you will mostly likely have to change street address, and possibly the phone number also. It is more efficient to tell SQL to change all of these fields with one statement than it is to issue an individual SQL statement to update each column. A complete statement would look like this:

```
UPDATE authors
SET phone = "510-555-1234"
address = "1542 Market St."
city = "San Fr0ancisco"
state = "CA"
Zip = "92111"
WHERE au_id = "274-80-9391"
```

Since you are not changing the authors name or contract status you do not have to include these columns.

DELETE

The DELETE statement is used to delete unneeded rows from a table, not to delete information from single columns. SQL allows you to delete rows from only a single table at a time. Generally, a DELETE statement should be a qualified statement, selecting specific rows to be deleted from a table. An unqualified statement, or one that is poorly qualified can inadvertently delete all of the rows in a table. The following SQL statement can be used to delete all publishers who are not located in the United States:

```
DELETE publishers
WHERE NOT country = 'USA'
```

This query works once you have either deleted all of the records in other tables which are linked to the records to be deleted or have shifted these links to another publisher. In the pubs database both the employee and the pub_info tables are linked to the publishers table through the pub_id column.

SQL does not allow you to delete records that are *dependent* on values that exist in another table. These other tables are often called *child* tables because they are dependent on a value contained in the *parent* table. These relationships will be discussed fully in Chapter 5.

Transactions and SQL

In Microsoft SQL Server, *transactions* are a set of procedures that must be completed at one time. Once a transaction begins, it must be fully completed or completely undone. All business procedures can be reduced to a series of transactions. A bank cashes a $100 check for a customer. The bank processes two transactions:

- Reducing the customers checking account for the $100.

- Increasing the banks cash account for $100.

Both of these transactions must be completed so that the banks books remain in balance. All SQL statements, except a simple SELECT statement, are transactional. Microsoft SQL Server guarantees that a transaction will be completely processed or it will not be processed at all. For example, if you want to increase the price of all business books in the pubs titles table by 25%, you would issue an UPDATE statement:

```
UPDATE titles
SET price = price * 1.25
WHERE type = business
```

If the server goes down after this transaction begins, but before it has processed all rows in the titles table, what happens? Once the server comes back up, and before the database is ready for use, Microsoft SQL Server will rollback all incomplete transactions—as if the UPDATE transaction had never been started. This is how Microsoft SQL Server can guarantee that a transaction will be completely processed.

There are three transaction commands that Microsoft SQL Server uses to decide if a SQL transaction has been started, completed or should be reversed:

- BEGIN TRANsaction. This statement is used to tell Microsoft SQL Server to group all of the subsequent operations—to begin a transaction.

- COMMIT TRANsaction. This statement tells the server to commit the operations in the current transaction. The transaction is completed and is to be written to the disk.

- ROLLBACK TRANsaction. This statement tells the server to reverse all transaction changes to the previous BEGIN TRAN statement.

- SAVE TRANsaction. This statement allows a user to set a save point within a transaction. If a transaction must meet specified conditions, it can be rolled back to the save point. It must then either be completed with additional SQL statements and a COMMIT TRAN statement, or rolled back to its beginning.

All SQL statements are implicitly begun and committed by the server. This means that you do not have to use BEGIN TRAN and COMMIT TRAN statements around each statement. If you are only processing short statements that are single transaction then a BEGIN TRAN and COMMIT TRAN statement are probably not necessary.

When you do not use a BEGIN and COMMIT TRAN statement in a transaction, Microsoft SQL Server assumes that each transaction has an implicit BEGIN and COMMIT TRAN statement. SQL Server implicitly commits each transaction as it is completed. A transaction such as our earlier bank example, though, should have a BEGIN TRAN and a COMMIT TRAN statement surrounding it. Otherwise it could be possible for only half of the transaction to be completed. For example:

```
implicit BEGIN TRAN
UPDATE customer_account
SET balance = balance - 100
tran_id = 3456
WHERE cust_id = "151545 3456"
implicit COMMIT TRAN

implicit BEGIN TRAN
INSERT bank_cashacct (tran_id, amount, cust_id)
VALUES (3456, 100, "151545 3456")
implicit COMMIT TRAN
```

If the server goes down before the second COMMIT TRAN then only the first half of this transaction, up to the first COMMIT TRAN will be written to the disk and the records changed accordingly. The second half of the transaction would be rolled back. Any multiple transaction that should all be written to the permanent file at one time should always be start with a BEGIN TRAN and end with a COMMIT TRAN statement. This will ensure that the entire transaction will be written or none of it will be. This same bank transaction should be written like this:

```
BEGIN TRAN
UPDATE customer_account
SET balance = balance - 100
```

```
tran_id = 3456
WHERE cust_id = "151545 3456"
INSERT bank_cashacct (tran_id, amount, cust_id)
VALUES (3456, 100, "151545 3456")
COMMIT TRAN
```

By using a BEGIN TRAN and a COMMIT TRAN statement around the transaction SQL Server guarantees that the entire transaction will be properly written to the permanent disk file. Now the server would automatically roll this transaction back if it were to go down before it was completed.

The ROLLBACK TRAN statement would be used in place of the COMMIT TRAN statement if you wanted to reverse all of the changes that had been made in the transaction since the BEGIN TRAN statement.

Summary

In this chapter, you have learned about SQL Server as a relational database management system. Specifically, you have learned:

- How a relational database system, such as SQL Server, stores data in tables, columns, and rows.

- You have been introduced to the way that SQL Server uses primary and foreign keys to relate data in one table to the data in another table.

- You have become familiar with the concepts of the Data Definition Language, the Data Manipulation Language, and the Data Control Language.

- You have seen how commonly used commands such as; SELECT, INSERT, UPDATE, and DELETE are used.

- Finally, you have seen how to change the sort order by using the ORDER BY clause, and to change the names of columns in a results set with an alias.

Chapter 3

Logical Structures

IN THIS CHAPTER

- Devices
- Database Objects
- Database Sizing
- System Catalog

Microsoft SQL Server uses several different types of *devices* when creating the structure used by the server to store all of your information. When you install Microsoft SQL Server, several structures are automatically installed along with the program. Many of these structures are system devices and are used by SQL Server to provide information that all users require to build new databases—information about who has access to the various databases, where a database may reside on a physical disk and how it is to be stored, when and where information is to be sent to a dump device, and many other types of special structures.

Most of the structures that you will use are composed first of a device and then objects within the device. You will become more familiar with them throughout this chapter.

Devices

A SQL *device* will generally come in one of two flavors: the *database device* and the *dump device* or *backup device*. Both consist of a real physical storage area, usually a file on a hard disk, that is used by SQL to store information.

Database Devices

A database device is used by SQL Server to store some or all of the information required for an individual database, and may include its transaction log. Commonly, the transaction log will be placed on a different device, making dumps of the log much easier. When you install Microsoft SQL Server, several database devices are also installed, including; master, MSDBData, and MSDBLog. Each database device becomes a physical file with the same name you give to the device and a file extension of .DAT; for example *master.dat*.

You can place many database objects, an individual database, along with its tables, permissions, views, and other objects, into any single database device. As will be discussed in later chapters, it is always good practice to place a database transaction log on a separate database device. You are limited only in the size of the database device, and this can be increased if necessary, provided you have the required disk space. You should make it a simple rule never to place new database objects in the master database device. This device is used by SQL Server to store the master, model and tempdb system databases and their transaction logs. The pubs database is also stored on the master database device if you install it. When you first install Microsoft SQL Server, only the master database device is created, and it is also set as the default device. It is highly recommended that you turn off the default setting and create additional database devices to store new user databases. When you create a new database, always specify the database device to indicate where to store the data. If you do not, then Microsoft SQL Server automatically select the first available default device with room for the new database. Devices are selected in alphabetical order. In the next few steps you will learn how to turn off the default setting on the master database device and then create a new database device:

1.   Open the Microsoft SQL Enterprise Manager and choose a server to connect to. Open the Database Devices folder, and then double-click on the master device. You will see the Edit Database Devices dialog box displayed.

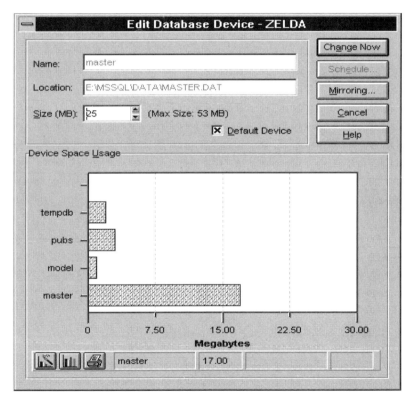

Figure 3.1: Use the Edit Database Devices dialog box to increase the size of a database device, set the default device option, and change other options.

2.   Click the **D**efault Device check box to clear it. This will reset the master database device's default setting to "defaultoff". This will help to ensure that a user will not place objects into the master device. Click the **OK** button to save this setting.

3.   Now click the Database Devices folder again to select it and then click the right mouse button, displaying a shortcut menu.

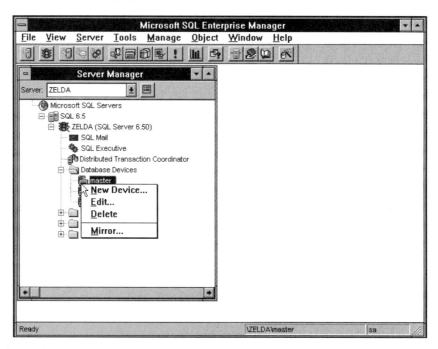

Figure 3.2: Use this shortcut menu to create new database devices, to edit existing devices and to refresh the display after you have created a new device so that it is displayed in the tree.

4.   Select the **N**ew Device option, displaying the New Database Device dialog box.

The New Database Device dialog box is used to name the device, and to tell SQL Server where the device is to be located and how large to make it. You can also set this new device to be a default device and create a mirror for it. A mirror is a duplicate copy of the database which can be used as a backup if the original file's database device fails for some reason. The graph in the lower half of the dialog box shows you the disks that are available for you to place your new device; use the scroll bar to view additional drives if necessary. The bars indicate the space that is available on each disk. The number of disks shown and the size of the graph's X-axis is dependent on the number and sizes of the disks in your server.

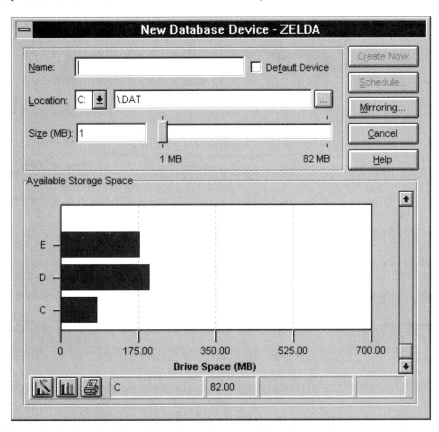

Figure 3.3: Use the New Database Device dialog box when you need to create additional database devices.

5.   Type **dataDB** as the name for your device in the **N**ame text box. Now click the De**f**ault Device check box to set this database device as the default device for a new database to be placed. Next, select the drive that you want to use to place your device, choosing from the **D**rive list box. If you have only a single hard disk with one partition you will only have drive "C" as an option. You must then decide where on the disk you specifically want the device to reside by selecting a path from the **P**ath text box. If you are placing the new device on the same disk that contains Microsoft

SQL Server then the path \MSSQL\DATA\ is automatically selected for you. You can change this selection if you want to place the device in another directory. To change directories, click the button marked (...), beside the location text box, and select a directory and/or drive from the displayed dialog box. Type 30 as the size for your device in the **S**ize(MB) text box, or click on the slider bar to choose the size. You must use whole numbers in this box.

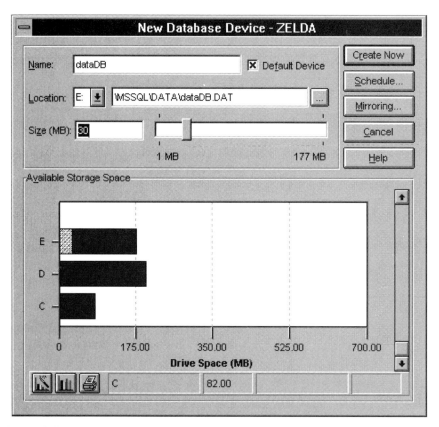

Figure 3.4: Here is the completed New Database Device dialog box. Notice how the size of the new device is indicated on the bar for the selected disk in the graph.

6.   Click the Create Now button to save the new database device. When SQL Server successfully completes the building process, a dialog box will be displayed. Click the **OK** button to close this dialog box. If you do not want to create the new database device now, you can click the Schedule button, displaying the Schedule

dialog box. Then choose a time when the server will be less busy so as not to disturb other users while the building and initialization process is being completed on the new database device. For a very large device, this can take several hours and use many of the server's resources.

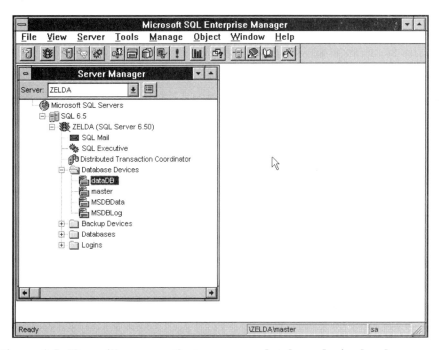

Figure 3.5: You will now see that your new database device has been added to the list of Database Devices for the selected server.

When creating a new database device you can place it on any existing drive on the server. SQL Server does not support database devices located over the network on another machine. While you can not place a database device on another computer's hard disk, you can place it on any existing local drive, and in any directory on those drives. You are not limited to placing a SQL Server database device on an Windows NT NTFS formatted drive volume, you can also use a DOS FAT formatted volume. If you plan to use a disk compression scheme to wring more space from your drives, you can use only compressed NTFS volumes for database devices—with a resulting performance penalty.

You can not move a database device once it has been created. You must backup all of the databases located on the device, drop it and recreate it in a new location. While you can move the physical file that is the database device in File Manager, SQL Server will not be able to use the database device, nor any databases located on it.

Backup Devices

Backup devices are used by Microsoft SQL Server to store backup copies of databases and transaction logs. In previous versions of Microsoft SQL Server, backup devices were called dump devices, and they are still referred to as dump devices by most other SQL programs. It is very important that you create one or more backup devices and use them regularly. One of the worst things that can happen to a database administrator is to have a hard disk fail and not to have dumped, or backed, up the files recently. If you have a media failure, you can use the latest backup to restore the database. A restore operation will usually involve the latest full backup of the database and one or more incremental backups of the transaction logs.

Backup devices can be created as disk files on the same or a different hard disk, a tape drive, or a diskette (floppy) drive. Unlike a database device, SQL Server does support the use of a networked tape drive or hard disk as a backup device. In order to use a tape drive as a backup device you must have set up the drive using the Windows NT Setup option in the Main group.

Backups consist of two different types: *full* and *incremental*. A full backup creates a copy of all of the allocated pages in your database, all database system tables, and the transaction logs. You should be aware that a full backup of a user database does not backup the system tables that are specific to the master database. The master database should be backed up every time you make any change to a database which is reflected in one of the master databases system tables. This would include such actions as creating a new database, changing the size of a database, and adding a transaction log.

An incremental backup simply copies the transaction logs. The transaction logs contain all of the transactions that have been processed since the previous dump transaction command. Normally when you backup the transaction log, Microsoft SQL Server also automatically truncates the log at the same time. This means that all of the transactions that have been backed up will also be deleted from the transaction log.

You can always create only full backups, ensuring yourself of a complete backup of everything. This does not relieve you of the necessity of performing the incremental backup. A full backup does not truncate the transaction log, and eventually this log will fill up with transactions that have been copied in a previous backup. Once the transaction log becomes full, all new transactions will be halted until you clear out the log.

Every organization should be sure that someone has the responsibility for performing backups regularly and properly. Microsoft SQL Server gives default rights to perform backups and restores to the system administrator, and to the database owner. Another login name can be granted backup and restore rights by either the system administrator or the database owner. Either the system administrator or the database owner can schedule automatic backups to run at regularly scheduled times. This is an excellent way to ensure that regular backups are performed, and can help prevent performance degradation to users by scheduling the backup during a period when the system is less busy.

In previous versions of Microsoft SQL Server, backups to the same device with the same name would automatically overwrite the older file. This is known as a *destructive backup* and resulted in the deletion of the older file. This had the potential of leaving you with no backup at all if a dump was accidentally interrupted. Since SQL Server 6.0, this operation has changed so that the new dump will be appended to an existing file, regardless whether on disk or on tape.

Dump devices, backup and restore processes will be discussed more fully in Chapter 11.

Database Objects

A database object is the primary container that holds other commonly used user objects such as tables, views, stored procedures, and rules. The database owner has primary responsibility for creating the objects that populate their database. Permission may be granted to someone who acts as a database developer to create and manage the objects within a database.

Before you can place a table or other database object on a database, you must first either select an existing database or create a new one. Databases are contained within one or more database devices, just as a table is contained within a database. Unlike a table, the actual database can be spanned across more than one device—the transaction log portion of the database is often placed on a separate device. Create a new database by following these steps:

1.   Connect to a server by clicking its icon in the Microsoft SQL Server Enterprises Manager window. Now right-click your mouse on the Databases folder so that the shortcut menu is displayed and choose New Database from the menu. You will now see the New Database dialog displayed.

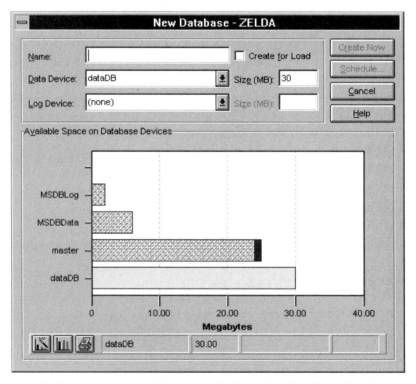

Figure 3.6: Create a new database easily by using the New Database dialog box.

2.   Type **Inventory** in the **N**ame text box. Since you have previously set dataDB as the default device, it has been selected in the **D**ata Device list box, and you don't need to change this unless you are creating a table that is to be stored on a different database device. Enter **10** as the size in megabytes for the database in the **S**ize (MB) text box.

You can't make the new database larger than the total available space on the database device. The maximum space available is displayed in this text box. Later, you can edit the new **Inventory** database and add more space on additional devices if you decide that the database needs to be larger.

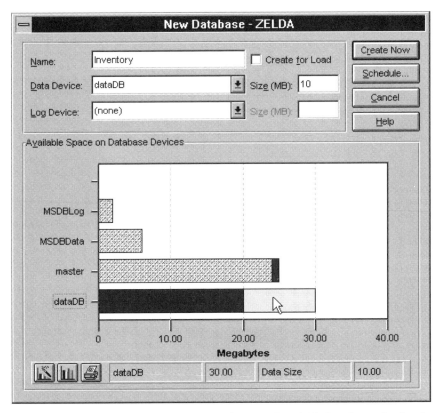

Figure 3.7: Notice how the graph bar for the dataDB database device has been split into two parts. It is now divided into a Data Size and a Free Space segment.

If you decide that you want to place your new database on a database device that does not yet exist, you can create a new database device by selecting new in the **D**ata Device list box. The New Database Device dialog box will be displayed and you simply have to finish entering the necessary information for the new device, just as you did in the previous section of this chapter. When you click on the Create Now button, you will be returned to the New Database dialog box to complete the creation of the database.

3.   Create a log device for this database so that you can easily dump all of the transactions that occur. Select <new> in the **L**og Device list box; the New Database Device dialog box will be displayed. Type Inventorylog in the **N**ew text box. Select the appropriate drive and path in which to store your log file using the **D**rive list box and the **P**ath text box. Enter 2 in the **S**ize (MB) text box to create a log file that is 2MB in size. Click the **OK** button to save your new log file and return to the New Database dialog box.

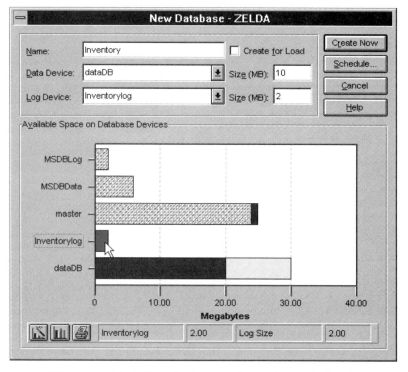

Figure 3.8: The completed New Database dialog box. Notice that the new log device has been added to the graph, and that the bar is a different color. This is because it is a log device.

There are many recommended ways to determine the size ratio between a database and its transaction log. A general rule of thumb is approximately 25% transaction log to database size. For a database that will have a very high rate of transactions or have very large transactions, you will need to increase the size of the transaction log to ensure that it does not fill up.

4.   Click the **OK** button to complete the new database. You will now see the new Inventory database and the Inventorylog database device displayed in the Server Manager window.

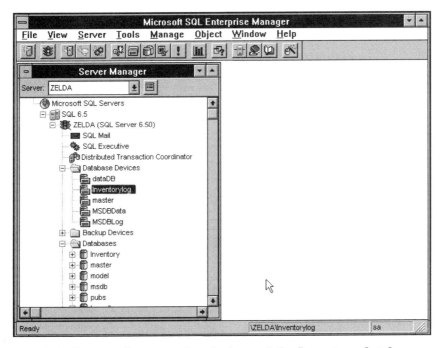

Figure 3.9: The new Inventorylog device and the Inventory database are now displayed in the SQL Server Enterprise Manager window.

Tables

Microsoft SQL Server uses two types of tables; system tables and user tables. Some system tables are stored within each database and are called database catalog (or system) tables, while others known as system catalog (or master system) tables are contained only within the master database. System tables are used by Microsoft SQL Server to keep track of user database objects, including table constraints, permissions, users, groups, and aliases.

> **Note**
>
> Whenever you make changes to the system tables you should be sure to back up the master database. This will ensure that your most current changes are available in case of a media failure. If you do not back up the master database, your only option in the unhappy event of a disk crash is to rebuild the master database from the Microsoft SQL Server CD. This will require you to rebuild or reload each of the user databases again so that their information is included in the master database's system tables. You will not be able to use any of the user databases until this possibly lengthy processes has been accomplished. Remember, the system tables in the master database include all of the information about user logins, permissions, database location and size.

The table object is the object that users will become most familiar with. The table is used by Microsoft SQL Server as the storage object for all data. You can have many tables in each database. Tables are generally used to store one type of data such as; customers, vendors, inventory items, orders, purchases, or purchase line items. Tables can be created to store any type of information. Any user who has been granted permission by the database owner can create tables in a database. Of course, if you are the system administrator or the database owner you do not need to have specific permission to be granted to add tables. You can easily add a new user table to an existing database by following these few steps:

1.   Click on the Inventory database in the Server Manager window, selecting it as the database in which you want to add a new table. You can open the Manage Tables dialog box by doing one of the following:

- Select **M**anage from the main menu and then choose **T**ables from the drop-down menu.

- Click the plus symbol to the left of the Inventory database icon, and then click the plus sign to the left of the Objects icon. Now right click on the Tables icon and select **N**ew Table from the shortcut menu.

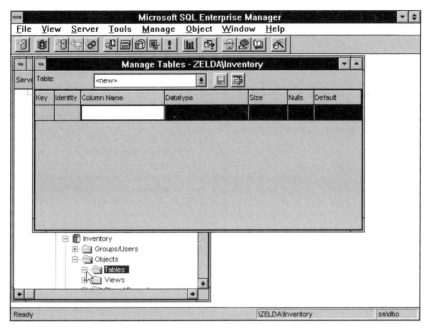

Figure 3.10: Use the Manage Tables dialog box to create and edit table definitions.

2.	Create the first field in your new table by entering the following information into each of the listed columns:

Column Name	item_id
Datatype	int

3.	Fill in the next several rows as indicated in the table below:

Column Name	Datatype	Size	Nulls	Default
item_id	int	"leave blank"	"leave blank"	"leave blank"
item_description	varchar	30	"leave blank"	"leave blank"
vendor_id	int	"leave blank"	"check mark"	"leave blank"
qty_onhand	int	"leave blank"	"check mark"	"leave blank"
qty_onorder	int	"leave blank"	"check mark"	"leave blank"
cost	smallmoney	"leave blank"	"check mark"	"leave blank"
retail_price	smallmoney	"leave blank"	"check mark"	"leave blank"
discontinued	bit	"leave blank"	"leave blank"	"leave blank"

Remember, the note in the Nulls column "check mark" indicates that you are to leave the default check mark in place. This will allow SQL Server to accept a null value in this column. The notation "leave blank" means that you are not to add anything here, in some cases SQL Server will not allow you to make an entry. The two columns "cost" and "retail_price" use the datatype of smallmoney because it has a range of ±$214,748.3647 which is more than adequate for most inventory items. If this was a table of capital goods or the items to be sold consisting of specialized machinery, you might want to use the datatype money as it has a much larger range.

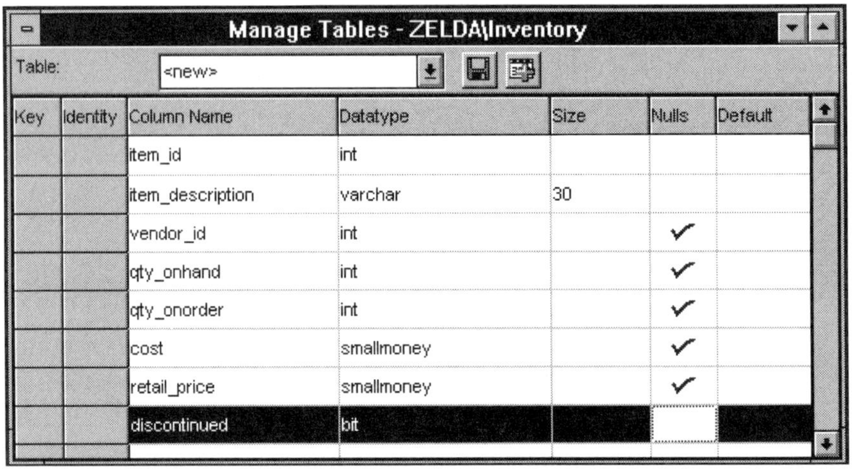

Figure 3.11: This is how the Manage Tables dialog box should now appear.

4.   Click on the Advanced Features button. The bottom half of the Manage Tables window now includes a new set of options that can be used with many of the fields that you have created. These options are used to set identity properties, primary keys, and other features to help ensure that the data entered into your tables is both consistent and correct. The concepts behind, and the uses for these advanced features will be discussed more fully later in Chapter 5.

5.   Be sure that the Primary Key/Identity tab is selected. In the Primary Key box, select the list box arrow button to display the list of columns available for use as a primary key. Only those fields whose datatype allows data to be entered which would be unique can be designated as a primary key. You cannot use a field which allows null values to be entered in the field. Only two columns meet these requirements as you will see when you click the button. Select the item_id column as

the primary key. Now click the **N**on-clustered toggle button in the Type box, and then click the **A**dd button.

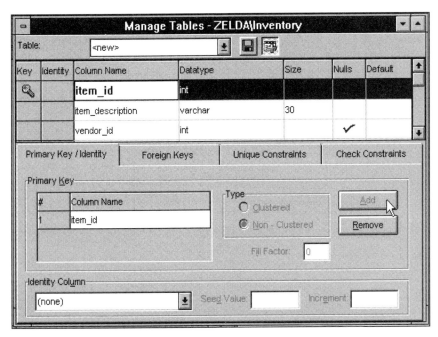

Figure 3.12: SQL Server adds the primary key designator in the Key column beside the item_id column. This icon helps you to quickly identify which column has been designated as the primary key.

6.   To complete a new table click, on the Save Table button. You will be prompted to enter a name for the new table in the Specify Table Name dialog box. Type **Products** into the text box and click the **OK** button. By opening the Inventory database, Objects, and Tables in the Server Manager window tree you will see the new table Products listed.

Views

A *view* is a different look at the data contained in a table or a group of related tables. You can use select statements on a view just as you would the table(s) behind the view. Views are often used to create a condensed version, or a window of a table, that can be used by group of users who do not need access to all of the information contained in the table.

For example, you may want to create a view of a personnel table for someone in the marketing department. A view can be created that will display selected employees, grouped by department or title, and include their education qualifications. You can leave sensitive information such as salaries, and dependent status out of the view. To the marketing individual, the view will be the same as if they were working with the real data in the table. Other reasons to create and use views could include:

- Allowing customers to browse through inventory tables, but not see your vendor and cost data.

- Compiling statistical information about customers or employees.

Like all other objects, a view can be created, dropped, and permission to use the view granted or revoked. A view can be used to add, delete, or update the underlying table information, but dropping a view has no effect on the table.

A view can be created very easily by using the SQL Enterprise Manager window from the ISQL/w window or from your front-end application. Both methods are similar, but are simply done in a different program. In the next several steps you will create a new view for the pubs table:

1.   Open the ISQL/w program and select the pubs database in the **DB** text box. Click the Query tab and type the following:

```
CREATE VIEW author_phonelist AS
SELECT last = au_lname, first = au_fname, phone
FROM authors
```

Note

You can use the alias function to change the column names displayed in the views result set from those used in the original tables so that they are easier to understand and reference in the view. Here the au_lname and au_fname columns have been renamed last and first, respectively. These names will be used to reference the columns whenever working with this view. When creating a SELECT view, some functions, such as ORDER BY, are not available to you. You can use these functions when you call the view to display the current results set, but not when creating the view.

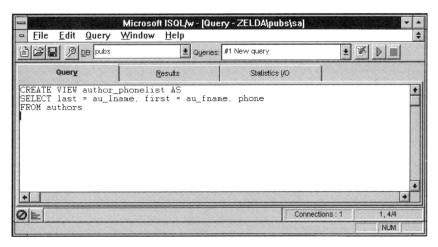

Figure 3.13: This CREATE VIEW statement will create a view of the authors table, showing only the last name, first name, and phone columns.

2. Click the Execute Query button to complete the statement. You will know that you were successful in creating the new view when you see the statement:

    This Command did not return data, and it did not return any rows.

3. Return to the query statement window, and type the following statement:

    SELECT *
    FROM author_phonelist
    ORDER BY last

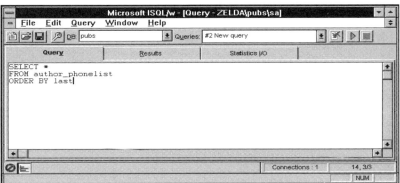

Figure 3.14: This SELECT statement will display the rows from the View author_phonelist. The names will be ordered by the "last" column.

4.   Click the Execute Query button to see the results set for the View.

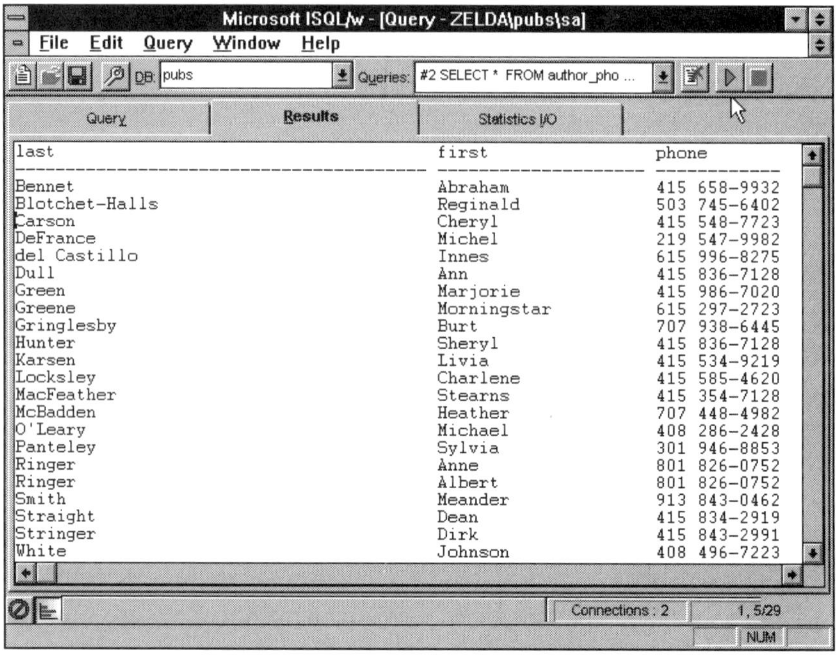

Figure 3.15: Here, the results set for the view is displayed, sorted by the values in the "last" column. Notice that not all of the author's names are displayed in this window. You must scroll down the window to view any additional names.

Views are an excellent way to allow users access to parts of a table or tables. Each time that the view is accessed a new results set with updated information is displayed; it is not static from the time it is created as a report would be, but is dynamic and always uses the most current information available.

You can also use a view to define a group of rows that will be displayed for a selected user or group. Unlike a table, where you can restrict access to specific columns, with a view you can also restrict access to selected rows. Since the view is based on a query, you can structure it so that only a selected group of rows is displayed in the view.

Cursors

Cursors are activated with a DECLARE cursor statement. You can build two types of cursors with SQL Server, dynamic and forward-only. Beginning with SQL Server 6.0, ANSI SQL cursors are server based, instead of based through DB-Library or Open Database Connectivity (ODBC) API's.

Cursors are most often used to provide a method for single-row operations to be performed in a results set from a query. Cursors can compliment the normal page-lock methods used in most queries when set operations are impractical, though with SQL Server 6.5's ability to use row-level locking, cursors are becoming less necessary. With a cursor, you can increase the granularity of your queries by allowing row-level functions, instead of page-level. Data in tables can be updated through a cursor, except in the case of a cursor declared with the keyword INSENSITIVE.

Note

Cursors should generally be used only when other methods that use a results set can not be found. The cursor places a substantial overhead burden on the servers resources.

As all objects that are used in SQL Server, the cursor must be named within a T-SQL statement. Cursors, like other objects, are restricted to names of no more than 30 characters, and no restricted characters. When you create a statement that uses a cursor, the usual procedure will follow this format:

- DECLARE cursor statement. This statement names the cursor, and uses a select statement specifying what tables and columns are to be selected for results set this cursor will work with. When using ISQL, ISQL/w, or SQL Server Enterprise Manager the statement must be executed by using a GO command, before the remaining parts of the statement can use the cursor.

- OPEN statement. This statement opens the declared cursor.

- FETCH statement. The FETCH statement specifies the conditions, if any, that must be met for a rows inclusion into the results set.

- CLOSE statement. This statement closes an open cursor. You must name the cursor which is to be closed.

- DEALLOCATE statement. This final statement removes the data structures created by the DECLARE cursor statement.

Unless specified otherwise with the fetch statement, cursors are forward-going only. This means that the cursor, when used with an INSERT statement, begins with the first row in a table and continues forward, from row-to-row throughout the results set. As the cursor moves to a new row, the row is locked and no other user is allowed to update the row. Once the cursor has finished and moved forward to the next row, it can be updated by another user, but the cursor never goes back to look at the updated information, unless you have allowed the cursor to scroll through the results set.

You can create a cursor that is able to scroll through a table by using the keyword SCROLL in the DECLARE statement. With the SCROLL keyword, your cursor can scroll both backward and forward, and even move to an absolute row number or specific number of rows from the current row. If data is updated in the underlying table, the next FETCH statement will return an updated results set.

A cursor that is declared with the keyword INSENSITIVE is not able to update the underlying table. When the INSENSITIVE keyword is used, a copy of the selected data is placed into a temporary table. The cursor then acts upon this temporary table. This is an effective method when you are using a cursor for creating a report and only need a snapshot of the current data.

Indexes

An index on a table in a SQL database acts just like any index that you use in everyday life. It is a tool that enables you to quickly search for some specific bit, or category of information. An index is a special object used by SQL Server to speed access to data contained in the table. Indexes create a method that SQL can use when performing a SELECT query so that every row does not have to be scanned for records. There are two types of indexes that you can use: clustered and nonclustered. The SQL query optimizer will decide if an index can be used to increase the speed of the query when it looks at the individual tables and data to be selected.

When you create an index, SQL Server places the index on index pages, while the actual data contained in the rows are stored on data pages. An index may consist of several layers of pages, until the lowest level index page points directly to the data page and the rows they contain. A new index can be built by using the CREATE INDEX statement, or by using the SQL Server Manager application. When you first create your indexes, it is better to build the clustered index before the nonclustered index. This ensures that SQL will not have to do the work of sorting and resorting a nonclustered index while the clustered index is being created. The next few steps show you how an index is created:

1.   Open the SQL Enterprise Manager window and then expand the Databases, Inventory, Objects, Tables folders. Select the Products table and then right-click your mouse, displaying the shortcut menu. Select Indexes from the menu, displaying the Manage Indexes dialog box.

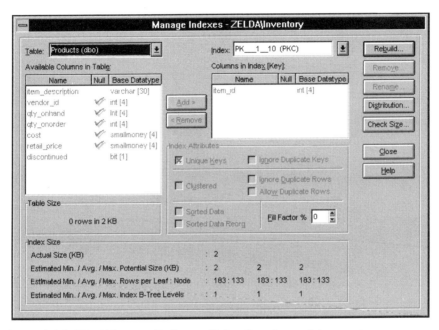

Figure 3.16: The Manage Indexes dialog box is used to create, remove, and edit indexes within the tables of your databases.

2.   Select (New Index) from the Index list box. This will clear the dialog box for a new index to be created. Type C_itemdescrip into the list box as the name for your new index.

3.   From the Available Columns In Table list box select the column item_description by clicking it once, then click the Add button to place the column name into the Columns In Index [Key] list box. Notice how the selected column is

removed from the first list box and placed into the second. This ensures that you don't accidentally try to use a column twice in a single index.

4.   In the Index Attributes box click the Clustered checkbox and then select the Allow Duplicate Rows button. This first option creates a clustered index, while the second allows the placement of duplicate values in the column such as, "#10 sheet metal screws."

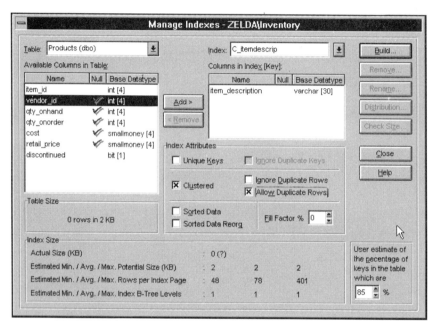

Figure 3.17: The Manage Indexes dialog box is now complete for the new index being created for this table.

5.   Now click the Build button. SQL Server will display another dialog box asking if you want to begin the build process now, schedule it later, or cancel the entire process. Click the Execute Now button to create the index. If the table contained rows of data, they would now be sorted and clustered together by the indexed column.

If you choose to build the index at a later time you will see another dialog box allowing you select a time and date to begin the process of building the index. If your database is currently being accessed by other users, it is suggested that you schedule this task for a time when the database is not normally being used.

6.   Click the Close button when you have built all of the indexes that you need at this time.

Once you have created a clustered index, SQL Server will not allow you to build another clustered index on the table unless you drop it first. Remember, the clustered index causes the rows of data to be physically sorted by the index order, so that like values are placed together.

Note

When you create a clustered index on a table be sure that you have the necessary free database space necessary. You will need approximately 120% of the table size in order to create a clustered index. This space enables the table and the index to both exist in the same database while it is being sorted.

Clustered Indexes

A clustered index means that the data in a table is physically stored in the index's order. There can be only one clustered index per table; after all, you can't force a table to physically order its rows on the disk by two different criteria. A clustered index may have several levels or leaves, with the last leaf being the data pages. Because a clustered index will usually have one or more less leaves than a nonclustered index it will tend to be faster. Figure 3.16 shows how a clustered index for finding a state can work.

With this clustered index on the state column, SQL Server creates the root page and stores a selected group of values and a set of pointers to the intermediate page, which in turn points to the beginning of each data page in the table. From there, SQL Server will scan the page to find the specific data requested. For example, to find the state "Iowa," SQL Server will look first at the root page and find that Iowa must exist between the values Alabama and Maine on the root page. Following the pointer for Alabama brings us to the intermediate page that begins with the value Alabama. Now scanning through this index page we find that Iowa is after the value Illinois. Following the pointer for Illinois to its data page, SQL Server now scans the data page and finds Iowa. Unlike scanning an entire table, scanning a single page at each step takes very little time.

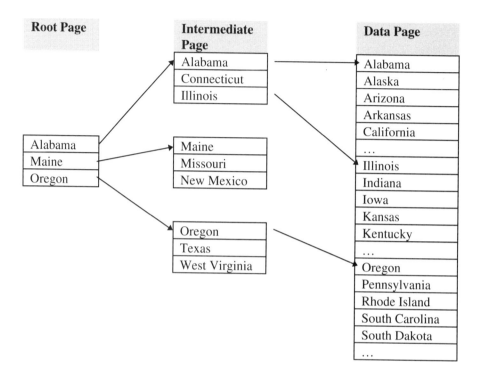

Figure 3.18: With a clustered index, SQL stores pointers that match the physical sort order of the data. The lowest index level leaf points to pages in the actual tables data pages.

Nonclustered Indexes

The nonclustered index adds an additional step or leaf in the process described above. An additional level of index is required for every row in the table to provide the necessary page pointers. Figure 3.19 shows how a nonclustered index works for finding cities in a table that is clustered by state names.

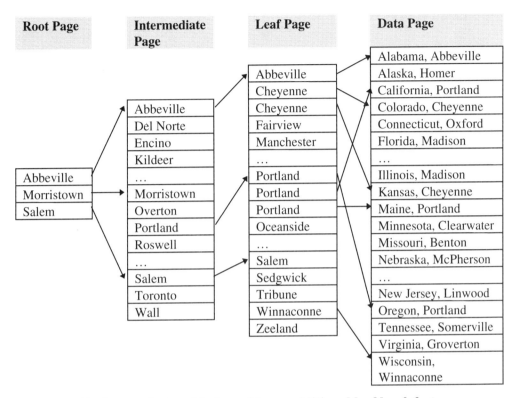

Figure 3.19: A non-clustered index adds an additional leaf level that keeps track of each individual row in a table and its row id.

Figure 3.19 shows how a nonclustered index on city name in a table which has a clustered index on the state name works. The Root Page is the highest level of the nonclustered index and contains only a relatively few entries. It is maintained in the table on its own index page and contains pointers to the first entry of each page in the Intermediate Page index level. This next level of the index has more entries and in turn pointers that point to the first item of each page in the Leaf Page index level. The Leaf Page index has one entry for every row in the table. As you add or delete rows in the table index entries are also added and deleted in the Leaf Page index. This level contains both an entry for each row in the table but also its row id which consists of both the page and row number for the row it points to.

Defaults

Instead of using a null value in a column, you can provide for a default value that will be automatically inserted if you do not specify a value for the column when inserting a new record. Default values are not retroactively applied to rows that already exist in a table. A default value is only inserted when you do not explicitly insert your own value, or null, into the column. Default values are often used for those columns which are often filled in with the same piece of data. For example, if 90% of your customers all live in the state of California, you may want to provide the State column with a default value of "CA." Then, whenever a new customer is entered into your database, SQL Server will automatically fill in the default value "CA" into the State column for this customer. The data entry clerk can override the default value whenever necessary.

Default values can be set when a table is created, or later by editing the table, or by using the CREATE DEFAULT statement. When you use the CREATE DEFAULT statement, you must also bind the default value specified to a specific column. This is a separate step and not done automatically.

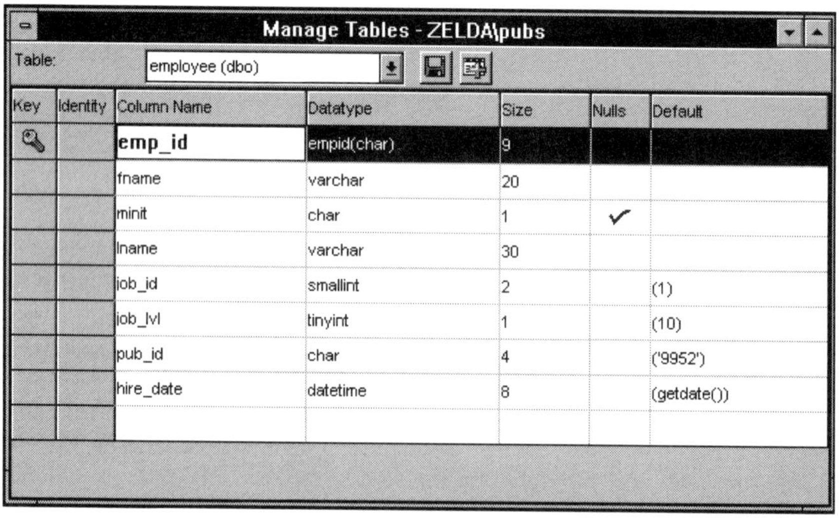

Key	Identity	Column Name	Datatype	Size	Nulls	Default
🔑		**emp_id**	empid(char)	9		
		fname	varchar	20		
		minit	char	1	✓	
		lname	varchar	30		
		job_id	smallint	2		(1)
		job_lvl	tinyint	1		(10)
		pub_id	char	4		('9952')
		hire_date	datetime	8		(getdate())

Table: employee (dbo) — Manage Tables - ZELDA\pubs

Figure 3.20: The employee table uses four default values as shown in the column labeled Default.

There are many uses for default values in a database. Whenever you have a table with a column which is often filled in with the same value, then set a default for the column using that value. Examples include: county, state, credit terms, or minimum hourly wage. You can probably think of many other uses for a default value, depending upon the database you may be using.

From the SQL Enterprise Manager window, open the employee table in the pubs database. As you can see here in figure 3.20, this table uses four default values.

The default values or expressions are shown in the Default column. Default values are entered enclosed within parentheses (). Notice how the various datatypes are entered; any type of number value is entered within the parentheses, while a char or varchar value will be entered enclosed in single quote marks within the parentheses. The column hire_date uses a different type of default value. The hire_date column uses datetime as a datatype and wants to have the current system date entered into this column. The expression **getdate()** is enclosed within the parentheses and tells SQL Server to go and fetch the current date on the servers system clock and enter that value into the column. A user adding a new employee to the table, can always override a default value by typing a different value into the column, if the have the appropriate permissions to do so.

You can easily create your own defaults by entering them into the Default column as you see in figure 3.20. Defaults created in this manner are T-SQL defaults and may not always work in another SQL database which is compatible only with ANSI-SQL.

The second method you can use to create a default value for a column is through the use of the CREATE DEFAULT statement. These defaults are ANSI-SQL defaults which you will be able to port to other ANSI-SQL compatible databases, and they are created in two steps:

1. Open the SQL Query Tool if you are in the SQL Enterprise Manager window, or open ISQL/w and type:

```
/* default publishers country value is "US" */
CREATE DEFAULT def_publ_country AS
'US'
```

This statement will create a default value of "US" for the country column, once you complete the process of binding the default to a column. If you were creating a default for a numeric datatype, or an expression, do not enclose the default value in quote marks.

2.   Execute this statement by clicking the Execute Query button.

3.   Now bind the default value to a specific table and column by using the stored procedure sp_bindefault like this:

> sp_bindefault def_publ_country, 'publishers.country'

Be sure that you surround the target, 'table_name.column_name' with single quote marks, otherwise SQL Server will assume that you are assigning this default to a user-defined datatype, and not to an existing table and column. Defaults created as shown above are ANSI-SQL defaults which you will be able to port them to other ANSI-SQL compatible databases.

Rules

Rules are used by SQL Server as a device for enforcing constraints on columns and user-defined datatypes. Rules help to ensure that the data entered into a table is consistent with the requirements of the database. A rule can be created that will ensure that only specific values can be entered into a column by restricting allowed values to a specified list of values from a table.

You can use any of the comparative operators that are allowed in a WHERE clause, but you must use an operator that is allowed with the datatype of the column for which you are creating the rule. For example, you can't use a LIKE operator with a numeric datatype.

There are limits to the functions that you can use when applying a rule. Rules can only deal with constant values, SQL Server functions, and edit masks. Rules are applied to data before an INSERT or an UPDATE. This allows SQL Server to check the data against the rules before actually inserting the new data or updating existing data. If the new information doesn't meet the rules, SQL Server will display a message telling you so.

Just like default values, rules can be created using the CREATE RULE statement or in the SQL Enterprise Manager window. Follow these steps to create a rule:

1. Open the SQL Enterprise Manager window and then expand the pubs database, then Objects, finally selecting Rules. Right-click on the Rules object and select New Rule from the shortcut menu, opening the Manager Rules dialog box.

2. Type **ssan** in the Rule list box as the name for the rule to be created. In the Description box type the following:

    @ssan like '[0-9][0-9][0-9]-[0-9][0-9]-[0-9][0-9][0-9][0-9]'

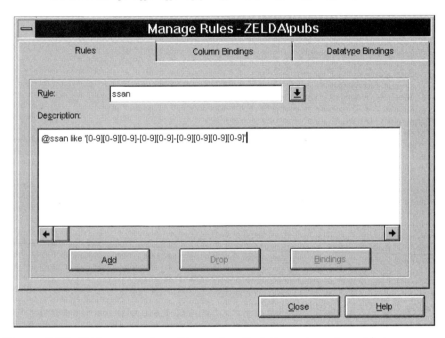

Figure 3.21: This new rule will require that the entry placed into a column is in the format for a U.S. social security number.

This rule will require the user to enter a series of three numbers followed by a dash, two more numbers, another dash and then four numbers. Any other entry will not be ruled as a valid entry and the INSERT or UPDATE will fail.

3.   Check the Add button to add this new rule into the list of rules for this database.

4.   Click the Column Bindings tab. If you want to select a different table to bind this rule, you will select one from the Tables list box. In this case the authors table is

the one we want. Click the button on the list box beside the column name au-id. You will see a list of rules from which you can select, and the (none) option. Click on the rule ssan(dbo) as the rule to be bound to this column, and then click on the **B**ind button to perform the bind function. This performs the same action that would be done if you use sp_bindrule function.

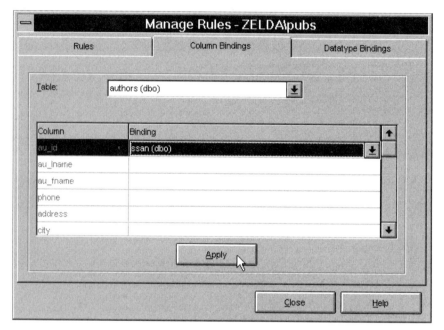

Figure 3.22: The ssan rule is now bound to the au_id column in the authors table, and will require the user to enter an authors ID number in a standard social security format.

5.   Click the **C**lose button, closing the Manage Rules dialog box. You will see the new rule listed underneath the Rules objects in the tree listing.

Triggers

Triggers are special objects that automatically activate when a specified condition is met. When the condition for the trigger is met, the trigger fires and the actions required by the trigger are performed. Triggers are most often used for enforcing complex referential integrity requirements that can not be met by using a set of simple constraints. Remember, constraints act on the table that they are attached to, while a trigger may be activated by the action of a single table, but can act across many tables, other databases, and even other servers. Triggers can be created that will execute a DLL within Windows NT, which in turn can access data from other programs, or pass information to other programs.

One example of a trigger is the ability to cascade updates and deletes of primary keys. For example, you have a vendor ID that is created from a combination of zip code and company name, and one of your vendors moves to a new location. The company name probably doesn't change, but the zip code very likely does. You can use a trigger to automatically perform a cascade update that will change the information in all tables that reference the vendor ID for the particular vendor so that they now reference the new vendor ID code. Using a trigger for this operation is much simpler than requiring a data entry operator to manually go through all of the tables in the database searching for each occurrence of the old vendor ID and update them—very likely missing one or more.

Each table can support a maximum of three triggers: one each for INSERT, UPDATE, and DELETE statements. A single trigger can support one or more statements, but you can only associate one trigger with each. Whenever a condition is met that fires a trigger, it is only fired one time for every statement that calls it. This means that if your statement modifies multiple rows of data, you must ensure that your trigger will act upon all the modified rows and not just simply the first or the last. A trigger can execute many functions and can be nested up to 16 deep. This means, that trigger1 can call trigger2, which in turn can call trigger3, and so forth, with trigger15 finally calling trigger16. The trigger can be constructed such that if all of the actions required by the trigger are not met, then the trigger will rollback the transaction. Be sure any trigger you create that rolls back a transaction sends an error to the user so they know the transaction was not processed.

There are several SQL statements that cannot to be used within a trigger:

- CREATE statements, including the creation of temporary tables.
- All ALTER table, and ALTER database statements
- SELECT INTO statements
- All DROP statements
- TRUNCATE table statements
- UPDATE STATISTICS statements

- GRANT and REVOKE permissions statements
- LOAD database and transaction statements
- RECONFIGURE any object statements
- DISK INIT, MIRROR, REINT, REFIT, REMIRROR, and UNMIRROR statements

Two special tables are used by triggers: *inserted* and *deleted* tables. These tables are views of the transaction log and are available only for the duration of the trigger. Once the trigger has completed its actions, these views no longer exist. A trigger that contains an INSERT statement stores the rows that are inserted into the table in the *inserted* table, while a DELETE statement stores the rows that are being deleted in the *deleted* table. An UPDATE statement acts if it is a DELETE statement followed by an INSERT statement. Triggers can use the inserted and deleted tables to determine if and how they should proceed with an action.

Triggers, like other database objects require a name, the table to which it will be attached, and the actions that will activate it. Triggers can be created by using the CREATE TRIGGER statement, or from within the SQL Enterprise Manager window. Only the database owner or the system administrator can create or drop a trigger, and these permissions cannot be granted to others. Create a simple trigger that will perform a cascade delete from the titles table to the titleauthor table by following these steps:

1.   Open the SQL Enterprise Manager window and select **M**anage, **T**riggers from the menu. You will see the Manage Triggers window displayed.

2.   Select the titles table from the Tables list box, and then type:

```
create trigger delete_titles on titles
for delete
as

if @ @rowcount = 0
return

/* cascade delete from titles to titleauthor table */
delete titleauthor
from titleauthor t, deleted d
where t.title_id = d.title_id
```

```
if @@error !=0
begin
print "Error occurred in deletion in related tables"
rollback tran
end

return
```

Some things to note about this trigger include:

The first part of the statement creates the trigger, specifying the table to which it is attached and on what it will trigger—delete, insert, or update.

The next part of the statement checks to see if any rows were altered. Remember, the trigger fires even if data was not altered, or deleted. With this statement if @@rowcount is equal to 0(zero), then the next action, return, is executed and the trigger action terminates. Otherwise, the trigger continues to the next statement.

The meat of the trigger tells it what to do. In this case to look at both the titleauthor and deleted tables, and if a value for title_id in the deleted table exists in the titleauthor table, then delete the corresponding row in the titleauthor table.

The final statements are used to trap errors that may occur. If SQL Server is not able to delete a row from the titleauthor table, then it will return the error message "Error occurred in deletion in related tables," and rollback the transaction. Remember, a trigger is fired from within a transaction. This means that the entire transaction, the deletion of a row in the titleauthor table, and the first part of the transaction when a row was deleted from titles are all rolled back.

3.   Click the Execute button to save the new trigger and bind it to the titles table.

Note

This trigger does not check for any dependencies that may exist between tables. Additional code will have to be written to affect all of the tables that reference the title_id column.

Stored Procedures

Stored procedures are database objects that are independent of individual tables, unlike triggers. They are a precompiled set of T-SQL statements, and can be built to use parameters passed to them, or to return status, rows, or output arguments back to the client who called the procedure. Stored procedures can call other procedures, or even themselves again, creating very complex systems. The stored procedure can add significant enhancements to your application.

SQL Server has many stored procedures already installed. All system stored procedures begin with **sp_** as the first part of its name. These system stored procedures are stored in the master database and are owned by the system administrator. Some of these procedures can be run from within other databases. When called from a database other than master, they will act on the tables of the calling database.

Another type of stored procedure is an *extended* stored procedure, some of which are also installed with SQL Server. Extended stored procedures are compiled within a dynamic-link library (DLL) file and are called and used in the same manner that any other stored procedure is used. Extended stored procedures can be used to call for and return information from a remote server, all the while being completely transparent to the client.

One reason to create and use stored procedures is that you can improve overall system performance by reducing the network traffic. The client calls to a stored procedure on the server and may pass some additional parameters that are required by the stored procedure. The SQL Server in turn runs the compiled version of the SQL statements and passes the answer or other information back to the client. Instead of having many SQL statements passing back and forth over the network, only the original call along with any parameters, and the results are passed over the network cable.

Stored procedures are called by name. If you do not use the stored procedures name as the first word in a SQL statement, you must proceed it with the keyword **execute**. Writing a stored procedure is a simple process that requires you to give the procedure a unique name, and then to write the SQL statements that are the heart of the stored procedure. These next few steps show you how to build a stored procedure that returns a results set displaying authors and the titles they have written:

1.	Open the SQL Enterprise Manager window, and then select **M**anage from the menu, and Stored **P**rocedures from the drop-down menu. You can also select Objects from the database in which you want to create the new stored procedure and right-click on it. You will see a shortcut menu; select the option, New **S**tored Procedure to see the Manage Stored Procedures window. From this window you will create new procedures and edit existing ones. You can of course, also use the ISQL/w program.

2.	Be sure that <New> is selected in the Procedures list box. Replace <PROCEDURE NAME> with the name for your new procedure, type au_pub_titles as the name for this procedure. The first line will now read:

```
CREATE PROCEDURE au_pub_titles AS
```

3.	Now move the cursor to the end of the line, press the Enter key to begin a new line, and type:

```
SELECT a.au_lname, t.title, p.pub_name
FROM authors a, titleauthor ta, titles t, publishers p
WHERE a.au_id = ta.au_id
AND ta.title_id = t.title_id
AND t.pub_id = p.pub_id
RETURN
```

4.	Click the Execute button. SQL Server will create the new stored procedure.

This stored procedure does not contain any that which require parameters to be filled in. When you do include such variables you must declare the datatype for the parameter. You can use any of the standard datatypes or any user-defined datatypes if they exist within the database where the stored procedure is created. A simple stored procedure as shown here contains the single parameter @au_lname.

```
CREATE PROC titles_by_author
(@au_lname varchar(40))
AS
SELECT a.au_lname, t.title
FROM authors a, titleauthor ta, titles t
WHERE a.au_id = ta.au_id
AND ta.title_id = t.title_id
AND au_lname LIKE @au_lname
RETURN
```

This stored procedure returns a results set that displays all books by the selected author, along with their last name. Using ISQL/w this stored procedure would be called like this:

titles_by_author *authors_last_name*

Simply include the last name of the author for whom you want to see a listing of titles as the parameter.

Identifiers

Defining the rules and conventions for identifiers, also simply called *names*, is one of the most important jobs you will have as you create your database schema. Consistency throughout the company database and across servers is very important. By using a consistent naming scheme, you will help to ensure that the foundation used to build your client/server structure will hold together. You want someone who is defining a new database object to be able to easily determine what name to use for the new object, while also ensuring that another user who accesses the object should be able to determine what is stored in it, or what function it will perform.

However you decide to enforce naming standards within your organization, be sure they are consistent across the entire organization. One of the things that you will have to determine is whether to use all uppercase, all lowercase, or mixed-case letters in naming schemes. And whether to use underscores between words, as in *customer_address* or if a mixed case convention is better, like *CustomerAddress*. Whatever you and your company decide, be consistent.

Identifiers define the conventions used to name the objects used in SQL Server, such as servers, databases, tables, views, indexes, procedures, triggers, and variables. There are several rules that SQL Server places on naming conventions, and then there are the business rules that you may apply to your own database. The rules that SQL Server places on identifiers are conventions that it requires you to use. You should also set your own naming conventions to be used within your own database.

Rules

SQL Serverhas several rules which are you are required to follow as you create names for the objects that you create, the servers that you set up and for any databases you create within a server. The basic rules include the following:

- Names are limited to maximum of 30 characters

- The owner of the database can use a name once per object. For example, a single database owner can not have a stored procedure named min_qty_onhand and at the same time have a constraint also named min_qty_onhand.

- The first character of a name can be any alphabetic character (a-z or A-Z) or the symbols; @ (at sign), _ (underscore), or # (pound sign). After the first character, you can use any letters, numbers, or the symbols $, #, _.

- The reserved symbols; @ and # have specialized meanings when used as the first character of an identifier: the @ symbol denotes a variable, as you learned in the previous section on stored procedures, while the # symbol means that the named object is a temporary object. An object that begins with a double pound sign "##" is a global temporary object.

- Embedded spaces are not allowed within an identifier, except under the rules of a quoted identifier, which is discussed later in this section.

You should limit the name of a temporary object to a maximum of 13 characters. SQL Server adds an internal numeric suffix to all temporary objects.

In addition to the rules required by SQL Server, you should consider some additional rules as you set your naming schemes for a production database:

- Do not use a database name for a table name, nor a table name for a column name. While these are strictly legal in SQL Server, it is not good practice.

- Do not use SQL Server reserved words as a name.

- When naming databases, be sure that your naming scheme can be used by the front-end client. For example, if you have many DOS-based clients the naming scheme should be no longer than eight characters so that it will easily map to the client.

- Keep database names short, but descriptive. The name should be descriptive enough that a user or programmer can tell which object they should be using, and not have to consult an object dictionary.

- Standardize your naming schemes. SQL Server is case-sensitive when naming databases.

- Do not use special or hard to type characters in a name. After all, you don't want your users or programmers to think about burning you in effigy every time they have to twist their fingers around the keyboard to enter a database name.

As Object Names

Each owner of an object, can use a name only once per object, but different owners can use the same object names within the same database. For example, Erik and Casey both have access to the CustomerDB database which is located on the server ZELDA, and have the ability to create new tables within this database. Both Erik and Casey can each create a table named *customer_tbl*. When an object's name is completely qualified it consists of:

[[[server].database].owner].object

This results in two objects which may appear to have the same name at the lowest level but actually have unique names:

ZELDA.CustomerDB.Casey.customer_tbl
ZELDA.CustomerDB.Erik.customer_tbl

Those parts of the fully qualified name in the first example, which are displayed within the brackets are optional. SQL Server assumes that the default value for owner is the current user, the default value for database is the current database, and the current value for server is the current server. This allows Erik to create a table with the same name that Casey used because the owner name will be different, creating a different qualified name. But if Casey, who is logged into the server ZELDA and into the CustomerDB, wants to access Erik's customer_tbl table, she would have to qualify the table name to *Erik.customer_tbl*. She must of course have already been granted permission by Erik as the table's owner to use his table.

Quoted Identifiers

The use of quoted identifiers is a feature that was added to Microsoft SQL Server 6.0, aligning its feature set more closely with the current ANSI standards. When using quoted identifiers, use double quotation marks (") to delimit keywords within a name—this is called a quoted identifier. While this is acceptable usage as far as the SQL Server's parser is concerned, it is not good practice. Whenever possible, if an object name uses a keyword, reserved word, or standard database terminology that may possibly become a keyword, try finding another word or term that can be used as the identifier. If this is not possible, then use the quoted identifier. A quoted identifier can be used as follows:

```
CREATE VIEW "view"
(au_lname, au_fname, phone)
AS
SELECT au_lname, au_fname, phone
FROM authors
```

Because the keyword *view* is reserved by SQL Server, you must enclose it within the double quotation marks in order to use it as an identifier, hence the name *quoted identifier*.

By using the SET command, you can turn SQL Server's ability to use a quoted identifier on or off. By default this setting is on, and you can then use a quoted identifier. If you turn it off, then SQL Server will not be able to see an object that uses a quoted identifier as a name. The above example will fail if you have not turned quoted identifiers on. The SET command must be used at the beginning of each SQL Server session, which will require access to objects that use quoted identifiers. The SET command is used as shown in this example:

```
SET QUOTED_IDENTIFIER on
go
CREATE VIEW "view"
(au_lname, au_fname, phone)
AS
SELECT au_lname, au_fname, phone
FROM authors
go
SET QUOTED_IDENTIFIER off
go
```

You can also use quoted identifiers on standard names, without setting QUOTED_IDENTIFIER to on. For example, you can create a table "Employee" and then refer to it as either "Employee" or Employee. If you set QUOTED_IDENTIFIER to on and create the table "Employee" with the double quote marks, you must then always turn QUOTED_IDENTIFIER to on, and use the table name "Employee" when referring or using the table.

In either case, creating an object name with QUOTED_IDENTIFIER set to on requires that you turn QUOTED_IDENTIFIER to on for every session when you will be accessing these objects. If you do not, SQL Server will simply display an error message telling you that you have not used the correct syntax near the object name. In other words, the object can not be found or accessed without first turning QUOTED_IDENTIFIERS to on.

Database Sizing

Determining the size of a database is one of the most difficult tasks you may be assigned. Invariably, the ultimate size of a database will be larger than originally estimated. The default size of all new databases is 2MB, which is the default size of the *model* database. The *model* database is one of the databases created by the Setup program when you first install SQL Server. Each time that you execute a CREATE DATABASE statement, SQL Server copies the model database and gives it the name that you specify in the CREATE statement.

SQL Server uses three units when designating storage for data objects:

- A *page*, which is equal to 2KB.
- An *extent*, which is eight continuous pages.
- An *allocation unit*, which is equal to 32 extents or 256 pages.

Remember, it is much easier to increase the size of a database than it is to decrease it. It is commonly accepted practice to start with a smaller database and increase its size as necessary. The easiest method of changing the size of a database is to use the SQL Enterprise Manager window. Follow these steps to adjust the size of a database:

1.   Open the SQL Enterprise Manager window, and then the Manage Database window. Remember, the Manage Database window can be opened by either:

- Selecting **M**anage, **D**atabases from the menu, or
- Right-clicking on the Databases icon and selecting **E**dit from the shortcut menu.

2.   Select the database whose size you want to change from the list on the Y-axis of the graph. A dotted-line box will surround the selected database name.

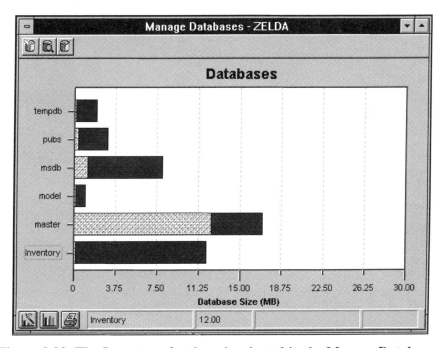

Figure 3.23: The Inventory database is selected in the Manage Database window.

3.   Click the Edit Database button to display the Edit Database dialog box. Click the **E**xpand button on the Database tab to increase the size of the Inventory database. To decrease the size of the selected database, you would click on the **S**hrink button.

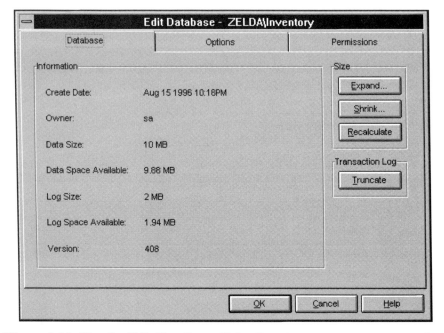

Figure 3.24: Use the Edit Database dialog box to reset many aspects of the selected database, including its size.

4.   The Expand Database dialog box is now displayed. Use the **D**ata Device list box to choose the specific database device on which you want to expand the Inventory database, in this case select dataDB. The maximum by which you can increase the database Inventory on this device is now displayed in the **S**ize(MB) box and is 20MB. Enter 10 as the number of additional megabytes to be added to the Inventory database. You can also expand the size of the transaction log by selecting and changing the options in the **L**og Device and **S**ize text boxes.

If you are using the default Windows NT colors, you will see the used space on each device displayed in blue, while available space is shown in red. The Inventory database is located on the master device by default. Selecting master in the **D**ata Device list box causes a number to be displayed in the **S**ize(MB) box. This is the maximum amount of space by which you can expand the Inventory database on the selected device. Remember, this number is the maximum amount of additional space to be added to the database, not the final size of the database. If you need more space you will need to choose a different database device. You are not required to keep a database on a single database device, but you can not add space to a database on more than one device at a time using this dialog box. Notice that when you select a device

86

and choose the space to be used, that SQL Server blocks that space out in green on the graph bar.

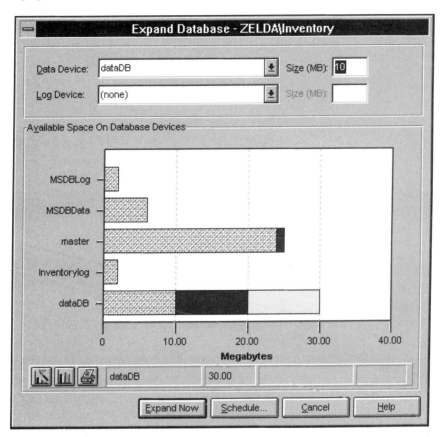

Figure 3.25: Use the Expand Database dialog box to increase the size of a selected database. You must choose the database device and how many megabytes to increase the size of the database.

4.   Click the **OK** button to save the changes you have made. You will be returned to the Edit Databases dialog box. Microsoft SQL Server will automatically recalculate the Data Size and Data Space Available figures. Click the **OK** button to complete the expansion of the Inventory database, and then close the Manage Database window.

Pages

A page is the smallest of the three units of storage used by SQL Server, and is 2KB in size. SQL Server makes use of five types of pages:

- Data or log pages. These pages are used to store the data contained in tables.

- Index pages are used to store index values.

- Text and images are stored on special pages. The data page contains a pointer, which links the page to a variable number of text/image pages that contain the actual data.

- The allocation page is the first page in each allocation unit. This page describes how the remaining 255 pages are used.

- Distribution pages contain a sample of data values contained in the table. SQL Server uses these values to determine which index to use with a query.

Each database is divided into 2KB pages, each page is assigned a logical page number beginning with 0 and increasing sequentially to the final page. This page number is part of each row ID number.

Extents

Each extent is made up of eight continuous pages, and 32 extents make up each allocation unit. This is the smallest unit in which a database can be divided. When a new table is created, it is first assigned one extent, or eight pages of space. As rows are added to the table, additional extents are also added to the table.

Allocation Units

Allocation units are the smallest unit by which a database can be created. The allocation unit consists of 256 continuous 2KB pages, which in turn equals to 512KB or ½MB in size. The first allocation page is logical page number 0, the next being logical page number 256. Each subsequent allocation page will be some multiple of 256.

System Catalog

Every DBMS system uses one or more data catalogs (also known as dictionaries), which are used to record information about the various databases, and all of the objects within them. This catalog is actually a database about the database. These tables are automatically created when you create the database, and are not normally visible to the user. SQL Server uses these tables to keep information about the database, its tables and other objects, and the users who have access to the database and its objects. These tables are maintained by SQL Server and should not be moved or edited by a user or database owner. Doing so may cause the database to become inaccessible.

The primary system catalog resides in the master database, and is most often referred to as the *system catalog*. This master catalog contains 13 tables which are unique to it. This system catalog's tables contain information of global concern to all of the other databases. This includes information about user logins, current system configuration, allocation and mapping of physical storage, and many other distinct pieces of data.

Each database also contains a subset of the system catalog, often referred to as the *data catalog*. This data catalog contains 18 tables. These tables contain information about the specific database in which they reside, and are concerned with items such as replication data, names and properties for each column of every table, information about constraints, and all of the other information that makes this a unique database. Whenever you create a new database, the data catalog is copied from the model database.

Summary

In this chapter, you have become familiar with the different types of objects used in an SQL Server database. Specifically, you have learned:

- How to create and edit a database device and backup device.

- How to create and edit databases. You have also learned to create and edit tables and views within these databases.

- The concepts of using, adding and changing indexes, and about the some of the different types of indexes used within SQL Server.

- How to create identifiers, or names, for the many objects that you use in SQL Server.

- Finally, you learned how to size a database, and then to later change the size of an existing database.

Chapter 4

Microsoft SQL Server Structures

IN THIS CHAPTER

- Server Architecture
- Processes
- Files

This chapter introduces you to the Microsoft SQL Server database structures and how they work together. Several topics will be considered throughout this chapter, including server architecture, single versus multiprocess databases, file usage, and buffers.

Server Architecture

Windows NT is Microsoft's first true application server. Windows NT, is a true 32-bit operating system, and including such features as preemptive scheduling, protected memory spaces, kernel-based architecture, and support for symmetric multiprocessing (SMP). SQL Server works through the native Windows NT architecture, enabling it to work on all platforms that are supported by Windows NT.

In this section, you will learn about several of the database files and devices that are created when you install Microsoft SQL Server. These are known collectively as system devices. A device is an operating system file and it contains one or more databases. SQL Server creates two types of devices: database devices and backup devices. A database device contains databases, whereas the backup, or dump device contains backups of databases.

Database Devices

A database device is a file in which you place databases and database objects. Whenever you create a new database, you place it in one or more database devices. If you have a very large database, you can allow it to span several database devices. Simple growth of a database can force you to expand its size, and if the database device is nearly full, you will have to use or create space on a different device.

When you install Microsoft SQL Server, the setup program creates three database devices: master, MSDBData, and MSDBLog. The master database device is located in the physical file MASTER.DAT, and this is where you will find the databases *master*, *model*, *pubs*, and *tempdb*. Setup also places the database *msdb* on the MSDBData device and the transaction log for *msdb* on the MSDBLog device, with filenames MSDB.DAT and MSDBLOG.DAT respectively.

Setup installs these files with the following default settings:

- The file MASTER.DAT is installed on your "C" drive by default. You can change this setting to a different drive during the setup procedure.

- Setup creates and uses the directory \MSSQL\DATA as the default path for the master device. You can also change this to a different directory.

- The directory and filename conform to the standard FAT 8.3 naming convention, even if you install the files on a NTFS drive volume. This helps to ensure compatibility with DOS-based operating systems.

- The default size of the master device is 25MB. You may want to increase this setting during the setup procedure to save yourself additional time later, if you have the necessary disk space. The only reason to increase the size of the master device now is if you will be creating a very large production database system with many tables and users, and each of these take up a row in several of the system tables located in the master database. You can always increase the size of the device later.

It is generally not good practice to use the master, MSDBData and MSDBLog database devices for *user* databases and objects. Create new database devices for user objects to be placed in. It is highly suggested that you remove the default setting from the master device, as was discussed in the previous chapter. This will ensure that a user does not accidentally place new objects on the master database device. When you create the database device for your users' application, enable the default setting for this device. You can require that users will automatically login to their default database and device, (see Chapter 3 for a detailed explanation of this procedure).

Backup Devices

Beginning with SQL Server version 6.5, dump devices are now called backup devices on the SQL Enterprise Manager tree, but the same commands and procedures that you may have used with version 6.0 still work. Backup or dump devices are used by SQL Server to store backups of both database and transaction log files.

When you install SQL Server, one backup device is automatically created, called diskdump. This is a disk-based backup device, and will be located at \MSSQL\BACKUP. When you perform your first backup, initializing the dump device, a new file, diskdump.DAT will be created. SQL Server will place all of your backups in this file. You can create additional backup devices and use a variety of media types, including disk, diskette, tape, optical drives, and removable media.

New backup devices can be created by following these steps:

1.   From the SQL Enterprise Manager window, select Backup Devices from the tree, and click the right mouse button, displaying a shortcut menu. Choose **New** Backup Device from the shortcut menu.

2.   By using the New Backup Device dialog box, you can create either a disk- or tape-based backup device. Type diskdump2 into the **N**ame text box. See how this name is appended to the location path in the text box below. The backup device name, like all other SQL Server objects, does not have to be an 8.3 format name, but it does have to meet SQL Server's rules for identifiers. If you are not sure of the path for your backup device, simply click on the Locate button (**...**) to the right of the **L**ocation text box. You can then use the Backup Device Location dialog box to select the path through a directory tree structure.

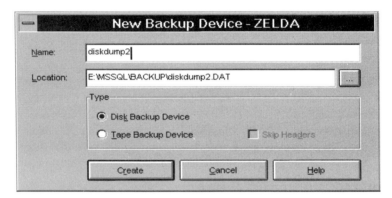

Figure 4.1: Create a backup device using the New Backup Device dialog box. Backup device names can be no longer than 30 characters.

3.   Click on the Create button and SQL Server will add the new device to the other Backup Devices shown in the SQL Enterprise Manager tree.

You will learn to use the backup and restore options in Chapter 11. A backup device can be created for a 5.25- or 3.5-inch diskette drive using the stored procedure sp_addumpdevice. When creating a tape backup device, the tape drive must already exist on the local machine. SQL Server does not support a networked tape device, but does support a networked disk device. If your only tape drive is located on a different computer than SQL Server, you can backup your data to a disk-based backup device and then copy the backup to the tape device during your normal backup schedule.

94

Processes

The Windows NT/SQL Server combination is a single-process, multithreaded database system, unlike many of the earlier client/server incarnations, which were multiprocess servers. There may be many different processes being run at any one time. A process can be either running or sleeping, and come in two varieties: client and server. Client processes are those which have been started from a client system, such as a query. A server process is most often an internal SQL Server process. With SQL Server 6.5, additional columns have been added to the *sysprocesses* table. This table contains information about processes that are currently running, or which have been run. The process which are currently being run can be viewed in the Current Activity window. From the SQL Enterprise Manager window, click the Current Activity button, or select **S**erver, **C**urrent Activity from the menu to view the current processes. Figure 4.2 shows the User Activity processes currently being run.

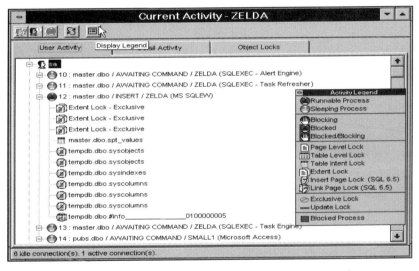

Figure 4.2: See several processes are running. Currently only one processes is runnable, while the rest are in a sleeping mode.

Each time a user logs into the server, a new client process is started. This process is automatically logged into the *sysprocesses* table, and will be displayed in the Current Activity window. The server can stop, or kill, a client process at any time. This may be necessary if a client process has blocked another process, and for some reason it can not be terminated at the client end.

When a client logs into SQL Server, it is assigned a Process ID, viewable in the Current Activity's Detail Activity tab. You can see the database to which the process is logged, the user name of the individual who is logged in, the computer from which they logged in, and whether the process is blocked and by which process it is blocked by. This final bit of information can be extremely valuable when deciding if a process needs to be killed. Long-running transactions may need to be terminated if they are preventing the transaction log from being truncated—potentially causing it to become full and so stopping all transactions from continuing.

A process that needs to be terminated, or killed, can be killed only by the system administrator. The kill command can not be transferred to another user. You can use either the kill statement, or use the kill button in the Current Activity dialog box to terminate a process. To kill a process using the kill statement, follow these steps:

1.   Determine the system process ID (spid) number of the process that you want to terminate, by executing the stored procedure sp_who. Open the ISQL/w application, selecting the master database and type **sp_who**, and click the Execute Query button.

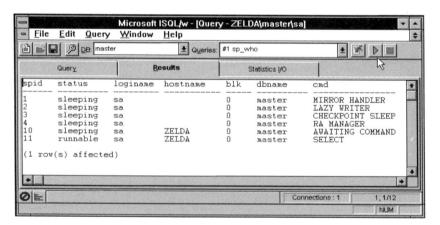

Figure 4.3: The results set for the sp_who statement. Notice the spid numbers located in the first column.

The stored procedure **sp_who** displays a results set that shows you several useful pieces of information. The first is all of the system process IDs currently open, and what their current status is—sleeping or runnable. The next two columns show who is logged to the process, and from what station the process is being run. The next column—blk—now displays the number 0 for all processes. If a process was blocking another process for continuing, its spid number would be displayed in this column on the row which is being blocked. For example, if spid 11 was being blocked by spid 10, then the number 10 would be displayed in the blk column for spid 11. If you, as system administrator, determined that spid 10 was a user process, such as an uncommitted transaction that had failed for some reason, you could terminate the process and allow spid 11 to continue.

2.   Click the Query tab and type **KILL 10**, in order to kill the process with ID number 10. If you are successful, you will see a message telling you that no rows were returned.

Follow these steps to kill a process from within the SQL Server Enterprise Manger application:

1.   Open the Current Activity window by clicking the Current Activity button, or selecting **Server, Current** Activity from the menu.

2.   You can terminate a process from any of the tabs, but the User Activity and Detail Activity are the more useful of the three. Select the process in the window and click the Kill Process button. A confirmation dialog box will be displayed, click the **Y**es button to kill the process, or the **No** button to stop the kill process and return to the Current Activity window.

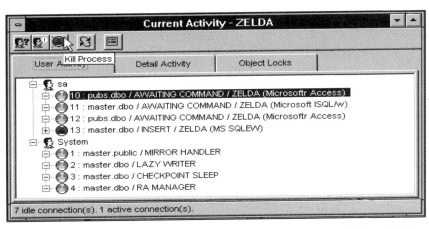

Figure 4.4: A process about to be killed in the Current Activity window.

There are several processes that can not be terminated by using the KILL statement or the Kill Process button in the Current Activity window. System processes such as

Mirror Handler, Lazy Writer, Checkpoint Sleep, and RA Manager, and any process running an extended stored procedure, can not be terminated.

Files

When the setup program is run, it creates a several databases on each of the three database devices that it creates. Each of these databases, except pubs, is required for the successful running of SQL Server. As you have learned earlier, database files can be locked at various levels, and can be either exclusive or shared. A shared lock is a read-only lock—while a transaction is being written to a table, the lock is escalated to an exclusive lock. Locks can be held on an entire table, or a part of a table. Table locks can be either an extent or a page. With SQL Server 6.5, row-level locks can be established for insert commands, whereas all other commands use page locks.

master Database

The master database is where all of the primary system tables reside. This is a required database, and also contains both stored procedures and extended stored procedures. There are thirteen tables that are unique to the master database. These tables include:

- syscharsets   This table has one row for every character set and sort order that has been defined for use with SQL Server.

- sysconfigures   This table has one row for each configuration option that can be set by an individual user.

- syscurconfigs   This table is similar to the sysconfigures table except that it contains only the current values, and also holds four entries describing the configuration structure. This table is built when queried by a user.

- sysdatabases   This table has one row for each database on SQL Server. The information includes data about the database's name, its owner, current status, and other information that can be used to recover a database.

- sysdevices   This table includes one row for each device installed on SQL Server. This encompasses all backup and database devices.

- syslanguages   This table contains a row for each language that is known to Microsoft SQL Server Server. If you are using U.S. English as the only language, then this table will be blank, as SQL Server always has this language available to it.

- syslocks   This table is created dynamically as required, and only exists in memory. All information about current locks held on tables is stored in this table. If the server goes down for any reason, all locks are automatically released.

- syslogins   This table contains one row for every authorized SQL Server user account.

- sysmessages   This table contains a row for each error or warning message that will be displayed by SQL Server. These error messages are displayed on the users screen.

- sysprocesses   This table contains information about both client and server processes currently running on SQL Server.

- sysremotelogins   This table has one row for each user logging in from a remote server, with permission to call stored procedures on this server.

- sysservers   This table contains a row for each server on which this server can call remote stored procedures.

- sysusages   This table has a row for each part of a disk allocated to a database.

model Database

The model database is created by the setup program and placed on the master database device along with the master database. This database is used by SQL Server as a pattern on which all new user databases are based. Whenever a new database is created, SQL Server copies the model and expands it to the size specified in the CREATE statement. A new database can always be larger than the model, but it can never be smaller.

The model database contains all of the system tables that are required for every user database. You can customize the model database so that it will include objects that you want to have as part of every table. Remember, if you make a change to the model database, every new database created after saving this change will incorporate these same modifications, so be sure that this is something that you want with every database and not just a modification necessary for a single database. Some commonly added objects that you may want to place in the model database are:

- Logins for users who are to be given access to all new databases.

- Custom user-defined datatypes, rules, defaults, constraints, and stored procedures.

- Default permissions for guest login accounts.

- Base tables used in all production databases.

It is highly recommended that you create and add all of the above options necessary to your own databases, to your model database before you begin to create new user databases. This will ensure that they all have the appropriate customized objects, and you will not have to go back, rechecking and adding objects to databases created earlier.

msdb Database

The msdb database is created by the setup program and is used by SQL Server as a storage place for task scheduling, event handling, alert notifications and, new with SQL Server 6.5, a place to record all backup and restore events. Backup and restore information is recorded even when a third party program is used to accomplish the task.

The msdb database is at the core of the SQL Server task scheduling center. In addition to logging backup and restore events, this database also logs all exception reports. If a problem occurs, it is the msdb database that checks the problem and notifies an operator of the problem. Windows NT can notify an operator of a problem or possible problem via e-mail or by pager. For a server with a 7X24 uptime requirement, the ability of the server to notify someone of a potential problem can be a lifesaver.

pubs Database

This is the sample database on which most of the examples used in the Microsoft SQL Server documentation are drawn from. You will also see the pubs database referred to in almost every book and article you may read about SQL Server. The setup program places the pubs database on the master database device.

You can use the pubs database as a training tool for new users or those users who want to gain more experience with various aspects of SQL Server without using live data. Many objects can be tested using the various tables contained in the pubs database.

The pubs database is not a required database and can be dropped if no longer needed. If you plan to use the pubs database as a learning tool, make a complete backup of the pubs database when you first install SQL Server. Then later, when the next user is in the training program, they can use a fresh copy of pubs.

Transaction Log Files

The SQL Server transaction log is one of the most important aspects of a DBMS that you will use. SQL Server uses a *write-ahead* log, which means that all transactions are written to the log before they are written to the database itself. This helps to ensure that the transaction logs can be used to recover the database. Each database has its own transaction log, which is a specialized system table named *syslogs*. It contains a serial listing of all modifications to all objects in the database, and is shared by all users of the database. The transaction log should always be kept on a separate device from your data files. This can help in two ways: dumps are easier to accomplish, and more importantly, if the database device which contains the data files goes down, the transaction log will remain intact.

You must ensure that the transaction logs are dumped on a regular basis, and that the log is of an adequate size for the number and size of the transactions performed in your databases. If a transaction log fills up, all further update, delete, and insert activity in any of the databases comes to a halt. A transaction log can fill up on any database, even the master or tempdb. The space required to keep a log file complete for modifications to a database can be substantial. This is due both to the overhead inherent in the logging procedure, and the data to be logged. When you first create your database, you must specify a size for it. This size figure can be very difficult to estimate at first, causing new administrators to often use a simple percentage of the database size, such as 10 or 25%. If you have enough experience with your data, you may be able to create some tests of the data to give you a more reliable number for the size of your transaction logs.

The data written to the transaction logs is automatically written to the database when a *checkpoint* is encountered. A checkpoint can occur in three circumstances:

- The database owner or system administrator manually issues a CHECKPOINT command.

- SQL Server executes a CHECKPOINT when the transaction log cache has reached a specified limit.

- SQL Server executes a CHECKPOINT when the specified *recovery interval* is reached.

Note

The recovery interval is the amount of time you determine that the database can remain down while SQL Server runs its recovery process in the event of an outage. If you determine that you can allow a ten minute interval to allow SQL Server to recover a database, then set this as the recovery interval. Remember, in a worst case basis, the recovery interval is the allowance for each database—if you have 20 databases, a 10-minute recovery equals a possible down-time of almost 3 hours and 20 minutes. Do not set the recovery interval too low either. The checkpoint process adds its own overhead penalty to the server, which will be especially noticeable with a high volume of transactions.

A checkpoint forces the transaction log to write all log pages that have been modified since the last checkpoint to the database device. This ensures that transactions which have been committed will be written to the database. The checkpoint can also force the transaction log to be truncated, if this option is turned on. When the log is truncated, all log pages whose transactions have all been committed are deleted from the transaction log. This process helps to ensure that the transaction log does not become full, stopping additional modifications to the database. An automatic checkpoint is issued by SQL Server approximately every 60 seconds—the actual interval is based upon the recovery interval and the number of transactions added to the log.

All transaction statements are written to the transaction log as they are received by the server. When a COMMIT TRANsaction is reached it flushes all of the *dirty* log pages from the log to the disk. A dirty page is a log page which has changed since the last checkpoint. When the COMMIT TRAN statement is reached only those statements that actually change data are written to the database. There is a short, but finite period of time when a transaction exists only in the transaction log. If the server fails before a transaction has been written to the database, but after the COMMIT TRAN statement has been logged, then the transaction will be rolled forward into the database during recovery. On the other hand, if the transaction has begun but not yet committed, then it will be rolled back during the recovery process.

You may wonder how an uncommitted transaction gets written to the log. The transaction log works in pages. More than one transaction may be written to a page, especially in multi-user environments. One user can easily overlap another user's transaction statements, causing SQL Server to write both BEGIN TRANscation statements on the same log page. The first user the commits their transaction, but SQL Server writes everything on that page to the transaction log, potentially creating an uncommitted transaction. Figure 4.3 illustrates how two transactions can be written, logged, committed, and either rolled forward or rolled back.

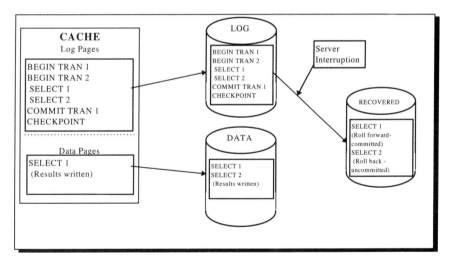

Figure 4.5: The checkpoint process saves data to the transaction log as pages. A transaction may be rolled forward or back during recovery, if the server fails.

A new feature of SQL Server 6.5 is that you can now choose a specific date and time through which transactions will be recovered. All transactions that occurred after the specified date and time will be rolled back, even if already committed. This recovery applies only to restores from a transaction log, not to full database or table restores.

Web Files

This feature is new to SQL Server 6.5 and allows you to create Hypertext Markup Language (HTML) documents, also called web pages, from information available in the databases on your server. These web pages can be viewed with any HTML browser. Microsoft SQL Server comes with the SQL Server Web Assistant, a new tool available from Microsoft that creates the HTML code for you. At this time, the Web Assistant is only available to servers on Intel-based computers, and only for use with SQL Server 6.5 databases. Using the Web Assistant with databases created with an earlier version of SQL Server will result in errors and a web page that will not work. The Web Assistant is really a front-end for the stored procedure **sp_makewebtask**. This stored procedure can be run from any Windows NT supported platform. There are two additional stored procedures used with generating HTML documents: **sp_runwebtask**, and **sp_dropwebtask**. These three new stored procedures have the following uses:

- sp_makewebtask is used to create the task that will produce the HTML document. This is the stored procedure that is run through the Web Assistant interface.

- sp_runwebtask is the stored procedure that actually creates the HTML document. When you run this stored procedure, it runs the task specified in the parameters.

- sp_dropwebtask is used to drop a previously created web task. You can specify either the task process name or the output file name when using this stored procedure.

The Web Assistant can be used to generate a HTML file as a one-time only or regularly scheduled server task. The Web Assistant can make use of SQL Server procedures, queries, and extended stored procedures, enabling you to create a web page that makes use of the most current information available at almost any time.

Using the Web Assistant is very simple method for creating a web page with information from your database. Some uses for this could be:

- Creating a web page where customers can browse through the items or services you supply and the prices for them.

- Building a web page on which your salespeople can view available inventory.

- Making a web page that can display updatable spec sheets for your products.

Note

Remember, you can set this task to run as often as necessary. Each time the task runs again, all of the information displayed on your web page is updated with the most current information contained in your database. This has the potential to save a company many thousands of dollars in printing and postage costs. Consider how many color flyers and spec sheets are printed, mailed and thrown away each year, and how many of these same flyers and spec sheets are out of date by the time they come back from the printer. You can have a completely up-to-date flyer and spec sheet on your web page that your customer can print for themselves if they want a copy, and they have the satisfaction of getting current information about your product.

The Web Assistant is used like this:

1.   From the Microsoft SQL Server 6.5 (Common) group, double-click on the SQL Server Web Assistant icon.

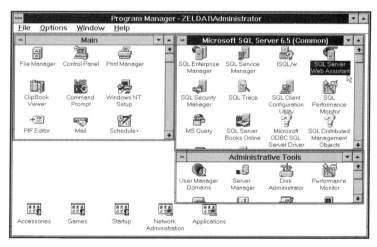

Figure 4.6: Your own SQL Server program group may have a different name, and the SQL Server Web Assistant icon may be located in a different position than you see here.

2.   Type the name of SQL Server from which you will be drawing information. This server is the one that has the database you want to use, not the server that may house your web site. If you are using SQL Server's security system, enter your Login ID and password in the appropriate text boxes. If you are using Windows NT's domain-managed security system, then click the checkbox to activate this option. Click the **N**ext button to open the next dialog box.

> **Note**
>
> Instead of entering the name of a specific server, you can type (**Local**) for the server on the computer that you are operating from. Be sure to also include the parentheses.

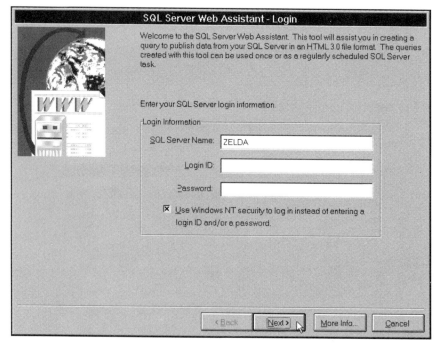

Figure 4.7: The first of several SQL Server Web Assistant dialog boxes you will use to complete your Web page. This dialog box requires login information.

106

3.   The next Web Assistant dialog box is used to select or enter a query on which your web page will be based. You have three options to choose from by clicking the appropriate option button:

- You can "Build a query from a database hierarchy," which means that you select databases and then tables by expanding the tree by clicking the plus sign (+) symbol beside the folder name in the upper list box displayed in this dialog box. Select individual columns for your query by expanding the table folder, and then clicking on specific columns. Specify criteria, such as ORDER BY, or WHERE clauses by typing the necessary information in the lower text box.

- You can "Enter a query as free-form text." This option allows you to enter a customized query by using T-SQL statements, stored procedures and extended stored procedures. If you are familiar with using T-SQL and programming this will give you the greatest degree of control.

- Finally, you can "Use a query in a stored procedure." This options allows you choose a stored procedure and add any arguments it requires.

In this example make the following selections:

- Select the "Build a query from a database hierarchy," option button. This is the default setting.

- Use the upper list box to expand the pubs database by clicking the plus sign (+) beside it, and then expand the authors table.

- Select the columns au_lname and au_fname.

- Expand the titleauthor table and select the columns au_id and title_id.

- Expand the titles table and select the columns title_id and titles.

- In the clauses list box, type the following statements:
```
SELECT au_lname, au_fname, titles
FROM authors, titleauthor, titles
WHERE authors.au_id = titleauthor.au_id
AND titleauthor.title_id = titles.title_id
ORDER BY au_lname
```

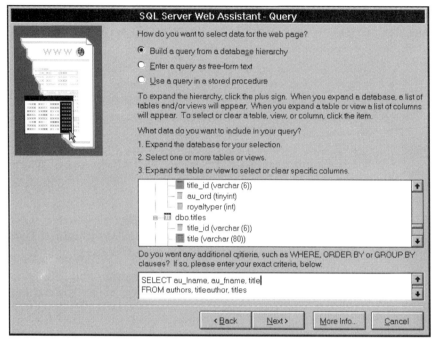

Figure 4.8: You now see several of the tables and columns selected in the upper list box and the WHERE clause entered into the bottom list box.

4. Click the **Next** button to display the next dialog box. With this dialog box, you will choose when the task you are creating will be run and turned into a HTML document. You have five options to select from:

- Now. Executes the script immediately upon completion. No arguments needed.

- Later. Executes the script at a specified date and time. You will be asked to supply a date and time.

- When Data Changes. This option causes the task to be automatically triggered when data is changed in a specific table and/or column. You must tell the Web Assistant which table(s) and/or column(s) whose changing data triggers the task to be run.

- On Certain Days of the Week. This selection allows you to update your web page on specified days of the week. You will be asked to supply both the days and a time for this action.

- On a Regular Basis. This scheduled task will be run again, after a specified number of hours, or days, or weeks. You will be asked how many and of what time unit is to elapse before this task will be triggered again.

The default selection is Now. Keep this option and click the Next button to move on to the next dialog box.

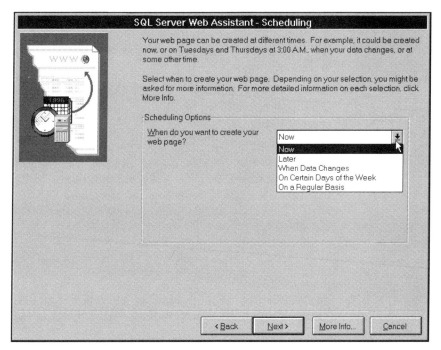

Figure 4.9: This dialog box is used to select when the sp_addwebtask is to be run.

5. This next dialog box asks for a number of different items:

- A name for the web document that you are creating. The default name given is C:\WEB.HTML. You must have the necessary permissions to create a file in the specified directory to create the file.

- A template file for the web page. A template provides the information requested in the next several options, making them unavailable. The default setting here is <no template file will be used>.

- The following information option enables you to enter the next several options.

  - Add a title for your web page by typing it into the text box. This title is displayed in the title bar of an Internet browser window.

  - Add a title for the results of the query. This title is displayed on the actual web page above the query results listing.

- The next three options allow you to add hot links to other web sites:

  - **No** is the first option, and does not allow you to add URL links to other web sites.

  - **Yes, add one URL and reference text**, allows you to add one URL link and the text which will be displayed on your web page.

  - **Yes, a**dd a list of URL's and reference text from a table, allows you to place several URL links and their reference text onto your web page. With this option you will create a query for a two-column table; the first column contains the URL address and the second column contains the reference text for the address.

For this example, make these selections:

- Leave the default filename. I have changed the drive setting in the example because I am not using the "C" drive for Windows NT.

- Type **Authors Listing** as the title for this web page.

- Type **Authors and Titles** for the query results title.

- Finally, keep the default **No** setting for including URL's with this web page.

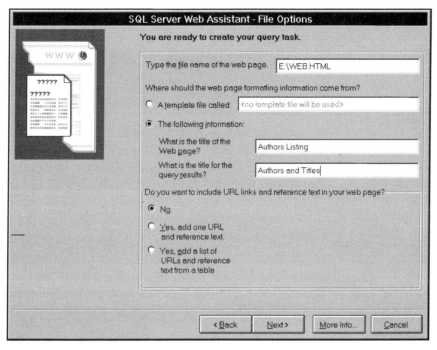

Figure 4.10: This dialog box is used to select a template, or to add titles and URL hot links to your web page.

6. Click the **N**ext button to display the final Web Assistant dialog box. This dialog box is used to choose these options:

- A header style for your query results title. The default option is HTML Header <H2></H2> which is a second-level header style.

- The font used to display the data resulting from your query.

- You can choose any or none of the checkboxes from the box at the bottom of this dialog box. Placing a check inside of the box turns the option on. These options include:

111

◆ Inserting a date and time showing when the data was last updated.

◆ Including the column name at the top of the results list. This option should only be used if the column has a meaningful name, not like au_lname. Remember, you can change column names in the query statement.

◆ You can also choose to limit the number of rows displayed on your web page. If your query results in more than one or two pages, you may want to limit the number of rows. Simply check the box and type a number into the text box.

For this example, leave all of the default settings except:

- Uncheck the box Include column or view column names with the query results.

- Check the Limit the query results to box and type 10 into the text box.

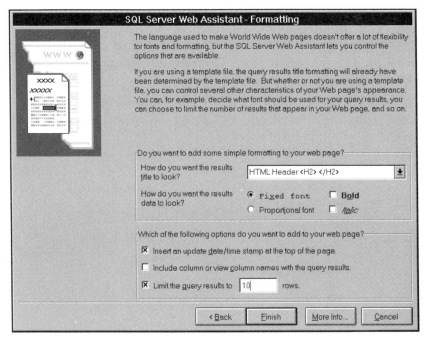

Figure 4.11: Use this dialog box to make the final settings for your web page.

7.   Click the **F**inish button to complete the task. You will see a last dialog box telling you that the task has been created and run, creating your web document. Click the **C**lose button to close this dialog box.

8.   You can view your web page by opening Windows NT's File Manager, finding the file \WEB.HTML and double-clicking it.

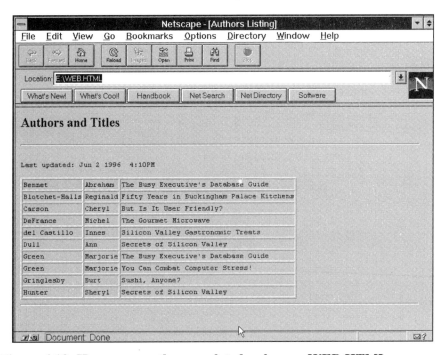

Figure 4.12: Here you see the completed web page WEB.HTML displayed in Netscape's browser.

Summary

In this chapter, you have learned to work with SQL Server's structures, processes, and file types. Specifically, you have learned:

- What is in the master, model, and msdb databases and what they are used for.

- How SQL Server uses processes and process IDs and how you can terminate one.

- How to use data and log files.

- How to use the Web Assistant application to create a web page from your database information.

Chapter 5

What Is Data Integrity?

IN THIS CHAPTER

- Entity Integrity
- Domain Integrity
- Referential Integrity
- User-defined Integrity

You are now familiar with the structure of Microsoft SQL Server. In this and the next several chapters you will learn how SQL Server works to help you do your tasks of being a system administrator.

Maintaining the integrity of the data contained within a database is one of the highest priorities of the database administrator. Data that has been corrupted or that is simply inaccurate from poor data entry can cost a business many thousands of dollars in lost time and revenue. Data integrity is important at all levels of database usage, from a small, single-user contact manager to a large, multi-user, multi-server, on-line transaction-processing database. This chapter covers how SQL Server can be used to ensure the accuracy and integrity of your data without depending on a client application.

There are several different types of integrity with which you must be concerned: entity, domain, referential, and user-defined. Each of these different types of integrity all work together to ensure that your data remains accurate and whole at all times.

Entity Integrity

Entity integrity is primarily concerned with how Microsoft SQL Server defines each row in a specific table as a unique entity. This form of integrity is usually enforced through some combination of PRIMARY KEY constraints, UNIQUE constraints, and indexes. Through the use of these constraints, SQL Server can help to ensure that each row of a table is indeed unique. With this form of integrity, you can be sure that you will not have a customer table full of duplicate customers, once for each time they may have placed an order. Without entity level integrity, you could easily have a table grow to many times the size that it should be, using valuable disk space.

Primary Key Constraint

The primary key constraint will be the object you will most commonly use to ensure entity level integrity. By definition, the primary key constraint is the column, or group of columns, that are used in a table to uniquely identify a specific row. A primary key constraint can never be null, must always have a unique index, and there can be no more than one primary key constraint per table.

You learned how to create a primary key constraint in Chapter 3, "Logical Structures," in the "Database Objects" section. Generally, you will find that it is advantageous to have a primary key column(s) in every table. The only exceptions should be very small tables, twenty rows or less, that are used primarily as lookup tables for sets of values. For example, you may have a discount table with two columns, one containing a discount code and the other containing a discount percentage. A table like this would not necessarily need to have a primary key constraint, but it easily could. Since this table will be referred to by another table, you may find that you get better results if the discount code column was listed as the primary key column for the table.

Primary key constraints can be defined when you first create a table or can be added later using the ALTER TABLE command, or from within the SQL Enterprise Manager window. When a primary key constraint is defined, SQL Server automatically builds a unique nonclustered index for the column values. You can change or specifically define the index as a clustered index if this better meets your requirements.

Primary key constraints can be defined at either table level or at column level when you are creating a new table. If your primary key is composed of more than one column, a composite primary key, then the constraint must be defined at the table level. Otherwise, you can define the constraint at a column level. The primary key constraint is applied at the table level only when it is added to an existing table. Remember, the primary key must uniquely identify every row in a table. If you do not have a single column which can do this, then you must either add a new column that can be so used, or you must select several columns that, taken together, can uniquely identify a row.

For example, a LAST_NAME column alone can not usually be used as a primary key because too many people have the same last names. For a small table, you may be able to get away with using a combination primary key composed of both the LAST_NAME, and FIRST_NAME columns. For a larger table with many names you will inevitably end up with two people with the same first and last names who are unique individuals, but to SQL Server they will be the same person and you will not be able to add the second person to your table because their entry would cause a violation of the primary key constraint. Your next best choice is the use of LAST_NAME, FIRST_NAME, and STREET_ADDRESS columns. I recommend using street over city or state because it is more likely that your database will have two or more John Smith's who live in Los Angeles, than two John Smith's both living at the same address. The best option is to include a column specifically to be used as an identity column in every table which needs a primary key constraint.

A primary key constraint can be dropped from a table using either the ALTER TABLE statement:

```
ALTER TABLE table_name
DROP CONSTRAINT constraint_name
```

Or you can use the SQL Enterprise Manager window by double-clicking the table to which the primary key constraint belongs, and then clicking the Advanced Features button. Select the tab of the primary key, if it is not already selected, and click the Remove button. Dropping a primary key constraint is not recommended, unless you incorrectly selected a wrong column for the constraint.

When using the bcp application to load a large block of data into an existing table, you may decide to drop the indexes before performing the bulk copy. If the data is already sorted in the clustered index order, than drop the nonclustered indexes, load the data, and then recreate the dropped indexes. If the data is not sorted by the clustered index, you can perform the load in one of two ways:

- Create the clustered index and then load the data with bcp. Once the data has been loaded, create the nonclustered indexes. Finally, update the statistics on the table. Or,

- Drop all indexes, if any have been created. Load the data using bcp, and then create the indexes, starting with the clustered index and then all of the nonclustered indexes.

UNIQUE Constraint

The unique constraint is similar in many ways to the primary key constraint with the exception that it does allow null values in the column. The unique constraint can be defined on any column which is not the primary key column, and does not have any rows with duplicate values in the column. You can use a maximum of 249 unique constraints per table. Its primary use is to enforce row-level integrity on non-primary key columns. The use of the UNIQUE constraint ensures that duplicate values will not be entered into the column.

The unique constraint, like the primary key constraint, can be defined at either a table or column level. If the unique constraint is applied to a single column, then it is applied at the column level. Conversely, if the constraint is applied to several columns, as in a composite unique constraint, then it is applied at the table level.

This constraint can be added when you are defining a new table with the CREATE TABLE statement, or you can add it later with the ALTER TABLE command. When a constraint is added to an existing table, it is applied only at the table level. A unique constraint can be dropped by using the ALTER TABLE statement.

Domain Integrity

Domain integrity refers to column level integrity, meaning that the information entered into a column must come from the set of values which are possible for this particular column. Domain integrity revolves around domain rules, column datatypes, and the CHECK constraint. Often, a foreign key constraint is part of the domain integrity, but this will be discussed in detail in the next section. Each column has an fundamental domain that represents the set of all possible valid values.

Domain Rules

Domain rules refer to those rules specifically bound to a column. Rules are used to help restrict the format of a value entered into a column. For example, a rule can be constructed that restricts values to a specific range of numbers, or to a list of specified items, such as brown, red, green, or Chicago, New York, Portland. You can use only one rule per column.

Rules are often used as a *mask* for data entry of information. A mask requires that data entered into a column follows a specific format. In the Rules section of Chapter 3, "Logical Structures," you created a rule for entering a U.S. social security number.

@ssan like '[0-9][0-9][0-9]-[0-9][0-9]-[0-9][0-9][0-9][0-9]'

Rules can be created by either using the Manager Rules dialog box from the SQL Enterprise Manager window or by using the CREATE RULE statement. In either case, a rule must be bound to a specific column. The rule can be bound with the sp_bindrule function, or from the Manager Rules dialog boxes Column Bindings tab. Both methods properly bind the rule to the specified column.

Rules can be dropped using the DROP RULE statement if they are not bound to a column. If you have already bound the rule to a column, you must first unbind the rule with the sp_unbindrule stored procedure.

Datatypes

Datatypes are used within the domain integrity structure as a method of ensuring that data entered in a column is of a specific type. SQL Server has several predefined datatypes which you can use when you define a column, and allowances are made for you to create your own specific datatypes.

The selection of the column datatype is extremely important. This will determine the type of data which can be placed in a column, and how long that data can be. Your selections will determine the space utilization of your columns, and will effect the performance, reliability, and manageability of your entire database. Once you choose a datatype for a column, you cannot change it again without first dropping the table and then rebuilding it and reloading the data. Doing this also runs the risk of losing some data if it is not compatible with the new datatype.

Datatypes must be applied to a column when the column is created. If you add a column to an existing table with the ALTER TABLE statement, you can use any datatype except for the bit datatype. The reason for this is that a column added to an existing table must be able to support a NULL value, since the rows already in the table will of course have NULL values for the new column. The bit datatype does not allow a default NULL value. The next several tables list the various default system datatypes included with SQL Server.

Table 5.1: Numeric Datatypes

Datatype/ General Type	Description	Example of Uses
Decimal [(p[,s])],or Numeric [(p[,s])]/ Numeric	These two datatypes are interchangeable, except that only the numeric datatype can be used with an **identity** column. This datatype stores an exact numeric value between $10^{38}-1$ through $-10^{38}-1$, and will require between 2 and 17 bytes of storage space. The precision p is for the maximum number of digits, both to the left and right of the decimal place which can be stored. The scale s represents the maximum number of digits to the right of the decimal point, and must be equal or less than the value of p.	Use the decimal or numeric datatypes for any column which will be used strictly for number values. Common uses are for quantities, miles traveled, etc.
float[(n)]/ Approximate Numeric	The float datatype is an approximate numeric value. This datatype has a precision of 15 digits, or as specified by n, and is stored in eight bytes. This datatype can include an exponent, and is entered as a negative or positive number X, followed by e or E, followed by another negative or positive integer Y. The number represented is the product of X and 10 raised to the power of the exponent Y.	The float datatype is most often used for those numbers which may have very large ranges but require the same precision, no matter if the number is large or small. Most commonly used for numbers expressed in scientific notation.
Real/ Approximate Numeric	The real datatype is similar to float. It has a precision of 7 digits, and a storage size of four bytes.	The real datatype is similar to the float datatype except that it has a smaller range and is stored in less space.
Int/ Integer numeric	This datatype stores only whole numbers with a range of -2^{31} through $2^{31}-1$ (-2,147,483,648 – 2,147,483,647). It is stored in four bytes.	The int datatype is used when only whole numbers need to be stored no fractional part of a number can be stored.

Table 5.1: Numeric Datatypes (cont'd)

Datatype/ General Type	Description	Example of Uses
Smallint/ Integer numeric	This datatype also stores only whole numbers, within the range of -2^{15} to $2^{15}-1$ (-32,768 – 32,767). It is stored in two bytes.	The smallint datatype is also used for any whole number within its range. Before using this datatype, be sure that its range will indeed fit all of the anticipated values.
Tinyint/ Integer numeric	This datatype stores whole numbers between 0 and 255, and is stored in one byte.	The tinyint datatype also stores whole number values. Again, be sure that this range will fit the data which will be stored.
Money/ Monetary	This datatype is used to store monetary values. When entering these values, type a dollar ($) sign preceding the value, otherwise SQL Server will assume this is a numeric value with four decimal places. Do not enter commas between numbers in a monetary datatype column. The range of values is from <$922,337,203,685,477.5808> through $922,337,203,685,477.5807. Precision is 0.0001 and is stored in eight bytes. Monetary values are rounded up to the nearest cent when displayed.	The money datatype can be used for most monetary values. Again, be sure that the 4 decimal place precision is adequate. If you are working with stocks and bonds pricing where values are expressed in 1/32's of a dollar ($0.03125), then 4 decimal places is not adequate.
Smallmoney / Monetary	The smallmoney datatype is similar in all aspects to money, except that it has a range from <$214,748.3648> to $214,748.3647, and is stored in four bytes.	The smallmoney datatype is used where a small range of monetary values are to be stored.

Table 5.2: Logical Datatypes

Datatype/ General Type	Description	Example of Uses
Bit/ Special	This datatype holds only the integers 1 or 0. Other values can be accepted into the column, but SQL Server will interpret them as 1. A bit datatype is most often used for Yes/No or True/False types of data. This datatype is stored in one byte.	The bit datatype is most often used to store yes/no, true/false types of data.

Table 5.3: Date Datatypes

Datatype/ General Type	Description	Example of Uses
Datetime/ Date and time	The datetime datatype is stored as two 4-byte integers. The first is the number of days before or after the base date of 1/1/1900, and the second 4-bytes is the number of milliseconds after midnight. Date values must be within the range of 1/1/1753 to 12/31/9999. Time values are accurate to within 3.33 milliseconds. You can enter either or both a date or a time value into a column with this datatype. Date values must be enclosed within single quote marks.	The datetime datatype is used for any column which is used for dates and/or time data. The most common usage is for date values. Use the datetime datatype to capture date information for order dates, ship dates, etc. You can use the value contained in a datetime column in a calculation, such as; add X number of days to the value in the ship date column to get an estimated arrival date.
Small-datetime/ Date and time	This datatype is less explicit than is the datetime datatype. The range of values for this datatype is between 1/1/1900 and 6/6/2079. Time accuracy is to the nearest minute. Date values must be enclosed within single quote marks.	The smalldatetime datatype is used in place of the datetime datatype when precision is not so necessary, or when the more restricted date range is adequate.

Table 5.4: Character or Text Datatypes

Datatype/ General Type	Description	Example of Uses
Char[(n)]/ Character	The char datatype can store a maximum of 255 characters. SQL Server stores the value entered as length n regardless of the actual number of characters entered. A char datatype can be NULL. Use this datatype when the data will be uniformly near the same length. If data entered into a char column is shorter than n, SQL Server will add trailing blanks to the data.	Use the char datatype to store any type of alphanumeric information of a fixed length. Common uses may include; customer IDs, product IDs, state abbreviations, zip/postal codes.
Varchar[(n)] /Character	This datatype can hold n to 255 characters, and is stored as the actual length of the data entered. Varchar can be NULL, but n must be a number between 1–255.	The varchar datatype is also used to store alphanumeric data. Use this datatype for variable length data such as names, streets, city, and descriptions.
Text/ Text, large	This datatype allows large amounts of text to be added, to approximately 2GB of data. This data is written to a special group of data pages and does not come under SQL Server's normal column limit of 255 characters. This column can not be used for variables or parameters in a stored procedure, nor can you use this column with an ORDER BY clause.	The text datatype is used for any long text entries. Most often used for long descriptions, telephone notes, or product summaries.

Table 5.5: Binary Datatypes

Datatype/ General Type	Description	Example of Uses
binary[(n)]/ Binary	The binary datatype can store a maximum of 255 bytes of fixed-length binary data. Regardless of the length of the data you enter into this column, it will be stored as size n. You must specify a number from 1–255 bytes as the value for n, but you can store 0 (zero) bytes in this column. Use this datatype when you expect that most values will be close to n in length.	The binary datatype is used to store binary information in bit patterns, not in hexadecimal format. Characters 0–9, A–F, and a–f can be used. Each binary string group must be preceded by 0x, like 0xAA. A length of 20 indicates that 20 two-character groups can be inputted into this column.
Varbinary [(n)]/ Binary	The varbinary datatype can also be a maximum of 255 bytes, but can be variable in length. Specify n between 1–255, as the maximum number of bytes which can be stored in this column. The actual storage space will the number of bytes entered into the column. Use this datatype when you expect NULL, or highly variable length values to be entered.	The varbinary datatype works like the binary datatype except that you can specify a variable data length for the column.
Timestamp/ Special Image/ Image	This datatype is used by SQL Server has nothing to do with the system clock. It is used to provide a unique version number for each row. When a row is inserted into a table, the timestamp is entered. Each time the row is updated, the timestamp is also updated by SQL Server. This datatype also allows large graphical files, up to 2GB in size. These files are also stored on a separate group of data pages.	The timestamp is a special datatype used most often to serialize row updates, enabling you to ensure that your users do not inadvertently update a row after another user has updated it. The image datatype is a special datatype which allows you to store images, often used for graphical representations of items, and digitized pictures.

When using the any datatype, if your data exceeds *n* in length, SQL Server will truncate the data without warning. Be certain that your data will not exceed length *n*, or that the data which may be truncated is not crucial to the database, or use a variable length datatype.

When using the datetime datatype, SQL Server allows you to enter a time without a date value. For example, entering a time of 6am will cause SQL Server to save this value as Jan 1, 1900 6:00:00:000AM. Entering a date/time value in this manner results in a value that will probably be meaningless to most queries. It is unlikely that most people will remember to search for a time value in the year 1900. It is highly recommended that you enter the current date along with a time value. Alternatively, you can create your application so that it will automatically add the current date and include the variable of the time the user enters.

Once a column has been created with a datatype and the table is populated with data, you can not change the datatype without first dropping the entire table and recreating it. You would then reload all of the data back into the table from the most current backup. With careful consideration of the change in datatype, you may or may not lose any data.

CHECK/NOCHECK Constraint

A CHECK constraint is either a table level, when more than one column is involved, or a column level constraint. It is used to validate information. Often rules and CHECK constraints can be used interchangeable, except that you can have more than one CHECK constraint per column. For example, the rule regarding social security numbers can be created as a CHECK constraint like this:

```
ALTER TABLE authors
ADD
CHECK CONSTRAINT CK_au_id
(au_id LIKE '[0-9][0-9][0-9]-[0-9][0-9]-[0-9][0-9][0-9][0-9]')
```

Like the rule, this constraint will ensure that an author's social security number is entered into the au_id column in the correct format, has the proper amount of numbers, and that all characters are numbers and not letters. Remember, the au_id has a datatype of varchar, which could allow letters instead of numbers.

By default, SQL Server will always check a value entered into a column against all constraints set on the column during an update, but there are circumstances when you may not want SQL Server to verify all constraints. For example, you may want to bulk load data into a table without SQL Server checking the information against the requirements of a CHECK constraint. You may also want to turn the CHECK constraint off when a column is added to a table with the ALTER TABLE statement. Use the WITH NOCHECK option so that the existing rows of data will not be checked against the new CHECK constraint. Use this option with caution unless you are already sure that your data conforms to the new CHECK constraint, or if your business requirements only need new data to conform to the constraint. To turn the CHECK constraint for au_id off, you would use the WITH NOCHECK option:

- **WITH NOCHECK,** this format is used when adding a CHECK constraint to an existing column and you do not want existing data to be checked against the requirements of the new constraint. The example below adds the CHECK constraint CK_au_id, but does not allow it to check data that already exists in the table.

    ```
    ALTER TABLE authors
    WITH NOCHECK
    ADD
    CHECK CONSTRAINT CK_au_id
    (au_id LIKE '[0-9][0-9][0-9]-[0-9][0-9]-[0-9][0-9][0-9][0-9]')
    ```

- **NOCHECK CONSTRAINT CK_au_id** is used to turn a CHECK constraint temporarily off. Use this option for bulk loading of new data into a table.

    ```
    ALTER TABLE authors
    NOCHECK CONSTRAINT CK_au_id
    ```

Only the system administrator, database owner, and table owner have permission to use the CHECK/NOCHECK options.

Referential Integrity

Referential integrity is a key function of a RDMS. By using SQL Server to perform as many of the referential integrity functions as possible, you reduce the possibility of errors in your database being introduced through a poorly written client application. SQL Server can be used to assign primary and foreign key relationships between tables and enforce these relationships before allowing a row to be inserted or updated into a table.

What is Referential Integrity?

Referential integrity is the property whereby all values entered into a foreign key column of one table have a corresponding value located in the primary key column to which they are related. The table which contains the primary key is often called the parent table, while the table with the foreign key is called a child table. A value can not be entered or changed in the foreign key column of the child table without a corresponding value existing in the parent table's primary key column, but a foreign key can contain a NULL value. For example, titles are related to their authors through the titleauthor table. The relationship is shown in figure 5.1:

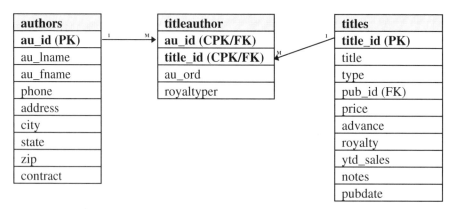

Figure 5.1: The relationships of primary and foreign key columns are shown between the authors, titleauthor, and the titles tables.

In the authors table the column au_id is the primary key (PK) column, while the titleauthor table uses a composite primary key (CPK) composed of both the au_id and title_id columns, and the titles table uses the title_id column as its primary key. The titleauthor table also contains two foreign key (FK) columns. The au_id column is a foreign key and related to the primary key au_id in the authors table, while the title_id column is a foreign key to the primary key title_id in the titles table. The primary key to foreign key creates the parent/child relations between tables. In the example shown in figure 5.1, the authors table is a parent table, as is the titles table.

The titleauthor table is a child table to both of the other two. Both the authors and titles table contain a primary key column, which is referenced as a foreign key column in the child table titleauthor. There are three basic relationships that can be defined through the primary/foreign key relations.

- One-to-One   This is a direct relationship between one primary key value of the parent table and no more than one related value in the foreign key column of the child table. This is relationship is not common in relational databases. An example of this relationship could be found between an employee and her department manager.

- One-to-Many   This relationship is the most commonly found, and exists when, for any single value in the primary key of the parent table, there can be one or more values found in the foreign key of the child table. An example of this relation can be found between the publishers table as the parent and the titles table as the child. For every one publisher, they may have many titles that they publish.

- Many-to-Many   This relationship is shown when for any one row in the parent table there can be one or more corresponding rows in the child table, and for any row in the child table there can be one or more corresponding rows in the parent table. *This relationship should be avoided because it can yield unpredictable results when querying the two tables.*

You may ask why a direct relationship between authors and titles is not created? The reason for this is that this relationship could easily be a many-to-many relationship. For every author there can be many titles, and for each title there can be many authors. This relationship should be avoided whenever possible, because it violates the primary key constraint in the titles table.

For example, the author Jack Smith has written three books: "How to fix a dishwasher," "How to fix a garbage disposal," and "How to fix a washing machine." His wife, Jane Smith, is co-author of the book, "How to fix a washing machine." Without the intervening bridge table, titleauthor, you would have two tables that would look like those in figure 5.2:

authors			titles		
au_id (PK)	au_lname	au_fname	title_id (PK)	title	au_id (FK)
1111	Smith	Jack	HR0001	How to fix a dishwasher	1111
1112	Smith	Jane	HR0002	How to fix a garbage disposal	1111
			HR0003	How to fix a washing machine	1111
			HR0003	How to fix a washing machine	1112

Figure 5.2: This relationship requires two rows in the titles table for the book, "How to fix a washing machine."

The many-to-many relationship requires extra rows in one or both tables. As you can see in figure 5.2, an extra row has been inserted into the table for the book, "How to fix a washing machine," to take into account that there are two authors, and as such—violates the primary key constraint by having two rows with the same primary key value. This duplicate entry of information is avoided when the bridge table titleauthor is used. The titleauthor table breaks the many-to-many relationship into two one-to-many relationships. The one-to-many relationship is much easier to use when constructing a query to retrieve selected rows from two or more tables, and does not violate the primary key constraint.

Defining Primary/Foreign Keys

Primary and foreign keys are defined for each table when you create the table with the CREATE TABLE statement, or are added with the ALTER TABLE statement. There is one caveat to creating primary and foreign key constraints. You must create the primary key constraint before you can create the foreign key constraint. Understanding this can help to shorten a potentially long frustration cycle. They can also be added to a table from within the SQL Enterprise Manager window. The T-SQL statements for a primary key would look like this:

```
ALTER TABLE authors
ADD CONSTRAINT au_pk_auid PRIMARY KEY (au_id)
```

You have the option to make this primary key constraint be a clustered or nonclustered constraint by placing the keyword CLUSTERED or NONCLUSTERED after the keyword PRIMARY KEY.

The procedure for placing a foreign key constraint is very similar. The T-SQL statements would look like this:

```
ALTER TABLE titleauthor
ADD CONSTRAINT ta_fk_auid FOREIGN KEY (au_id)
REFERENCES author (au_id)
```

Again, you add the constraint, name it, and tell SQL Server what kind of constraint you are creating. In the case of the foreign key, you must also tell SQL Server what table and column(s) are being referenced as the primary key.

The procedure for placing a primary and foreign key are different when you use the SQL Enterprise Manager window. The following steps apply whether you are creating a new table or altering an existing table. If you are placing a primary key constraint on an existing table, the procedure will fail if the data contained in the column(s) designated as the primary key does not meet the requirements, primarily that of uniqueness. You can not have duplicate values in a primary key column, and you can not turn this off with a NOCHECK option. Follow these steps to set primary and foreign key columns:

1.   Open the SQL Enterprise Manager window and select the pubs database. Expand the pubs database folder and then the Objects folder. Double-click the table folder titleauthor, displaying the Manage Tables window. Maximize the window, and click the Advanced Features button.

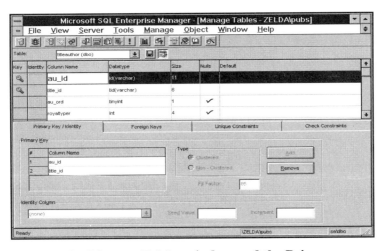

Figure 5.3: Use the Manage Tables window and the Primary Key/Identity tab to add, change, and delete primary key constraints.

You can see that this table has a composite primary key already set. If there had been no primary key constraint set on this table, you would select a column from the Column Name list box. You would then choose whether this constraint will be clustered or nonclustered by clicking the appropriate option button, and then finally click on the Add button.

2.   Click the Foreign Keys tab to set a foreign key and reference.

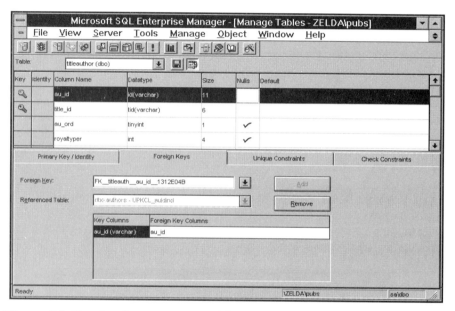

Figure 5.4: Foreign keys are set at this tab in the Manage Tables window.

This tab is used to set a foreign key relationship. Use the Foreign Key list box to name the new constraint, or select an existing foreign key constraint from the list box if you want to remove a constraint. Select the table whose primary key will be referenced by the foreign key of this table from the Referenced Table list box. Finally, choose one of the primary key columns from the referenced table in the Key Columns list and the corresponding column from the current table in the Foreign Key Columns. Columns do not have to have the same name in order to be part of a relationship, but they must have a corresponding datatype. For example, a primary key column can have an int datatype, while the foreign key column may have the smallint datatype. You could not relate a primary key with an int datatype and a foreign key with a char datatype.

A foreign key constraint can be quickly removed by selecting it in the Foreign **Key** list box and then clicking the **R**emove button.

Enforcing Referential Integrity

By creating a network of primary/foreign key columns you create a system to enforce the referential integrity of your database. There are two final pieces to ensuring that referential integrity is enforced, and they are called:

- *Cascading Delete*: This term refers to the deleting of all records that depend upon a value contained in another table. For example, in a order entry system if a customer is deleted, then all of their outstanding orders should also be deleted. Otherwise, you may end up trying to ship or post as a receivable an order for a nonexistent customer. The records in the orders table are dependent upon the presence of a corresponding customer.

- *Cascading Update*: This term refers to the ability of the database to automatically change the dependent rows to reflect a change in the parent table. For example, if a customer moves, you may need to change their customer ID. At the same time, you would also want to update all of the customer's outstanding orders, their account in the accounts receivable, and other similar tables with the new customer ID code.

Much of the work done to enforce this form of referential integrity has been confined to triggers in earlier versions of SQL Server. When an action that requires a cascading delete or update occurs, then the trigger updates or deletes the referenced records. With SQL Server 6.5, declarative referential integrity (DRI) can be used in the forms which have been discussed in this chapter. Information about each table is maintained in the system tables: *sysconstraints* and *sysreferences*. SQL Server now uses these tables to maintain the information necessary to enforce DRI for you. As you create PRIMARY, FOREIGN KEY, CHECK, UNIQUE, IDENTITY, and DEFAULT constraints, SQL Server is recording this information in one of these system tables and then using the data to ensure that information recorded in one table meets the requirements of the constraints placed on a column.

User-defined Integrity

All forms of integrity checking support the application of a user-defined business rule. User-defined integrity is always based on one of SQL Server's forms of integrity checking, and then enhanced further to support some specific need. You have already learned how to use and create both procedures and triggers. These are often used to enhance the integrity protection available to a database, but much of their abilities have been taken over by DRI.

One of the most commonly used forms of user-defined integrity is the creation of user-defined datatypes. While SQL Server comes with a number of datatypes, there may be business requirements for a datatype with a more precise definition. The user-defined datatype is not really a new datatype, it is only a new way to describe an existing datatype. You can use the stored procedure's **sp_addtype** to create a new datatype definition, and **sp_droptype** to delete a user-defined datatype. You can not drop a datatype that is currently bound to a column without first dropping the table, then dropping the datatype.

The simplest method to add a new datatype is from within the SQL Enterprise Manager window. Follow these steps to add an additional datatype:

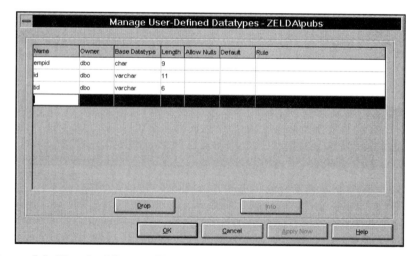

Figure 5.5: Use the Manage User-Defined Datatypes dialog box to add, edit, or drop all user-defined datatypes.

1.   Open the SQL Enterprise Manager window, and expand pubs, objects, and double-click on the User Defined Datatypes icon to open the Manage User-Defined Datatypes dialog box.

Several user-defined datatypes that are part of the pubs database are already shown. Once you build your own database this dialog box will be empty until you add your first datatype.

2.   Enter the following information into the indicated columns, being sure to press the Tab key to move from column to column. Do not use the Enter key.

- Type **ssan** in the Name column for the new datatype.

- The default entry of **dbo** (database owner) is the normal entry in the Owner column. This option cannot be changed without first dropping the datatype.

- In the Datatype column click the list box button and select **char** from the list. This option can not be changed later.

- Type **11** in the Length column as the maximum number of characters allowed for this datatype. This option can not be changed without dropping and recreating.

- The Allow Nulls column allows you to choose whether NULL values are allowed for this datatype—it is selected by either clicking it or pressing the Spacebar, a checkmark will be displayed in the column. This option can not be changed later.

- Select a default definition for this datatype in the Default column if applicable. The default must be created and named before you can select it for use with a user-defined datatype. The default is selected from the list box. This option can be added at a later time.

- Select a rule to be applied with this user-defined datatype from the drop-down list box in the Rule column. A rule must already exist to apply it to your new datatype. This option can be added at a later time.

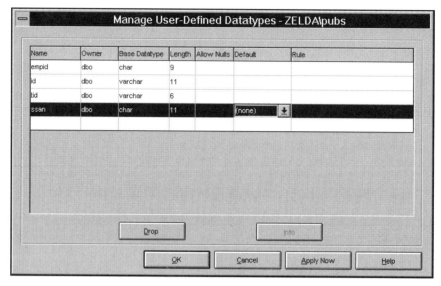

Figure 5.6: The Manage User-Defined Datatypes dialog box makes creating a new datatype a mater of filling in just a few pieces of information.

3.   When you have completed the new datatype, there are two options for you to complete and save it:

- **OK**. This option saves the new datatype and closes the dialog box.

- **Apply Now**. This button saves the new datatype and leaves the dialog box open so that you can create another datatype.

4.   Click the **OK** button.

If you decide later to drop a user-defined datatype, simply select it from the list of datatypes in this dialog box and then click the **D**rop button. You can also use the stored procedure sp_droptype.

On the Manage User-Defined Datatypes dialog box there is a button called **Info**. This button displays the User Datatype Info dialog box which is used to quickly display information about to which columns and tables a selected datatype has been used with. To view this information, simply select a datatype and click the Info button and you will see the User Datatype Info dialog box, as seen in figure 5.7.

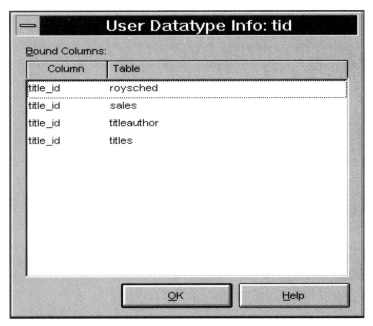

Figure 5.7: The User Datatype Info dialog box displays information about which tables and columns a user-defined datatype has been assigned to.

User-defined datatypes can be very useful in helping to enforce the integrity of a database that has many complex business rules. This is the function of each of the various parts of integrity enforcement.

Summary

In this chapter, you have learned how to ensure entity integrity, domain integrity, and enforce referential integrity. Specifically, you have learned to:

- Use the UNIQUE constraint to enforce integrity on columns which are no primary keys.

- Create and enforce primary key constraints on one or more columns.

- Use domain rules and datatypes to ensure the domains integrity.

- Check or not check new data copied into a table against a CHECK constraint.

- Use referential integrity to help ensure data consistency.

- Create relationships between tables using primary key and foreign keys in tables.

- Create special user-defined rules, procedures, and triggers to help enforce the integrity of the data in your database.

Chapter 6

Data Consistency and Concurrency

IN THIS CHAPTER

- Statements and Transactions
- Using Locks for Consistency

In this chapter, you begin to look at the more real-world application of SQL Server—the multiple-user database. So far, you have really only looked at SQL Server from the point-of-view of the system administrator. Now you will look at how SQL Server behaves when more than one user is accessing a database concurrently, all at the same time, and all trying to use the same tables, rows, and columns.

The potential problems inherent in a multiple-user scenario are immediately clear. For example, imagine several rental car agencies throughout a city, with a big convention just hitting town. There are a limited number of cars available, and it can be very easy to see two agents trying to rent a car to two different people at the same time. Using SQL Server, how can be sure that two agents do not accidentally both book the same car?

Through this chapter you will learn how SQL Server can be used to resolve this problem of keeping your data consistent with multiple concurrent users. In the second half of this chapter you will learn how a more complex problem involving data consistency—resolving how to allow some users to read a database while others are writing to it. The goal of using SQL Server is to allow the maximum number of simultaneous users (concurrency), while maintaining the correctness of your data (consistency).

Statements and Transactions

As you learned earlier in this book, a *statement* is a single T-SQL command, ranging from a simple UPDATE, INSERT, or SELECT statement to very complex statements involving many individual commands and modifying clauses such as WHERE and ORDER BY.

The next step in using T-SQL statements is turning these statements into *transactions*. Transactions consist of one or more T-SQL statements that are sent to the SQL Server by a client application. How much time a transaction takes is dependent on several items, including:

- When the user and client application send a COMMIT TRANsaction statement to the server. Remember, while SQL Server does write uncommitted transactions to the log and data files, these transactions can and will be rolled back if they are not accompanied by the specific T-SQL statement COMMIT TRAN, in the event of a server failure.

- The actual processing time required by the server's CPU.

- If there are any transactions blocking the transaction and preventing it from being committed.

Statements sent by separate users to the server do not have to be received at the exact same moment to be considered concurrent. Even when they overlap, there is always the potential for one statement to interfere with the other. In a multiple-user system, you can easily have two people reading the same row, both with the full intention of adding or changing the information contained in that row. As you will come to understand, this is a very important concept. Concurrency can create many potential problems if you are not prepared to resolve them before they begin. Windows NT, being a multithreaded operating system, automatically serializes each statement as it is received.

Using Locks for Consistency

SQL Server uses locks in order to ensure data consistency and allow for the maximum concurrency of users. A lock can come in several forms: exclusive, shared, or intent. These locks are over tables, pages, extents, and rows. You will usually find that read transactions acquire shared locks, while write transactions acquire an exclusive lock. Intent locks can be granted to read transactions when the users intent is to update the row. This ensures that another user will not be granted an exclusive lock on the data that the first user intends to update.

Understanding a Lock

Concurrency issues are solved by using locks. SQL Server holds several different locks which ensure which the greatest number of users can access the various tables and rows in a database, while providing a level of guarantee that data read by one user, with the intent of updating the information, will not be changed by another user. Once an exclusive lock has been granted to a user, SQL Server holds the lock until a COMMIT TRAN or a ROLLBACK TRAN statement is reached. If a deadlock is detected the transaction killed with the KILL statement.

SQL Server uses locks to prevent the problems inherent in the example of the car rental agency discussed at the beginning of this chapter. How does SQL Server prevent the rental of a car by two different agents? When the first agent, Casey, queries the database for available cars she finds a suitable blue, mid-size vehicle for her customer. While Casey's query is browsing the database, SQL Server holds an intent lock. This lock will allow other users to read the page, but not to acquire an exclusive lock. A second later, Eric queries the database for another customer, and is granted a shared lock on the database. Eric's query also finds that the same blue, mid-size car is available. As Eric talks to his customer, Casey finishes her rental agreement and commits a rental transaction. SQL Server grants Casey an exclusive lock and updates the database table by tagging the vehicle as rented and no longer available. Eric completes his rental agreement and commits it. This transaction fails because the selected vehicle has now been tagged as being rented, and Eric will have to find another car for his customer.

When building an application, you must be careful about allowing a user to create a single transaction statement that updates many rows in many tables. Long running transactions such as this can effectively block all other users from working in the database until the transaction has completed its actions. By ensuring that transactions are broken into smaller steps, you can help to eliminate this problem.

Shared Locks

In general, SQL Server holds *shared locks* for read operations, this being the least restrictive lock. Under most circumstances, a shared lock is held only on the page that is currently being read, such as when using a SELECT statement. Once the page has been read, the lock is released. SQL Server can hold many concurrent shared locks on the same table or same page.

While a shared lock is held on a page, other more restrictive locks are excluded from being formed. Once one user has a shared lock on a page, another user cannot be granted any form of an exclusive lock—which means that they can not write to or change the data on that page until the shared lock has been released. A shared lock can be escalated to an update lock, whereby a transaction updates a row. Once the transaction has been completed with a COMMIT TRAN statement, the next user who was trying to acquire an exclusive or update lock will be granted their lock.

Update Locks

An *update lock* is used by SQL Server when the user's intent is to modify the data contained on the page. An update lock is compatible with a shared lock. If an UPDATE transaction plans to make modifications to the data on a page which already is held by a shared lock, the transaction will be granted an update lock. Once the all shared locks have been relinquished, the update lock is promoted to an exclusive lock. Update locks are acquired during the initial read operation, and are held on a page level.

No other shared locks will be granted while an update lock is held. Update locks are used to prevent one of the common forms of deadlock, which will be discussed further later in this chapter. When a transaction is ready to actually write changes to a page, the update lock is promoted to an exclusive lock. The update lock also prevents *lock starvation*. Lock starvation occurs when many read transaction acquire shared locks on a page, preventing another transaction from acquiring an exclusive lock on the page. SQL Server services all locks on a first come, first served, basis.

The update lock allows maximum concurrency to your users on the page or table while ensuring a user that no one can change the data they are reading until they have completed their transaction. While the update lock is compatible with shared locks, only one update lock can be held on any one page at a time.

Exclusive Locks

The *exclusive lock* is the most restrictive of all the lock types SQL Server holds. No other user can place any type of lock on a table or page when an exclusive lock has been placed on it. Exclusive locks are used for all transactions that write data to a page; for example, UPDATE, INSERT, and DELETE transactions. Exclusive locks are held for the duration of the transaction and are automatically released once the transaction is completed.

What Is Lock Granularity?

The subject of *lock granularity* is concerned with how much of a table is held by the lock. Locks can cover a row, a page, an extent, or a table. The finer the granularity, the less real estate is covered by the lock. SQL Server can automatically escalate lock granularity from page to table if the number of pages locked by a single transaction falls above a set threshold or if the number of pages locked falls above a specified percentage of the pages contained in the table. A lock of any type uses the same number of overhead resources. SQL Server may determine at some point that it is more efficient to escalate a page lock to a table lock in order to conserve resources. The lock escalation threshold can be set using the stored procedure sp_configure, or from the SQL Server Enterprise Manager application. Follow these steps to change the lock escalation thresholds:

1.   Open the SQL Server Enterprise Manager application and select Server, SQL Server, Configure from the menu, displaying the Server Configuration/Options dialog box.

2.   Click on the Configuration tab to view the many configuration options available. Click the LE Threshold maximum row in the Current column. You can type any value that is shown in the Minimum and Maximum columns.

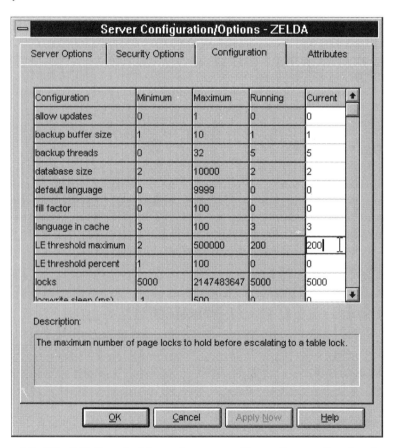

Figure 6.1: The LE threshold maximum configuration option has been selected.

The current value is 200. This means that once a query requests a lock on the 201st page, the lock will be escalated to a table lock.

3.   Move to the **LE threshold percent** to specify a percentage of the number of pages that must be locked by a transaction before a lock is escalated to a table lock. Type a value in the Current column of this row to change the value. The default value is 0%.

The LE threshold percent setting is especially helpful if you have many small tables that have less than 200 pages.

4.   Click the **OK** button to apply these changes, if any.

Row Locks

The smallest, or finest, lock is a row lock. The ability to lock a single row is a new feature in SQL Server 6.5, and is available only for INSERT transactions. Insert Row-level Locking, or IRL, allows you lock a single row during an INSERT transaction. It is especially useful for tables with a very high transaction rate where new records are inserted at the end of the file, and one of these conditions is applicable:

- The table does not have an index.

- The table uses a nonclustered index.

- The table uses a clustered index on a sequentially increasing key, such as an identity datatype.

When these conditions exist in a table, you will often have many users all trying to place an exclusive lock on the final page of the table as they insert a new record. This condition is called a *hotspot* and can cause a significant slow down in transaction rate when too many users have to wait while another transaction completes its insert. By locking only a single row, you can allow many concurrent users to complete their transactions on the same page without waiting.

> **Note**
>
> If a clustered index is used on a table, it must have the UNIQUE property if you want to be able to take advantage of insert row-level locking.

IRL must be specifically enabled by using the stored procedure **sp_tableoption**. You can enable IRL on an entire database, or for specific tables. When using the stored procedure to enable IRL, the new value takes effect immediately on all tables in the current database. Tables created after IRL is enabled must have IRL specifically enabled for each of them. Only the system administrator the database owner can enable IRL for all tables, while a user can turn off IRL for specific tables.

In order to provide better concurrency when using IRL, two new lock modes have been added to SQL Server.

- Insert_page. This lock mode allows multiple transactions to lock a page while each concurrently inserts data in its own row. The Insert_page lock is compatible only with other Insert_page locks, and it is held until the transactions are complete.

- Link_page. This lock mode is granted to the first transaction that determines the current page is full and that a new page will need to be allocated and linked to the current page. The Insert_page lock for the transaction is promoted to a Link_page lock, and blocks additional requests for Insert_page locks until the new page is allocated and linked to the current page.

Page Locks

The *page lock* is the default granularity locking level, and is the finest level available for all transactions except an INSERT transaction. A page lock can be exclusive or shared, and covers an entire 2K page, either a data page or an index page. When a UPDATE, INSERT, or DELETE transaction is about to write data to a page, it requests and holds an exclusive page lock, preventing any other transaction from writing to the page.

As already mentioned, SQL Server will promote a page lock to a table lock if the number of page locks in a table exceeds a set value. This value is set using the stored procedure **sp_configure**. When using **sp_configure**, you can customize several options that are used to determine when a lock will be escalated:

- LE threshold maximum. This value determines the maximum number of page locks that will be held on a table before escalating from page lock to table lock. The default setting is 200 page locks.

- LE Threshold minimum. This value determines the minimum number of page locks that must be held before escalating from page lock to table lock. This setting works in conjunction with the LE threshold percent value. This setting prevents a table lock being set by the server on very small tables where the LE threshold percent is easily reached. The default setting is 20 page locks.

- LE threshold percent. This value determines the percentage of pages which must be locked before requesting a table lock. The default setting for this value is 0 (zero), allowing a table lock to be requested only when the LE threshold maximum is reached.

As already discussed earlier in this chapter, both the LE threshold maximum and LE threshold percent can be changed within the SQL Server Enterprise Manager application, using the Server Configuration/Options dialog box.

Table Locks

A table lock is the coarsest lock level supported by SQL Server. Table locks are held by SQL Server when the server believes that a transaction will affect an entire table. Table locks can prevent lock collisions and deadlocks at the page level.

Like page locks, table locks can by either exclusive or shared. When an exclusive table lock is held by a transaction, no other transaction can obtain an exclusive page lock or row lock. In other words, when one transaction has an exclusive lock on a table, no other transaction can write to that table until the table lock is released.

A specialized form of a table lock that lower-level locks, such as a page lock, can obtain is called an *intent lock*. When a transaction is planning to write data to one or more pages of a table, it also acquires an intent lock on the table. This lock prevents another concurrent transaction from obtaining a table lock until the first transaction has completed writing to the pages it is modifying.

Deadlocks

Deadlocks are special situations where two (or more) transactions cannot proceed until the other releases a lock it is holding. Neither transaction can proceed because of the other, creating a deadlock. If a deadlock occurs, SQL Server will automatically roll back the transaction that requires the least amount of processing time, sending error message 1205 back to the client application. When this error is received by the client application, the following message is displayed:

> Your server command (process id#%d) was deadlocked with another process and has been chosen as deadlock victim. Re-run your command.

Once SQL Server rolls back the deadlocking transaction, the other transaction is free to place a lock on the resource and complete the process it started. Client applications should always check and trap for error 1205, being sure to resubmit the transaction to the server. Of course, a well written application will not allow deadlocks to occur in the first place. If deadlocks are frequent, recheck how you have set up the locking system in your application.

Update locks are commonly used by SQL Server to prevent deadlocks. When two transactions are both reading a page, one may obtain an update lock if it intends to change data on the page. This prevents the first transaction from escalating their shared lock to an exclusive lock until the other transaction either completes its transaction or is demoted to a standard shared lock.

Using Locks with SELECT

You can customize how locks are used with the SELECT transaction. When lock options are stated in a transaction, they override the default lock formations.

Table 6.1: Lock Options with Select

Lock Option	Description
HOLDLOCK	When selected, this option tells SQL Server to hold a shared lock until the transaction which has specified the HOLDLOCK has completed its work, instead of automatically releasing the lock as soon as the page, view, or table is no longer required.
NOLOCK	This option tells SQL Server to reject all lock requests, holding no shared or exclusive locks. When this lock option has been selected it is possible to read uncommitted transactions or data on pages which are about to be rolled back. This option is also called "dirty reads."

Table 6.1: Lock Options with Select (cont'd)

Lock Option	Description
PAGLOCK	This is the default setting, and requires SQL Server to use shared page locks.
TABLOCK	This option requires SQL Server to use shared table locks. Other users are able to read the table, but no one can update the data contained in the table until the transaction that set the TABLOCK has completed its work on the table. If used in conjunction with the HOLDLOCK option, TABLOCK will be held until the entire transaction has been completed.
TABLOCKX	This option instructs SQL Server to place an exclusive lock on the table. This lock will prevent others from reading or updating the table until the transaction has finished.
UPDLOCK	This lock option uses update locks instead of shared locks when reading a table, holding the update lock until the end of the transaction. This allows you to read data without blocking others from reading the table. By using this option you are assured that data is not changed in the table until after you have completed your transaction.

Setting Transaction Isolation Level

Similar to setting the locking level in a SELECT transaction, you can also set the isolation level for an entire SQL Server session by using the SET statement. The transaction isolation level specifies the default locking level for all SELECT statements during the users current session. Once you log off of the session the isolation levels return to their default settings, and will have to be reset again when you login if you require a different isolation level.

Only one option can be specified in the SET statement, and it remains the default setting for the current session unless explicitly changed.

Table 6.2: Setting the Transaction Isolation Level

Transaction Isolation Level	Description
READ COMMITTED	This is the default method used by SQL Server. Use this option in the SET statement to return the locking behavior back to the default mode.
READ UNCOMMITTED	This mode allows no shared or exclusive locks, and allows "dirty reads" uncommitted data, also called phantom reads. You cannot be assured that data once read will not change when reread during the same transaction. Phantom reads are those where a transaction has rolled back, giving you a value that logically never existed.
REPEATABLE READ or SERIALIZABLE	These are identical terms. Nonrepeatable and phantom reads are not possible when this option is set.

Summary

In this chapter, you have learned several techniques to ensure that your data remains consistent, while at the same time allowing the maximum number of concurrent users. Specifically, you learned:

- To use exclusive, shared, intent, and update locks on tables, pages, extents, and rows.

- How to set the lock granularity in the Server Configuration/Options dialog box.

- That SQL Server uses update locks to prevent deadlocks from occurring.

- To customize a SELECT statement for a locking level.

- To use the SET statement to set the transaction isolation level.

Chapter 7

Startup and Shutdown

IN THIS CHAPTER

- Starting Microsoft SQL Server
- Options for Startup
- Shutting Down Microsoft SQL Server

Before other users can work with a SQL Server database, SQL Server must first be started. If a user tries to login to the database when the server has been stopped or not yet started, they will receive an error telling them that the connection failed.

There are many reasons for shutting down SQL Server: upgrades, full off-line backups, loading a database, or making changes to a databases structure, and many other reasons. Once SQL Server has been stopped or shutdown, it must be started before users can gain access to the information contained in the databases.

Starting Microsoft SQL Server

Microsoft SQL Server runs as a *service* under Windows NT. Services can be configured to start automatically when Windows NT starts, manually started, or disabled. Configuration is normally done in the Services dialog box, which is accessed in the Control Panel. You can also select a server in the SQL Enterprise Manager window and make configuration changes from there.

In multi-user DBMS system, which is what SQL Server is meant to be operated as, it is best if SQL Server is started as an automatic service when the server is booted. If you did not set SQL Server for automatic startup when you ran the Setup program, it can be easily done with a few simple steps.

1.   Double-click the SQL Enterprise Manager icon to open its window. If the SQL Server service has already been started you will see the green light visible on the server stoplight icon. If the light is red the SQL Server service has not been started, and if it is yellow than the service has been paused. If the server is not started, right-click on the SQL Server stoplight icon, and select **S**tart from the shortcut menu.

The same actions can also be performed from the main menu by selecting **S**erver, SQL Server, **S**tart, or by clicking the Stop/Pause/Start Server button on the toolbar.

2.   Right-click the SQL Server icon and select **C**onfigure from the shortcut menu. You will now see the Server Configuration/Options dialog box. Select the Server Options tab and click the Auto Start Server at Boot Time checkbox. The server service will be added and/or changed to automatic in the Windows NT Services Manager.

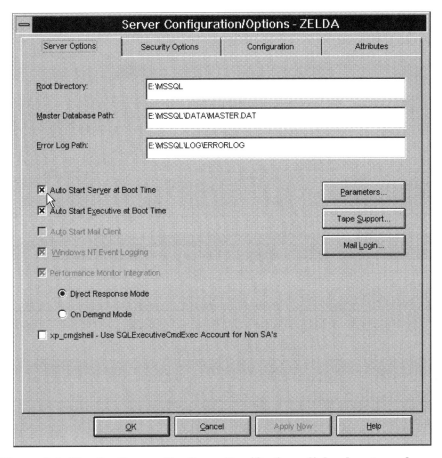

Figure 7.1: Use the Server Configuration/Options dialog box to make adjustments to many server options.

3.   Click the **OK** button to save your changes to the server configuration.

4.   Click the Control Panel icon in the Main program group, and then the Services icon to view the Services dialog box. Scroll through thc list until you find the listing for the MSSQLServer service. You should see the Status listed as Started, and the Startup option as Automatic.

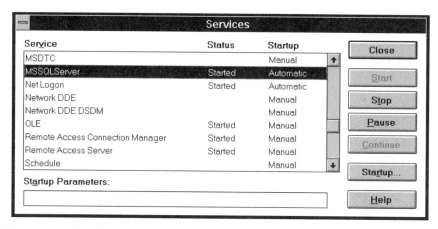

Figure 7.2: The Services dialog box can be used to view or change a services Status (Started, Stopped, or Paused), how it starts up (Automatic, Manual, or Disabled), and add additional parameters where required.

5.   Click the Close button to close the Services dialog box.

Note

You can also set the Startup parameter within the Services dialog box by clicking the Startup button and then selecting the Automatic option button in the Startup Type group.

Options for Startup

SQL Server can be started with several options. It can be run in a single-user mode, or in the normal multi-user mode. You have already learned how to start the SQL Server and to set it to run automatically upon system bootup.

The default options set when you first installed SQL Server are stored in the Windows NT Registry, and are used every time SQL Server is started, whether as a service, from the command line, or from the SQL Enterprise Manager window. You can also start the SQL Server by doing one of the following:

- Starting the service from the Services applet in the Control Panel.

- Typing **net start mssqlserver** from any command line prompt.

- From an operating system command line prompt running the SQL Server application SQLSERVER.EXE, using the following option switches:

   ♦ -c   Starts SQL Server separately from the Windows NT Service Control Manager, shortening the startup time.

   ♦ -d   This switch must be followed by the fully qualified path for the MASTER database device.

   ♦ -e   Follow this switch with the fully qualified path for the error log file.

   ♦ -f   Starts SQL Server in a minimum configuration. Often used when resetting options that have prevented the server from starting.

   ♦ -m   Starts SQL Server in a single-user mode. Often used when repairing or upgrading the server software or databases.

   ♦ -n   Causes the Windows NT event log to be bypassed. It is recommended that when this option is selected you use the -e switch, or no SQL Server events will be logged.

   ♦ -p   This option lets you specify the level of precision that will be supported by decimal and numeric datatypes. The default setting is a maximum precision of 28. You can specify a precision level from 1 to 38. If no precision level is specified when the -p switch is used, the maximum level of 38 will be used for both decimal and numeric datatypes.

   ♦ -r   Use this option to start SQL Server using the mirror file for the MASTER database device if it has become damaged.

   ♦ -s   Selects an alternate set of startup parameters held under the alternate key name in the Registry. This option can only be run from a command-line prompt.

   ♦ /T   Starts SQL Server with a specified trace flag. A trace flag is used to start the server with nonstandard parameters. This switch should be set using an uppercase T. A lowercase t, while accepted by SQL Server, sets additional internal trace flags used by SQL Server support engineers.

   ♦ -x   Disables keeping both CPU time and cache-hit ratio statistics and allows maximum performance.

The first two methods start SQL Server as a Windows NT service, while the third method does not. With SQL Server started independently of the Service Control Manager, you cannot use SQL Enterprise Manager to start, stop, or pause SQL Server as a service. Also, all system messages will print in the window used to start SQL Server. All command-line options will take priority over default options set in the Registry. Finally, you must shutdown the server before logging off of the Windows NT network.

Shutting Down Microsoft SQL Server

For certain jobs, such as upgrading the server software, loading a database from a backup and transaction logs, or making changes to the structure of a database, you will need to shut down SQL Server and then restart it in a single-user mode. This ensures that no user can access the database and update records that may be in a state of change. Shut downs can be scheduled, allowing you to send a message to all users currently logged in, or they can be performed immediately with no warning to users. In this section you will learn how to shut the server down, and how to pause the server.

Pausing the Server

If SQL Server has been started as a Windows NT service, you can pause it before shutting down. Pausing the server allows users who are connected to finish their current tasks, but does not allow new connections to be established. SQL Server can be paused from either the stoplight application by clicking the **P**ause option, or from the command line window with the statement:

```
net pause mssqlserver
```

Generally, it is good practice to pause the server before shutting it down. After pausing, you can send a message to all users that you plan to shut the server down in a specified amount of time. This way all of your users can complete their work and log off in an orderly manner.

Shutting Down the Server

Under most circumstances, SQL Server is considered to be a 24X7 (24 hour by 7 day) server, and is running around-the-clock. When you do need to shut it down, the process can be accomplished from either the local machine on which SQL Server is running, from another server, or from a client workstation on the network.

SQL Server can be shut down using the command line statement SHUTDOWN, which will disable all new logins to the server. In addition, all users currently logged in to the server are allowed to complete their transactions and procedures, all database checkpoints are executed, and then the SQL Server executable program stops. Only the system administrator login remains active after SHUTDOWN has finished. This shut down is orderly and ensures that data integrity is maintained.

You can also use the statement SHUTDOWN WITH NOWAIT. This shut down option should not be used unless there is some type of emergency and the server must be shut down immediately. This option shuts the server down, with no regard to current server processes being run. All transactions are stopped, and will be rolled back upon restarting SQL Server during the normal recovery operations. Checkpoints are not executed, and the server will need to do much additional work to recover when restarted. While data integrity is not compromised, it can cause much anxiety among your users who have been cut off from the server without warning. As the system administrator, you can be sure that you will receive many excited phone calls if you shut the server down in this manner.

If SQL Server has been started from a command line window, you can stop the server by pressing Ctrl+C from you keyboard. This will also shutdown the server via an orderly shutdown.

You can also use the graphical stoplight icon, SQL Service Manager, within the Microsoft SQL Server program group, or click the stoplight icon on the SQL Enterprise Manager's toolbar. From either place you can stop, pause, or start SQL Server. Figure 7.3 displays the SQL Server Service Manager dialog box with its stoplight interface for starting, stopping, or pausing the server.

Figure 7.3: With the SQL Server Service Manager dialog box, you can stop, pause, or start the SQL Server service.

SQL Server must be shut down for you to perform several common management tasks:

- Resetting many configuration options. While there are some configuration selections that can be set with the server running, most do require that the server be shut down. Changes in memory allocation and some system resources do not take effect until SQL Server is restarted.

- Deleting some transactions from the logs. When a client application is disconnected without committing or rolling back a transaction that has been written to the log, you will need to remove the transaction in order to truncate the log. When the server is restarted, normal recovery will mark these transactions for roll back.

- Setting trace flags. Specialized server trace flags are set during SQL Server startup. These flags can be used to access DBCC and additional monitoring processes.

- Configuring a mirror device for the master device. A mirror device must be created and the server restarted before the mirror is activated.

Only the system administrator, and other users who can use the system administrator login, have permission to use the **SHUTDOWN** command. This function cannot be granted to another user.

Summary

In this chapter you have learned to bring SQL Server to an orderly shutdown and restart. Specifically, you have learned:

- To manually stop and start SQL Server.

- To set SQL Server for automatic startup.

- To pause the Server before shutting it down.

Chapter 8

Managing Database Space

IN THIS CHAPTER

- Planning Database Space Requirements
- Expanding a Database
- Shrinking a Database
- Dropping Database Devices

As a system administrator one of your jobs is to ensure that SQL Server makes optimal use of the disk space that is available to it. This includes not only being sure that there is enough disk space for SQL Server and the associated data files, but that they are distributed across the disk(s) such that recovery can be easily facilitated.

Planning Database Space Requirements

Planning the space requirements for a new database is very important. As you create a database device, physical disk space is allocated to the device. If you allocate too little space, you will have to allocate additional space, if there is room available. If you allocate too much space, you may take much needed expensive disk space from other databases. Remember, SQL Server allocates disk space using three different storage units:

- A 2KB page

- The extent, composed of 8 continuous pages

- The allocation unit, composed of 32 extents, or 256 pages

The minimum size that you can allocate for a database is one allocation unit, or one-half MB. While this is not a great deal of space by today's standards, it can be very easy to allocate all of your available disk space if you have several heavily used databases. The final size of a database is the total of all data fragments, plus the size of all log fragments. A fragment is a part of a database contained on a database device and is a minimum of one allocation unit in size. A database can consist of both data and log fragments scattered across several devices.

When creating a new database or allocating additional space for an existing one, you will decide not only on how large the database will be, but also how large the transaction log should be. When first creating a database, a rough guideline is that between 10 to 25% of your database's size should be allocated to the transaction log. Once the database has been tested and is placed into production, you should be able to more accurately assess the necessary size of the transaction log. Some of the factors that you will need to consider as you decide on the size of your transaction log are:

- The number of transactions processed between dumps.

- The length of time you have set for the recovery interval.

- The average size of transactions, or the amount of data updated by average transactions.

- How often very large transactions are processed.

This last point is made primarily because a poorly written transaction can potentially cause a transaction log to become full between dumps without coming to the COMIT TRAN statement, bringing the entire database to a grinding halt.

The transaction log should always be placed on a separate database device from its database file. The better option is not only on a separate device, but a device that is located on a different physical disk. The reason that you want to locate the transaction log on a separate device is so that the transaction log can be dumped and truncated. This allows you to keep the log backup files as up-to-date as possible and as small as possible, by removing the inactive part of the log—all transactions from the last DUMP TRANSACTION statement up to the last uncommitted transaction. If you keep both the log and database together on the same device, you can not dump the transaction log by itself, you have to do a full backup of the entire database. This is a much more time consuming process than dumping just the transaction log.

Note

After making any changes to the size of an existing database, be sure to backup both the database you changed, and more importantly, the master database.

Sizing the Database

When you create a database, there are several parameters you supply to SQL Server, one of which is the initial size of the database. If you do not tell SQL Server how large a database to create, then SQL Server will create a database of the same size as the model database. Remember, SQL Server will copy the model database and insert all of its tables into your new database. With SQL Server prior to version 6.5, the smallest database that could be created was 2MB in size. SQL Server 6.5 reduces this to 1MB, allowing you to place databases on floppy disks as removable media.

Space for a database can be allocated across as many database devices as necessary. This is often done when the device on which the database currently resides becomes full, or if you want to locate different parts of the database on different devices. Database devices must exist on one of the servers local drives SQL Server does not support database devices across networked drives.

The default size of a database is controlled by the greater of the model database size or the value of **database size** in the **sysconfigures** table. For example, if your model database is 1MB in size, the default setting and the database size value has been set to 6, your new database will be created with a default size of 6MB, unless you specify a different value. A database cannot be created smaller than the model database. Remember, when SQL Server creates your database, it copies the necessary system tables from the model database and places them into your new database, and then extends the size of your database to your specified size or to the larger of the database size value or the model database size.

The default database size value is changed using the stored procedure **sp_configure**:

```
sp_configure "database size", 6
reconfigure
```

The **reconfigure** statement is required to make the changes in the sysconfigures table. Only the system administrator can use **sp_configure** with parameters and effect a change. SQL Server must be stopped and then started again for all but dynamic values to take effect. You can also increase the size of the model database so that it is 6MB in size. The recommended method is to change the database size value with **sp_configure**. This is the easiest adjustment to make, and you do not have to give over additional physical disk space for the model database.

You can also change the database size value from the SQL Server Enterprise Manager application, by opening the Server Configuration/Options. The database size configuration is an option available on the Configuration tab. If you change the value of the database size, you will have to stop and then restart SQL Server before the new value will take effect.

When creating a new database, you can specify a different size for it, rather than use the size of the model database, or the value specified in database size. This is how to specify the size of a database when using the T-SQL CREATE statement:

```
CREATE DATABASE inventory
ON business1 = 10
```

This statement will create a new database with the name *inventory*, one database device *business1*, with a size of 10MB.

You can also use the SQL Enterprise Manager window to create a new database, and if necessary, a new database device. Using the SQL Enterprise Manager is a very simple way to create a new database or a new database device. See Chapter 3, "Logical Structures," for a complete description on how to create new databases and devices with SQL Enterprise Manager.

Sizing the Transaction Log

The size of your transaction log is very important to the well-being of your database and information. If the log is too small, it may become full before a checkpoint is reached and the log dumped and truncated, bringing all modifications to data to a halt. If it is too large it will unnecessarily use up valuable disk space.

In almost all normal cases, you will want to create a separate database device on which to place the transaction log. The only exception to this rule is in regards to the master database. Its log cannot be separated, nor placed on a different device other than its default placement on the master database device. By using separate devices, you give yourself much additional flexibility and security because:

- Under normal database usage, SQL Server truncates, or clears the log only after an incremental backup has occurred. When the data and transaction log are not separated, SQL Server can only perform full backups, requiring the system administrator to manually truncate the log after each full backup. This is both inefficient of your time and negates some of the important features available to you with SQL Server.

- By separating the log and data areas of a database you can gain some additional performance advantages, especially if the different devices are on separate physical disks and/or controllers in the server.

- Recovery can be expedited and is more assured if the logs are separate from the data. With complete transaction logs and incremental backups, you can be assured of recovery possibly even to the last transaction. With only full backups of all of your data, you can only recover up to the point when the last full backup was performed.

The actual size of your transaction logs will depend on several factors:

- How frequent incremental backups are performed. The more frequently incremental backups are done, the smaller the required transaction log.

- The volume of simultaneous updates by multiple users. The larger the number of simultaneous updates, the larger the transaction log should be. If many updates are performed at once, it is possible to fill the transaction log, which in turn prevents all transactions from being completed.

- Numbers of long transactions. The transaction log can quickly become full if large amounts of data are being updated or inserted in a single transaction. Remember, the data does not get written from the log to the data rows until after a transaction has been committed. With a large, single transaction you may need to have a transaction log larger than the data areas. It is always recommended that large transactions be broken into several smaller ones. You can then dump the log after each.

- The normal activity level of the database. If a database has a high level of normal activity, the transaction log will probably need to be correspondingly larger to ensure that it does not become full before the next incremental backup and clearing of the log.

Transaction logs can be created along with their data areas with the CREATE DATABASE statement, or they can be added later using the ALTER DATABASE statement. You can also, of course, use the SQL Enterprise Manager window and the Manage Database dialog box as you learned earlier in Chapter 3, "Logical Structures."

When creating a new database with separate data and log areas, the T-SQL statement looks like this:

```
CREATE DATABASE inventory
ON business1 = 10
LOG ON business1log = 3
```

This statement creates a new database *inventory* with a data area of 10MB in size on the device *business1*, with the transaction log located on the device *business1log* and a log area of 3MB. This gives you a database with a total size of 13MB.

When altering an existing database so that the log area is separate, when originally created with shared data and log areas, you have one additional step to perform. The stored procedure **sp_logdevice** is required for SQL Server to move the **syslogs** system table which contains the transaction log onto the new device before you can use the DUMP TRANSACTION statement. The T-SQL statement would look like this:

```
ALTER DATABASE inventory
ON business1log = 5
GO
SP_LOGDEVICE inventory, business1log
GO
```

This statement alters the database *inventory* by adding a new 5MB segment on device *business1log*. The **sp_logdevice** then moves the transaction log to the new segment. All new transactions will be located on the new device. You must dump the transaction log to ensure that no log pages remain with the data pages of the database.

Expanding a Database

After a database has been used for some time, it may begin to fill up the space it has been allocated. Before this actually happens, you will want to allocate more space to the database. Space can be allocated on any available database device. You can expand a database across one or more devices, and the task can be accomplished using either T-SQL statements or from within the graphical SQL Enterprise Manager window. Databases can be expanded while SQL Server is running and the database is in use, it will not adversely effect your users.

There is one exception to the statement that you can allocate space for a database on any available device, and that is for the master database. The master database can only be expanded on the master database device. It can not be placed on another device. If you need to expand the master database and there is not enough room on the master device, you will need to increase the size of the master device first and then expand the master database.

On the Same Database Device

In most cases, you will expand a database on the same device on which it currently exists—though this is not a requirement. When expanding a database, you can use the T-SQL ALTER DATABASE statement, or work within the SQL Enterprise Manager application window. An ALTER DATABASE statement would look like this:

```
ALTER DATABASE inventory
ON business1 = 15
```

This statement adds an additional data segment to the database *inventory* with a size of 15MB This additional segment is added to the databases original size. The size of the inventory database after this ALTER DATABASE statement has been run will be the original size plus the new 15MB segment.

While the size of a database can be changed with the **ALTER DATABASE** statement, you may find using the graphical SQL Enterprise Manager window easier, as shown in these steps:

1. Open the SQL Enterprise Manager window and select **M**anage, **D**atabases from the menu. You will now see the Manage Databases dialog box. From this window you can begin the process of creating new databases, or to expand or shrink existing ones.

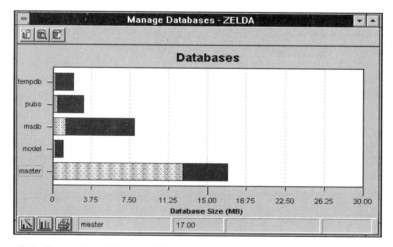

Figure 8.1: From the Manage Databases window, you can add and alter the various databases on your server. If you do not see a database on the graph, there will be a scroll bar on the right side of the graph, use it to view additional databases.

Note

Notice the information displayed in the status bar at the bottom of the Manage Database window as you move the mouse pointer onto the different graph bars. When you place the pointer onto one of the graph bars, the database name is displayed in the status bar. Alongside the name as you move the pointer along the graph bar you will see either Used Space or Free Space and the megabytes for each.

---

2.   Select the **pubs** database by moving the selector box from **master** to **pubs** on the graphs Y-axis. Now either click the Edit Database button on the toolbar, or double-click the database name or the database's bar on the graph to display the Edit Database dialog box.

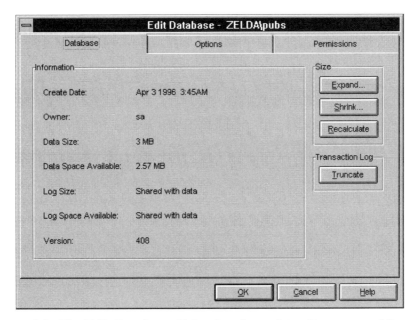

Figure 8.2: The Edit Database dialog box is used to alter many of the properties, including the size of a selected database.

This dialog box has three tab buttons, each of which are used to alter or add different aspects of a database.

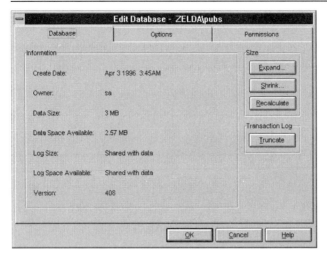

The Database tab, shown here in figure 8.3, is used to alter the size of the selected database, by either expanding or shrinking it. Both the **Expand** and **Shrink** button display another dialog box for the purpose of altering the database size. When expanding the database, you will also select the database device on which to place the additional extension. The **T**runcate button allows you to truncate the databases log file. When you use this option, all of the inactive log entries will be deleted without being dumped to a backup device. The **R**ecalculate button allows SQL Server to recalculate the available space in the database. You should always use this option before shrinking a database, to ensure that SQL Server has complete statistics for the current size of the database, and enable you to ensure that you will have complete information when you decide how to expand your database.

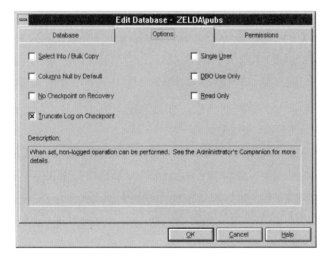

The Options tab, shown here in figure 8.4, displays a dialog box with several options. Each of these options effect the entire database. **Select Into/Bulk Copy** allows you to add large blocks of data into the database without logging each transaction. **Columns Null by Default** specifies that all columns added to a new table will allow NULL values unless otherwise specified. **N**o Checkpoint on Recovery prevents a checkpoint from being recorded during recovery. **T**runcate Log on Checkpoint is a default setting, and the only setting you can set for the master database. It specifies that the transaction log will be truncated when a checkpoint is reached. Single **U**ser sets this database to allow only one user at a time. **D**BO Use Only allows only the database owner to use the database. **R**ead Only allows users to read, but not to alter, records.

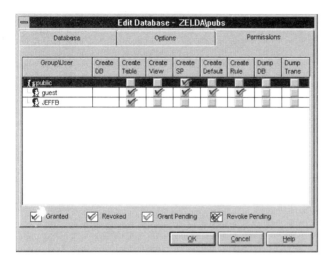

The Permissions tab options, shown here as figure 8.5, enable you to grant or revoke CREATE and DUMP permissions for various statements to those users who have been granted access to the database. From here, you can restrict the abilities of selected users from creating databases, tables, views, stored procedures, default values, and rules. You can also restrict who can dump the database or the transaction log. These restrictions can be placed on either an individual user or on an entire group of users. Use this tab option to easily select users or groups, and what permissions you either want to grant to them, or to restrict them from accessing. Simply select a specific user or group from the list in the first column and then click the check box to grant a permission in the various option columns. To revoke a permission, click the check box to remove the checkmark. The option will be displayed as a checkmark with the red international symbol for no, the circle with a slash through it.

3.   Click the Database tab if not already selected. The options available in this dialog box are those concerned with expanding the size of your database, where to place the new segments of the database, and truncating the log file. Click the **E**xpand button.

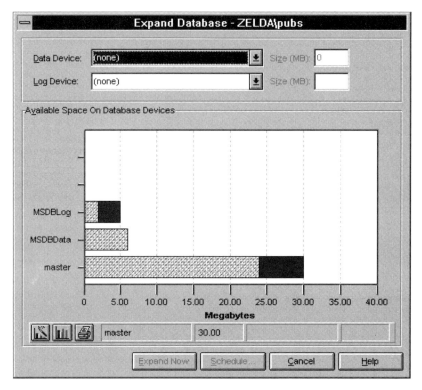

Figure 8.6: From the Expand Database dialog box you can view both available and used space and choose which database devices on which to expand the selected database. You can even create a new database device here. This dialog box also displays information about each device as you move the mouse pointer through and along its bar.

4.   From the **D**ata Device list box, select master as the database device on which to expand the pubs database. Notice how the Size(MB) text box changes from 0 to 6 and the Free Space part of the master databases graph changes color. It now displays the Data Size color, and this will also be shown in the status bar if you run the mouse pointer over it.

There are three icon buttons in the status bar that are used to customize some of the features of the graph:

- The first button is used to change some of the graph properties: labels, display solid colors or textured colors, display a graph legend, and choose graph types.

- • The second button changes some of the bar graph options, including: graph mode, which turns on or off the information displayed in the status bar, and the graph orientation–horizontal or vertical bars.

- • The third button gives you some printing options, including: print colors, date/time or graph legend inclusion, and font selection.

5. In the Size(MB) text box, type 2 as the amount of new space you want to add to the pubs database. See how the master databases bar changes again, now showing three segments: Used Space, Free Space, and Data Size.

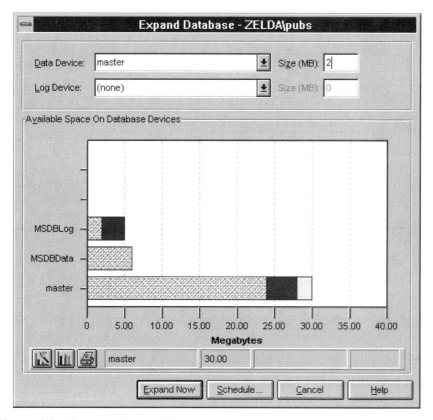

Figure 8.7: Here the Expand Database dialog box shows the additional space added to the pubs database pictured on the master database's bar of the graph.

6.   Click the Expand Now button, and SQL Server will expand the pubs database on the master database device now.

> Clicking the Schedule button will display a Schedule dialog box. You can then choose when the expansion will occur. Use this option when you have users working in the database and there is a time, such as after hours, when SQL Server can proceed with this action and not interfere with normal business operations. If you are only creating a small extension to a database, the perceived delays by your users may not be significant, but if you are planning a very large expansion of your database, it may take SQL Server several minutes to several hours, depending upon your server's platform, memory, and number of users, to complete this task.

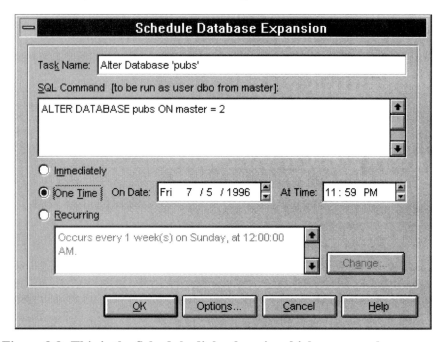

Figure 8.8: This is the Schedule dialog box, in which you can choose a specific time for this task to run.

You will now be back at the Edit Database dialog box. Notice that Data Size now equals 5MB, the original 3, plus the 2 you just added, and that the Data Space Available now equals 4.57MB.

On Other Database Devices

As a database grows, you may want to expand the database over different devices or onto more than one device. With a database that has a very high rate of queries and updates, you can gain some performance benefits by placing parts of the database on separate hard disk drives and disk controllers. The process of adding a new database segment, either data or log, on a different device is the same as you have already learned. The only difference is that you name the new device instead of the device the database or transaction log was originally placed on. The T-SQL statement to expand a database across two devices is also very similar to the one you used to expand the same database on one device, and looks like this:

```
ALTER DATABASE inventory
ON business1 = 15, ON business2 = 10
```

This statement adds two data segments to the database *inventory*. The first 15MB segment is placed on the device *business1*, and a second segment of 10MB is placed on device *business2*. These additional segments are added to the databases original size.

You can also use SQL Enterprise Manager to expand a database across different or multiple segments. The process is the same as shown in the previous section of this chapter. When placing a segment on a different database device, you will select the new device, instead of the original device, in step 4 and then continue with steps 5 and 6. When adding new segments on more than one device, you simply repeat steps 4, 5 and 6 for each new segment, selecting the appropriate device.

Shrinking a Database

At times you may find that a database has not grown as you had originally anticipated and you want to recover the disk space which was allocated to the database. You can not shrink a database so that is smaller than the model database or to a size which is not a valid number of allocation units. Nor can you shrink the database so that it is smaller than it now is. For example, if your database contains 5MB of actual data, you cannot shrink it so that it will fit in a 4MB database, without deleting 1MB of data first. A database can be shrunk using the T-SQL statement DBCC SHRINKDB or from within the SQL Enterprise Manager window.

When using DBCC SHRINKDB you should use a two-step process. The first is to check how small you can make the database, and the second is actually shrinking the database. Use ISQL/w and enter the following statement:

```
USE pubs
GO
SP_DBOPTION 'pubs', 'single user', true
GO
DBCC SHRINKDB (pubs)
GO
```

You will see a results of these statements in the Results window, like this:

```
Current size of database      Size database can be shrunk to
-------------------------------   -------------------------------------------
1536                          1024
(1 row(s) affected)
```

As you look at the statement, the first one tells SQL Server that you want to work with the pubs database. You could have selected pubs in the **DB** list box and then you would not have had to added this statement line. The next statement with the stored procedure **sp_dboption** sets the database into a single user mode, this is required when shrinking a database. The final statement DBCC SHRINKDB displays the current size of the database and the minimum size to which you can shrink it. Whenever you use the DBCC SHRINKDB statement without a size appended to it, you will see this type of a results.

Note

Before shrinking a database, backup both the master and the database that will be shrunk before you actually perform the shrinking. This will ensure that you can recover your data if anything untoward happens during the process.

The smallest you can shrink the pubs database is to 1MB in size, and it can be accomplish with this statement:

```
USE pubs
GO
SP_DBOPTION 'pubs', 'single user', true
GO
DBCC SHRINKDB (pubs, 1024)
GO
```

If you receive the message that no rows were returned and their are no error messages, than everything should have proceeded normally and the database will now be shrunk to your specified size. If you do receive error messages, be sure to check each and see what may need to be done.

Shrinking a database from within the SQL Enterprise Manager is a very simple task:

1. Open the SQL Enterprise Manager window and right-click on Databases. Select Edit from the shortcut menu to display the Manage Databases dialog box.

Note

If you do not see the database you wish to shrink in the graph, use the horizontal scroll bar that is available, and scroll up or down until you do see the database name and bar. This scroll bar is only available if there are more databases than can be displayed within the graph area.

2. Select the pubs database. You can edit this database by either double-clicking it or selecting it and then clicking the Edit Database button. This will display the Edit Database dialog box which you learned to used earlier in this chapter in the section "Expanding a Database." Notice the totals for the Data Size and Data Space Available in this dialog box and then click the Shrink button.

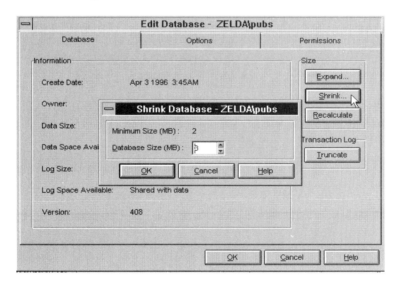

Figure 8.9: By clicking the Shrink button you can use the Shrink Database dialog box to select a new size for the selected database.

The Shrink Database dialog box will display the minimum size to which you can shrink the database, and displays the current size of the database in the spinner box labeled **D**atabase Size (MB).

3.   Type **2** as the reduced size of the pubs database and click the **OK** button. SQL Server will shrink the database and then recalculate the Data Size and Data Space Available figures in the Manage Database dialog box.

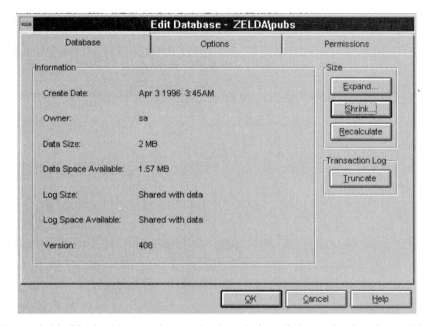

Figure 8.10: Notice the newly recalculated size of the pubs database. If you watch closely, you will see the figures change.

4.   Click the **OK** button to complete the shrinking process.

If you want to expand the database back to its original size, see the "Expanding a Database" section earlier in this chapter.

Note

Be sure to backup the master database after shrinking a database so that you are ensured that all of the necessary information about the database is permanently saved.

Dropping Database Devices

One of the normal functions as system administrator that you will have to routinely perform is the dropping of unused database objects and devices. Dropping unused devices helps you to free additional valuable disk space on your server. Only the system administrator has permission to drop devices and this permission cannot be granted to another user, nor can the database be in use by a user when it is dropped. You will have to set some rules and standards as to what to consider available for dropping.

Some of the reasons you may decide to drop a database device could be:

- The database has been replaced by a newer, faster version of the application and all necessary data has been dumped to the new device.

- The database may be a temporary testing or teaching device that can be dropped once their function is no longer necessary.

Dropping the device from SQL Server does not also delete the device's operating system file, you must still delete the file from File Manager or a command line prompt. Dropping a device removes its entry from the *sysdevices* table in the master database. Database devices can be dropped using the stored procedure sp_dropdevice or from within the SQL Enterprise Manager. The stored procedure would look like this:

```
sp_dropdevice pubs, DELFILE
```

The optional statement DELFILE tells SQL Server to delete the operating system file after dropping the device. If you do not want to delete the physical file, then do not use the DELFILE statement. You cannot use this stored procedure to drop a database device if it still has any databases in it. You must first drop any existing databases before you can use the stored procedure sp_dropdevice.

There are two methods you can use to drop a database device from within the SQL Enterprise Manager window, the simplest being:

1.   Open the SQL Enterprise Manager window, connect to the server and open its Database Devices folder. Right-click on the device you want to delete and select **D**elete from the shortcut menu.

Figure 8.11: From the Delete Non-Empty Device dialog box, you can see a list of all data and log fragments that are contained in this device. Each item listed in this dialog box will be dropped along with the device.

2.   Click the **D**elete Device button if you really do want to delete this device and everything that is stored on it. Click the **C**ancel button to return to the SQL Enterprise Manager window without making any changes.

3.   Use File Manager to delete the operating system files for the dropped database device. Remember, the database device will have the same name as the device listed in figure 8.8, with the extension .DAT.

Summary

In this chapter, you have learned to plan the size and locations for both databases and their transaction logs. Specifically, you have learned:

- How to size both a database and its transaction log.

- How to expand a database and transaction log.

- To shrink a database or transaction log.

- And to delete a database device and any databases or transaction logs that may exist on it.

Chapter 9

Optimizing Performance

IN THIS CHAPTER

- Optimizing Memory Usage
- Optimizing Disk Performance
- Using Segments
- The Multithreaded Server
- Optimizing Queries
- Dropping Databases

Other than the everyday tasks of maintaining databases, client access, and other such tasks, a system administrator will attempt to tweak and tune SQL Server to improve the performance of the database as a whole. This is not a single procedure, but a continuous process that involves several of SQL Servers subsystems: memory, physical disks, database segments, and queries. In this chapter, database performance has to do with the speed with which your clients can access information contained in a SQL Server database. This can be a very complex topic, with some specialists devoting years to mastering the craft.

Optimizing Memory Usage

This chapter will provide an overview of the subject and some of the steps you can use to improve the performance of your SQL Server database. In the Windows NT operating system, much of the memory configuration is done by Windows NT and the operating system administrator, who often is not the same person who is the SQL Server system administrator.

How much memory is made available to SQL Server is determined by a number of factors, including:

- How much physical memory is installed in the computer?

- Is the server used for any other purposes, or is it dedicated exclusively to SQL Server's use?

- How much physical disk space is available?

- Will the server be participating as a replication server?

System Memory

As you consider memory, you must consider how Windows NT uses memory and how it allocates that memory for SQL Server to use. Windows NT configures the available memory, reserving approximately the first 12MB to its own operating kernel and services. The amount of memory required by Windows NT will grow as your needs for resources for SQL Server also grow, as Windows NT has to accommodate additional threads, page tables, and other memory needs. The next portion of available memory is available for executable programs, such as SQL Server. The physical memory available to you in your server is allocated based on a determination by SQL Server's setup program when you first installed the program. Setup will automatically appropriate 4 to 8MB of memory in servers with less than 32MB of RAM, or 16 or more MB in systems with 32MB or more.

Win32 applications, such as SQL Server, can make use of Windows NT's Virtual Memory Manager, allowing the application to make use of virtual memory. Virtual memory is a combination of both physical RAM memory and hard disk space used by the PAGEFILE.SYS file. To ensure the best possible performance, SQL Server can lock memory for its own use, potentially causing other applications to receive "out of memory" errors. If this does occur, you may need to adjust downward the amount of memory assigned to SQL Server. If the server is assigned more work than simply a server for SQL Server, you may have to give less memory than SQL Server optimally wants, unless you add additional RAM to the computer.

The memory allocated to SQL Server is divided into several parts. The first is the part that is used by the SQL Server executable program. This memory is not configurable, nor adjustable. The next part is configurable and is used by SQL Server's kernel and internal structures. The final, and largest part, is the cache. The cache is composed of two parts: procedure and data. The procedure cache holds stored procedures, triggers, views, rules, and defaults. The data cache holds the data SQL Server believes will be needed next. The size of the procedure cache can be changed, which has the effect of changing the data cache at the same time.

SQL Server provides several tools for you to use to help you decide how to tune your server's memory. The primary tools are DBCC MEMUSAGE and several of the statistics available from the SQL Performance Monitor.

DBCC MEMUSAGE will give you a detailed report on how SQL Server is using the memory it has been provided. This report is divided into three sections: Memory Usage, Buffer Cache, and Procedure Cache. DBCC MEMUSAGE can be used from within the ISQL/w program. An abbreviated version of the report looks like this:

Memory Usage:

	Meg.	2K Blks	Bytes
Configured Memory:	16.0000	8192	16777216
Code size:	1.7166	879	1800000
Static Structures:	0.2559	132	268336
Locks:	0.2861	147	300000
Open Objects:	0.1144	59	120000
Open Databases:	0.0031	2	3220
User Context Areas:	0.7505	385	787002
Page Cache:	8.9232	4569	9356608
Proc Headers:	0.2148	110	225212
Proc Cache Bufs:	3.6074	1847	3782656

This is the memory usage section of the report. Notice how all of the parameters are shown first in megabytes, then 2K pages, and finally in bytes—the first two columns are generally the more useful. The most important things that you want to note on this report, as far as memory configuration is concerned are:

Be sure that *Configured Memory* is the same size that you set when configuring the memory option for SQL Server using sp_configure, or from within SQL Enterprise Manager. In this case it is 16MB or 8192-2K pages.

Proc Headers and *Proc Cache Bufs* when added together equal the size of the procedure cache. Here the procedure cache is 3.8222MB or 1957-2K pages.

The *Page Cache* is the same as the data cache. It is 8.9232MB or 4569-2K pages.

Buffer Cache, Top 20:

DB Id	Object Id	Index Id	2K Buffers
1	5	0	187
1	3	0	41
1	1	0	21
5	5	0	20
1	5	1	10
1	1	2	9
1	99	0	9
2	3	0	8
1	2	0	6

1	6	0	6
1	36	0	4
5	1	0	4
5	2	0	4
5	3	0	4
5	5	1	4
1	6	1	3
2	2	0	3
5	1	2	3
5	99	0	3
1	45	255	2

The second part of the report lists the first 20 largest objects, tables, and indexes, which are being held in the buffer cache.

Procedure Cache, Top 20:

Procedure Name: sp_MSdbuserprofile
Database Id: 1
Object Id: 1449056198
Version: 1
Uid: 1
Type: stored procedure
Number of trees: 0
Size of trees: 0.000000 Mb, 0.000000 bytes, 0 pages
Number of plans: 2
Size of plans: 0.171600 Mb, 179936.000000 bytes, 90 pages

Procedure Name: sp_helpdistributor
Database Id: 1
Object Id: 1372531923
Version: 1
Uid: 1
Type: stored procedure
Number of trees: 0
Size of trees: 0.000000 Mb, 0.000000 bytes, 0 pages
Number of plans: 2
Size of plans: 0.042969 Mb, 45056.000000 bytes, 24 pages

Procedure Name: sp_MSforeach_worker
Database Id: 1
Object Id: 1337055799

Version: 1
Uid: 1
Type: stored procedure
Number of trees: 0
Size of trees: 0.000000 Mb, 0.000000 bytes, 0 pages
Number of plans: 1
Size of plans: 0.037066 Mb, 38866.000000 bytes, 20 pages

The final part of the DBCC MEMUSAGE report lists the largest 20 objects stored in the procedure cache, though only the first three are shown here. If an object has been duplicated in the procedure cache, all of its aspects are lumped together and only listed once in this report. You may often have duplicated objects. A precompiled version of an object is listed as *trees*, while compiled versions are listed as *plans*.

You can also use the SQL Performance Monitor to check selected performance statistics. This can be shown as a live graph, allowing you to monitor how well SQL Server is using the resources that are available to it. You should run these tests while the server is under a normal working load, otherwise you will get results which will probably not be representative of your system.

One of the easiest and least expensive ways to improve the performance of SQL Server is to add additional physical memory. By using SQL Performance Monitor, you can determine if this will actually help in your situation or not. New memory is primarily used by SQL Server as additional buffer cache, which consequently may improve the cache hit ratio. The cache hit ratio is a statistic which shows how often, as a percentage, SQL Server finds the data it needs to be available in the data cache. The more often, or the higher this ratio, the less often SQL Server has to go and read this information from disk. Since disk reads are many times slower than reading the same information from the data cache, disk reads are much more expensive than are memory reads in terms of performance. The SQL Performance Monitor is used like this:

1.   Double-click on the Performance Monitor icon. You may find it in the Microsoft SQL Server program group, or in the Administrative Tools program group. You will now see the Performance Monitor window displayed.

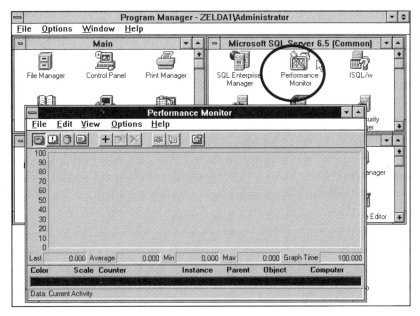

Figure 9.1: The Performance Monitor icon is circled here, and its window is now open. No performance statistics have yet been selected.

2.   Click the Add counter button on the toolbar, select **E**dit, **A**dd To Chart from the menu, or press keyboard shortcut Ctrl+I to open the Add to Chart dialog box.

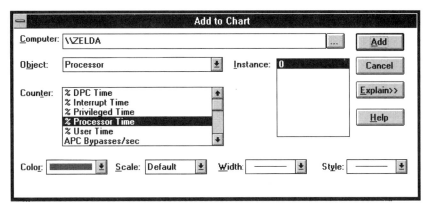

Figure 9.2: From the Add to Chart dialog box you can select from many different groups of counters, depending upon the type of information that you want to get.

> **Note**
>
> When you install SQL Server, setup adds several groups of additional counters to the Performance Monitor are unique to SQL Server. If you want an explanation of a specific, counter click on the Explain button. You will see a small extension added to the bottom of the window where a description of the currently selected counter will be displayed.

3.   From the Object list box, select Memory. You will now see a new list displayed in the Counter list. Select Page Faults/sec from the list now displayed in Counter list box, and then click the Add button. Notice that the Cancel button changes to a Done button. Click it once you have added all of the counters that you currently want to view. Click it now.

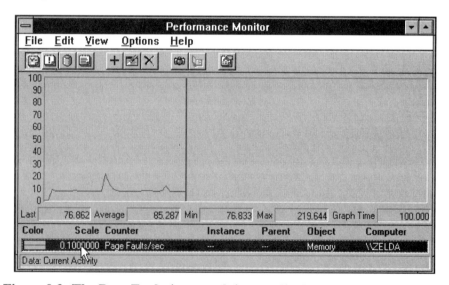

Figure 9.3: The Page Faults/sec graph is now displayed. This counter can help you to decide if your memory configuration is optimized for SQL Server.

The Performance Monitor can run in the background so that you can periodically check current statistics. You can display more than one counter at a time on the graph, and you can adjust the frequency at which the Performance Monitor will update the graph. A setting of between 1 and 3 seconds is usually adequate for most statistics. If you want to view the graph over a longer period of time, click the Option button on the toolbar and reset the value for **I**nterval to a greater number of seconds. The value shown in figure 9.3 for Graph Time is the number of seconds for the Performance Monitor to complete a sweep from one side of the graph to the other. You can also decrease the time interval to values of less than one second, but note that a short time interval adds a measure of overhead to the graph. Once you set the time interval too small, such as one tenth of a second, some of the counters will jump to 100 percent, and you may add a degree of unstability within Windows NT itself, possibly causing a system crash.

Allocating Memory

Once you have gathered your information you can make some adjustments to SQL Server's memory allocations. There are two parameters which you can change: memory and procedure cache. The memory parameter is the amount of memory which SQL Server will request from Windows NT. Windows NT will allocate as much of this memory from real physical memory, allocating any remaining amount from virtual memory.

SQL Server uses the first part of the allocated memory for its own executable code, its kernel, and internal structures. Another 5% of the remaining memory is allocated towards miscellaneous overhead incurred by the server. The remaining 95% is divided between procedure and buffer cache.

Both the memory and procedure cache settings can be changed from within the SQL Enterprise Manager window. Recheck the Performance Monitor statistics after making changes, especially increases to the memory parameter. If you see that the number of page faults increases, then you have allocated too much memory for SQL Server's use and are causing the system to resort to the paging file for data. Causing SQL Server to read from the paging file results in actual disk reads, and consequently is much slower. Reconfigure these two parameters like this:

1.   Open the SQL Enterprise Manager window and right-click on the server icon. Select **C**onfigure from the shortcut menu. You can also use the menu bar and choose **Server**, **SQL Server**, **Configure**, displaying the Server Configuration/Options dialog box.

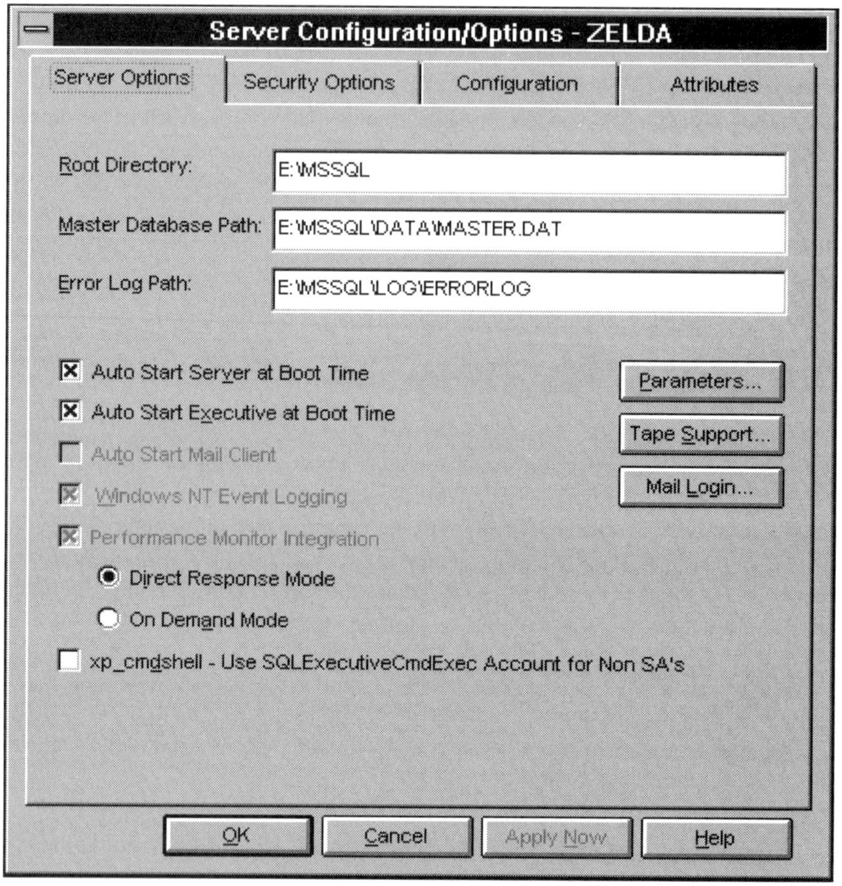

Figure 9.4: The Server Configuration/Options dialog box is used to change many options and configuration parameters, including memory and procedure cache size.

2.   Click the Configuration tab and then scroll down the list of configuration parameters until you find memory. The parameters are listed in alphabetical order.

The Configuration tab is divided into four columns. The first column lists the minimum values for the parameter, while the next column lists the maximum value. The third column lists the currently running value, while the fourth, Current, column is the column you can use to change a parameter.

3.   Select the memory parameter by clicking the value displayed in the Current column. Replace the current value of 4096 with the new value 8192. This new value means that after SQL Server has been stopped and restarted, it will request 16MB of memory from Windows NT. Remember, the value you enter for memory is the number of 2K pages, not the number of MBs required.

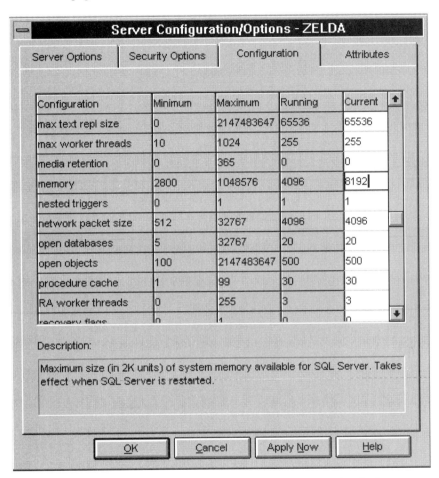

Configuration	Minimum	Maximum	Running	Current
max text repl size	0	2147483647	65536	65536
max worker threads	10	1024	255	255
media retention	0	365	0	0
memory	2800	1048576	4096	8192
nested triggers	0	1	1	1
network packet size	512	32767	4096	4096
open databases	5	32767	20	20
open objects	100	2147483647	500	500
procedure cache	1	99	30	30
RA worker threads	0	255	3	3
recovery flags	0	1	0	0

Description:

Maximum size (in 2K units) of system memory available for SQL Server. Takes effect when SQL Server is restarted.

Figure 9.5: From the Configuration tab you can change both the memory and procedure cache sizes.

Note: If you inadvertently set an invalid memory configuration (usually by over-committing memory), SQL Server may not be able to start. You can start SQL Server in a minimum configuration using the **-f** switch. This is done within Windows NT's

193

Control Panel and the Services Manager applet. The **-f** switch is used as a startup parameter.

The procedure cache parameter is expressed as a percentage of the memory remaining available to it and the buffer cache. As you can see in figure 9.5, the procedure cache is set at 30%, with a valid range from 1–99%. A new setting in either or both of these parameters will not take effect until SQL Server has been stopped and then restarted. Some of the other parameters can be changed and these settings will take effect immediately after closing the Server Configuration/Options dialog box if you click on the Apply Now button.

> **Note**
>
> Setting the memory option too high may cause the system to have to read from the paging system, while setting it too low will cause poor overall SQL Server system performance because it does not have access to the resources it wants.

4.   Apply your changes to the memory parameter by clicking the **OK** button. Now stop SQL Server by using the stoplight button on the toolbar, displaying the SQL Server Manager dialog box. Click the red light button to stop the server, and then click the green light to restart the server once again. Once the server service has started, click the **D**one button to close the dialog box. Your new settings will now be in effect.

If you want to see how much memory is available, you can rerun DBCC MEMUSAGE to see the new settings in the Memory Usage part of the report.

Optimizing Disk Performance

Once you have optimized your available memory for SQL Server, you can now look at your disk subsystem. Under most circumstances your I/O system is not as much of a bottleneck as is the actual disk access. The first piece of information you need to know is, do you have one hard disk for SQL Server, or do you have two or more?

The problem with a single disk system is the collision between disk reads requested by a user needing data from a table, and disk writes from the log writer. As a database becomes busier, the potential for collisions between conflicting I/O requests will become more frequent, resulting in slow performance.

There are not many things that can be done to speed up a hard drive's access speed, short of replacing your drives with faster ones. This can get expensive very quickly. One of the easiest, and least expensive things you can do is to separate data and log files, placing them onto separate database devices. The assumption is that these devices are also on separate physical disks. Even better is to separate the disks by using two controllers. By reducing the competition of the log and data files for the narrow access available for I/O access to the relatively slow disk drives, you can help to improve the performance of the entire system.

There are several methods for getting around the problems of optimizing the performance of the disk subsystem. The best option is the use of a Redundant Array of Inexpensive Disks (RAID) subsystem, which will be covered further in Chapter 11, "Backups and Disaster Recovery."

The next best option is with the use of software-based disk striping. Windows NT allows you to create stripe sets across several disks. A stripe set allows you to create a single logical volume across several disks. When you use this option Windows NT allows you to create separate partitions on from 2 to 32 separate disks, which are then combined as a single volume. You cannot place more than one member partition from any stripe set on any one disk. A hard disk may contain more than one partition which are members of different stripe sets. Then, as a database is read or written to, it is placed as stripes across all of the disks in the set. This form of disk writing and reading provides a relatively inexpensive way to balance the I/O load of a database.

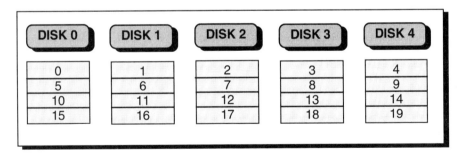

Figure 9.6: A striped set composed of five disks. As a database is read or written it will be evenly distributed across all of the members of the set.

An older technique that can be used instead of striped sets is to simply separate the data, index, and log files onto separate drives. The idea behind this is that separating these files onto their own disk will help to balance the I/O load across the several disks. The problem is that it places a greater burden on the system administrator, that of balancing the load. This means that the system administrator must manually adjust the locations of each of these files or segments, and routinely monitor their activity—making additional changes as necessary. Also, as a database becomes larger, or even at different times of the day, the database activity may change. One table may become significantly larger than the table it has been balanced against, or one table may be heavily accessed early in the day, and the second is accessed later in the day, resulting in the uneven load you were trying to eliminate.

Using Segments

Simply put, a segment is a group of named disk areas. A segment is specific to a database, in other words, separate databases can not share a segment. Segments can be created for the use of a specific table, an index, or a log file from the database. You can even split a table so that parts of it reside on different segments, enabling you to better balance the I/O load across several disks.

One of the advantages of segments is that an object placed on it can not grow beyond the segment, unlike an object on a device which can grow to the full size allocated to the device. For example, if you have a table whose growth you want to limit, placing it on a segment effectively limits its growth to the maximum size of the segment. This is a feature which is not available with either RAID or with striped sets.

To segment your data, or not to segment—that is the question. And generally, the answer is no. Segments have their uses but do add to the system overhead. Only a very small percentage of SQL Servers need to use segmentation.

With that said, why would you want to use segments? The primary reason of course, is to improve the overall performance of disk access. Splitting a table from its nonclustered indexes can help to improve performance by allowing parallel access to both the table and the index. You may also want to place large text and image columns from a table onto a separate segment. This can help improve the performance of a heavily read table. You cannot separate a clustered index from its table. If you move a clustered index to a new segment, the table and its data will automatically follow the index to the new segment. The converse is also true—a clustered index will follow its table to a new segment.

The following segments are predefined and created whenever you create a new database:

- DEFAULT   This segment stores all database objects that are not specifically allocated to one of the other two.

- LOGSEGME NT   All database logs are stored on this segment.

- SYSTEM   This segment stores all of the system tables for a database.

Like other database devices, of which a segment could be considered a device of a device, you can create, alter and drop any segment.

The Multithreaded Server

The concept of threads was introduced in Chapter 1, "An Overview of Microsoft SQL Server." SQL Server uses native Windows NT operating system threads for all work performed.

One of the features added to SQL Server 6.5 is the ability to associate a thread with a specific processor in a Symmetric Multi Processor (SMP) system with four or more processors. The term used is *thread affinity*. By configuring the affinity mask option, you can select certain processors which will receive work from groups of threads.

By using thread affinity, you can often improve throughput of data by taking worker threads from certain processors that are busy and placing them on processors with unused cycles. In a SMP system, Windows NT uses processor 0 for all I/O processing, so this processor is often very busy. Without thread affinity, many additional processes may be placed on this processor instead of one that has less work, slowing the overall system throughput and degrading performance. Windows NT also places all delayed process calls (DPC), usually associated with the work required by a network interface card (NIC), on the highest numbered processor. If for example, you have a server with two NICs, and eight processors, then one NIC will have its work placed on processor 7, while the second NICs work will be placed on processor 6. That leaves five processors on which you can balance SQL Server's work load.

Threads are associated with a processor by using the **SRV_THREADAFFINITY** option parameter. The thread affinity mask uses a number 1 in a bit designation for the processor to turn the processor on. A 0 indicates that this processor will not accept input from SQL Server. For example, Table 9.1 shows some of the affinity masks options for a four-processor system:

Table 9.1: Sample Affinity Masks

Decimal Value	Binary bit mask	Will allow SQL Server threads on processor
1	00000001	Allows SQL Server threads on processor 0.
3	00000011	Allows SQL Server threads on processors 0 and 1.
6	00000110	Allows SQL Server threads on processors 1 and 2, isolating processor 0 for I/O use, and processor 3 for DPC uses.
7	00000111	Allows SQL Server threads on processors 0, 1, and 2, isolating processor 3 for DPC use.
14	00001110	Allows SQL Server threads on processors 1, 2, and 3, isolating only processor 0 for I/O use.
15	00001111	Allows SQL Server threads on all processors.

This example of an affinity mask in a four processor system will set processors 1, 2, and 3 as being available for SQL Server's threads:

```
sp_configure 'affinity mask', 14
```

This system will now pass no thread requests to processor 0, isolating it for the use of the I/O subsystem.

Note

The affinity mask option is only available on SMP systems with more than four processors. Trying to run this stored procedure parameter on a system that does not meet these requirements will result in a message telling you the option is not available and may be an advanced option.

Optimizing Queries

One of the key areas to concentrate when working on the performance tuning of SQL Server is being sure that your queries are properly optimized. If you have a query, or several queries, that return the data requested but do so without using the benefits of good optimization, your applications will be slower than they should be. Some of the greatest benefits when tuning SQL Server's performance are realized in:

- Building a database with a logical design.

- Creating tables designed for the specific information they are to contain, and including no extraneous data.

- Adding indexes that can be used by a query.

- Designing queries that use available indexes and return limited results sets.

- Removing indexes that slow down updates.

- Limiting the number of columns used in a query to only those that provide the required information.

Always be sure that a query makes use of a good index. Queries that simply scan an entire table and then return most if not all of the rows to the user are an inefficient use of network bandwidth and SQL Server's own abilities. Create queries that make use of indexes in the WHERE clause, so that only the required information is returned, versus constructing queries that return a wide range of data to the client for additional browsing.

When building a query on a table that contains a composite index, be sure to use the first column of this index as a part of the WHERE clause for the query. If instead you build the query so that only the second or subsequent columns of the composite index are used in the WHERE clause, ignoring the first column, the optimizer will not be able to use the index. Remember, it is a composite index composed of all member columns, not just selected ones.

Cost-based Optimization

SQL Server uses a cost-based optimizer to determine the best method of accessing information for the client application. The optimizer determines the best method of joining tables, and which indexes will be used. The query optimizer looks at all possible paths and chooses the one which results in the least cost. Cost is most simply put as time. The optimizer will choose the path that will require the least pages to be read, the smallest amount of I/O, and the fewest of all resources. Once it has weighed all of these factors, the plan that costs the least will be used.

You may wonder how the optimizer can make such decisions based on so little information. The answer is through the use of statistical information kept on each table. These statistics provide the optimizer with data on how information in the table is distributed and how its indexes are used. These statistics must be updated periodically, or eventually the optimizer will be making decisions based on outdated information. You should update these statistics after truncating and repopulating a table, bulk loading of data into a table, or a heavy period of adding and updating the data contained in the table.

Gathering Statistics

Statistics can be viewed for any index by running the DBCC SHOW_STATISTICS statement. DBCC is SQL Server's "DataBase Consistency Checker." By periodically checking the statistics for all, or a sample of often used, indexes and tables can help you to know how often you should update the statistics recorded for your database. The DBCC SHOW_STATISTICS is used like this with the indicated parameters:

> DBCC SHOW_STATISTICS (table_name, index_name)

You must specify both the name of the table where the index exists and the name of the index. View the statistics for the index maintained on the au_id column in the authors table by following these steps:

1.   Open SQL Enterprise Manager, opening the Databases folder. Select the pubs folder and then select **Manage, Indexes** from the menu.

> **Note**
>
> You must have the exact name of the index, not simply the name of the column on which the index is built, in order to display or create statistics about it. Remember, you can use a column in more than one index.

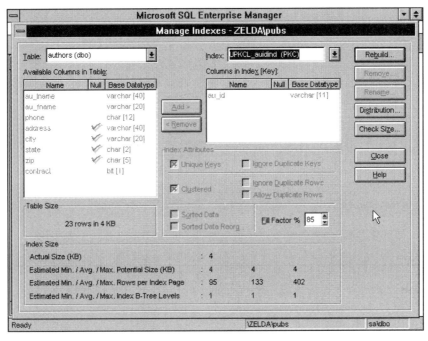

Figure 9.7: From the Manage Indexes dialog box you can find the name of any index.

2.   Write down the name of the index "UPKCL_auidind" so that you can refer to it later. Now that you have the name of the index you want to view statistics on, close this dialog box.

3.   Open the ISQL/w application and connect to the server.

4.   Select pubs in the **DB** list box as the database to use, and then type DBCC SHOW_STATISTICS (authors, UPKCL_auidind) into the query window.

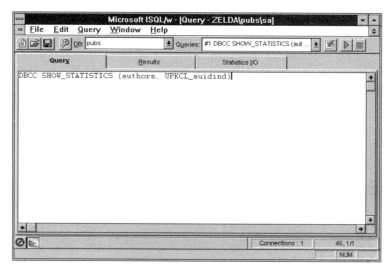

Figure 9.8: Use this DBCC statement to view current statistics on the specified index.

5.   Click the Execute button, or press Ctrl+E, to execute the statement and view the results.

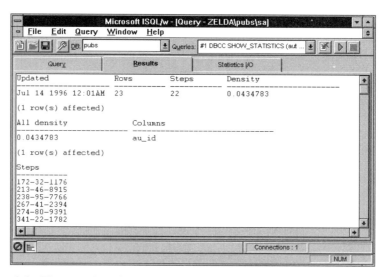

Figure 9.9: The results of the DBCC SHOW_STATISTICS statement for a selected index.

As you can see in the results window, all of the statistical information contained on the distribution page for the selected index and table are displayed. The first piece of information you should notice is the date that the statistics were last updated. This will give you an indication of how good the statistics are. This example shows the statistics for a primary key index. As you remember, a primary key constraint allows for only unique values to be entered. This is indicated if you multiply the values listed as *Rows* and *Density* (23 * 0.0434783) and get the product of 1.0, indicating that each value is unique in this index. The closer to 1.0 that the Row * Density reaches, the more likely that the index will be used. If a query were run on the authors table, and it further used a WHERE clause specifying that a certain value was to be displayed, then it would be very likely that the query optimizer would use the index.

Looking at a nonunique, composite index, you will see a different set of statistics. These statistics were taken from a customer database which has a composite index based on the customer's last name and first name columns. Running the DBCC SHOW_STATISTICS statement on this index resulted in a completely different group of statistics. Since the index is not unique, its selectivity is based on how the data is distributed, and the estimated chances of duplicate values within the data. Here you see that the selectivity (Rows * Density) is 41.7, indicating the likelihood of 42 duplicate values.

Look at the *All density* values, which display more accurate statistics for the selectivity of each column or group of columns. The selectivity value for the C_Lname column is 155.8, which indicates that there is a high likelihood of duplicate values. The selectivity value for the composite index, C_Lname + C_Fname is only 13.9, indicating relatively few potential duplicate values (14) and a corresponding likelihood that the optimizer would use this index.

Updated	Rows	Steps	Density
Jul 14 1996 12:01AM	5456	56	0.0075823
(1 row(s) affected)			

All density	Columns
0.028559	C_Lname
0.00254891	C_Lname, C_Fname
(2 row(s) affected)	

Steps
Andreasen
...
Zachary

The distribution pages where these statistics are kept are created when you run the UPDATE STATISTICS statement on a table that contains data with one or more indexes, or when you add an index to an existing table. Each distribution page contains all of the statistical information for a single index.

Updating Statistics

Statistics on the indexes of your tables should be checked and updated periodically, especially for those tables through which many transactions are posted. These statistics are automatically updated each time you create or re-create an index on a table that is already populated. When you decide to manually update statistics, you can use the following T-SQL statement in the ISQL/w query window like this:

UPDATE STATISTICS table_name index_name

The table_name parameter is required as this statement runs on the specified table. You can also run this statement from another database, if you add the database/owner parameter also. The index_name parameter is optional. When you use the index_name parameter, then only the statistics for the specified index are updated. Otherwise, all of the statistics for the named table will be updated. When these statistics are made or updated, a sampling of key values in each index is taken and the distribution of these key values is recorded. The optimizer then uses this information to help it make decisions on how a query will be optimized and then run. When this statement is executed it returns no rows or data.

You can also both view and update an index's statistics from within the SQL Enterprise Manager. Follow these steps to see how:

1.   Open SQL Enterprise Manager, opening the Databases folder. Select the pubs folder and then select **M**anage, **I**ndexes from the menu. You will now see the Manage Indexes dialog box displayed.

2.   Select the index that you want to view or update statistics in the **I**ndex list box, such as the primary key index UPKCL_auidind, and then click the Distribution button.

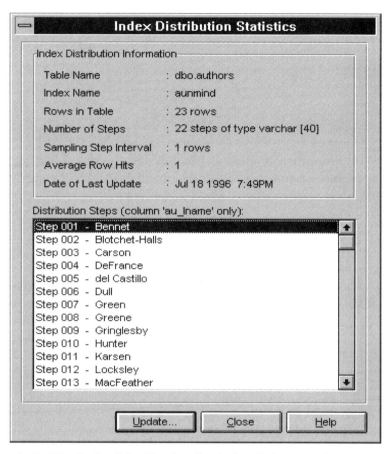

Figure 9.10: The Index Distribution Statistics dialog box lists most of the statistics kept on the indexes distribution page.

3.   By clicking the Update button you will be given the choice of updating the statistics for the selected index or for all of the indexes in the selected table. You will also be able to choose to perform the update now or to schedule it as a task for execution at a selected time.

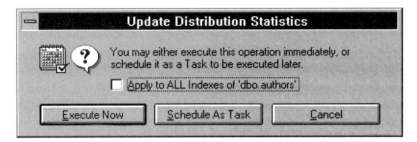

Figure 9.11: From the Update Distribution Statistics dialog box, you can choose to update a selected index, to update all indexes of the current table, and when to execute the update procedure.

4.   Click the checkbox **A**pply to ALL Indexes of 'table_name' to update the statistics of all indexes in the selected table. Click the **E**xecute Now button to update statistics immediately, or click the **S**chedule As Task button to execute this procedure at a selected time. If you choose to schedule this as a task, you will see a dialog box that will allow you to set the time for the procedure to be executed.

5.   Click on the **C**lose button to return to the Manage Index dialog box and then again to close this dialog box also.

The statistical information is not all displayed in the same fashion as when displayed used the DBCC SHOW_STATISTICS statement in ISQL/w. One of the things that you will first notice is that the density statistic is not shown. So how do you know if an index is a "good" index and will be used by the optimizer, or not?

The *Average Row Hits* statistic gives you this information. The number displayed here is the average number of rows that would be returned by a query that meets these qualifications:

- A WHERE clause is used on the indexed column.

- The clause is qualified equality which searches for a specific value.

- The equality is based on the first column of a composite index.

The closer the Average Row Hits number is to 1, the more likely that the index will find the information requested by the query. When the number of rows in the selected table exceeds 200, then one of the subjective ratings shown here is also displayed:

- Very Good (more than 1 row but less than 0.5% of the rows)

- Good (more than 0.5% of the rows but less than 1% of the rows)

- Fair (more than 1% of the rows but less than 2.5% of the rows)

- Poor (more than 2.5% of the rows but less than 5% of the rows)

- Very Poor (more than 5% of the rows)

These ratings give you a subjective estimate of how many rows will be returned, based on a query using the first column of the index with a qualified equality clause. The estimate is shown as a percentage of the rows returned from the total rows in the table. These ratings can be used to give you a rough estimate of how well a given index will be used by the query optimizer, and will not always be an accurate indicator for all indexes.

Clustered Indexes

A clustered index is a special index object where the bottom or leaf pages of the index are the actual data pages. Only one clustered index can be created per table. After all, you can't have a table whose physical row order is the same as two different columns, unless the columns are identical—in which case, why was the second one created?

Clustered indexes are most often used on columns whose values are grouped together, for example a *department* column. A clustered index would then group all employees who work in the same department together within the table. This would help to speed those queries which sort information by department, or select records from a specific department. Often a significant increase in speed is seen because once the query finds the first matching records, the remaining matches will be found in the adjacent rows. Whenever possible, use a clustered index in the WHERE clause of a query. The optimizer will be sure to use this index and be able to maximize performance against it.

When working with a clustered index, you are not required to specify an equality in the WHERE clause. The clustered index also works very well with a query that returns a range of values. Ranges can be selected by using range operators in the WHERE clause. Range operators include:

BETWEEN, <, >, >=, and <=

The range operators are often used in expressions, which can also include AND and OR operators. For example:

```
SELECT * FROM authors
WHERE state BETWEEN 'CA' AND 'KS'
```

This query will select all rows whose values in the *state* column is between the values 'CA' and 'KS' inclusive. The other range operators are most often used with numeric values and data types, but can be used with alphanumeric columns also.

Using Nonclustered Indexes

Unlike a clustered index, rows are not physically ordered by the index, which can result in a slower overall access to the data and a return of information from a query. Nonclustered indexes contain pointers to the data rows on the leaf pages of the index. Also unlike a clustered index, you can have as many as 249 nonclustered indexes per table. While using indexes can result in an overall increase in speed of a queries returning a results set and a reduction in the I/O cost of the query, creating and maintaining indexes adds to the server overhead.

Be sure to use indexes where they will be helpful, but do not necessarily create an index on every column and combination of columns for every table. When a nonclustered index is available to be used in a query, the optimizer must choose between using the index and simply performing a table scan. When the index is used, SQL Server must read the index, which is contained on logical index pages, and then the actual data pages. When querying a smaller table, the optimizer may decide not to use the index, relying on a simple table scan. The reason behind this is that the number of page I/O operations required to read the nonclustered index pages and then the data pages becomes greater than the table scan, especially if the optimizer determines that the indexes are not useful for this query.

Creating Useful Indexes

The query optimizer determines the usefulness of an index by the selectivity of the WHERE clause in the query. This selectivity is based on an estimate of the percentage of total rows to be returned to the client. The statistics recorded on the distribution pages are used to appraise the available indexes, estimate the number of page I/Os required by using various indexes, and the select the plan which will require the fewest number of page I/Os.

You can help the query optimizer by closely examining the WHERE clauses of the queries sent to SQL Server. The WHERE clause is the primary place the optimizer looks for information about how best to perform the query. After all, this is the place you limit the query. By using a column that contains an index in the WHERE clause, you can speed the results set to the client. Alternatively, if a column is used in the WHERE clause and the query is often used, consider placing an index on this column to help the optimizer.

Another way to make your indexes useful to the query optimizer is to build *narrow* indexes. A narrow index is one which covers as few columns as possible. While a nonclustered index can include up to 16 columns, a wide composite index like this can require many I/O page reads to use the index. The query optimizer could easily decide that a table scan would be cheaper in terms of numbers of I/O page reads. A wide, composite, nonclustered index would be used if a query were constructed so that all of the columns from both the SELECT list and WHERE clause are included in the index. When this occurs, SQL Server does not have to read down to the data pages because the required information is contained on the index pages. Due to the overhead required to maintain an index like this, especially in the hope that the optimizer will use it, it is best avoided. The speed and efficiency in using more numerous, narrow indexes will generally provide you with greater performance, and a higher likelihood that the optimizer will use the indexes.

Avoid creating a composite index whose first column is invariably not used as the first column in the queries WHERE clause. For example, the authors table from the pubs database has a composite index created from the au_lname + au_fname columns. The following query statement shows a WHERE clause that will make use of this index, and two examples of clauses which will not:

```
SELECT au_id, au_lname, au_fname FROM authors
WHERE au_lname BETWEEN 'DeFrance' AND 'Karsen'
```

This query does make use of the index aunmind.

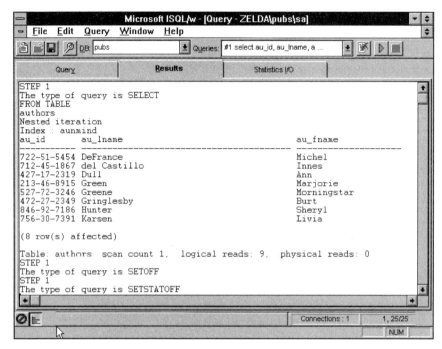

Figure 9.12: The query plan shows the use of the aunmind index, along with the number of reads that were required.

```
SELECT au_id, au_lname, au_fname FROM authors
WHERE au_fname BETWEEN 'Livia' AND 'Michel'
```

With this query statement, the optimizer uses a table scan because there are no useful indexes. Since the WHERE clause uses the second column from the composite index aunmind, the optimizer has determined that a table scan will use fewer I/O reads than trying to work with the index. Notice the number of reads that this scan uses compared with the number required in the previous query, where the index was used.

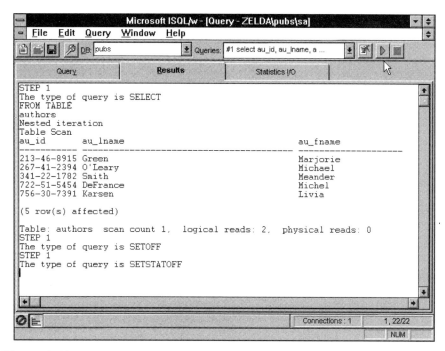

Figure 9.13: The optimizer has chosen to use a table scan for this query.

    SELECT au_id, au_lname, state FROM authors
    WHERE state NOT LIKE 'CA'

This query also will not use the composite index aunmind, but will perform a table scan as the least costly method of showing the results set of rows which do not equal the value 'CA.'

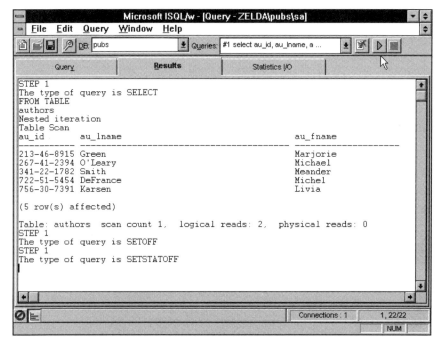

Figure 9.14: The results set for this query show that only 2 reads were required.

With careful attention to how you build indexes and then use them in queries, you can help SQL Server's optimizer increase the speed with which results are returned to the client.

Dropping Databases

Like devices, you may want to drop a database without dropping the device(s) on which it is located. This is just as easy as dropping the device. You may for example, decide that the pubs database, or a pre-production database is no longer necessary and you want to recover the space on the device You can easily drop an entire database with just a few simple keystrokes or mouse clicks. When you drop a database, SQL Server drops all of the data, database objects, and logs for this database, and then all references to it from the master database's tables. Only the system administrator or the database owner can drop a database, and no one can be using the database at the time it is dropped.

A database can be dropped using the DROP command like this:

```
DROP DATABASE test1
```

Alternatively, you can also drop a database from the SQL Enterprise Manager window in just a few steps:

1.   Open the SQL Enterprise Manager and connect to the server. Open the Databases folder and select the database to be dropped.

2.   Right-click on the name of the database to be dropped and select **D**elete from the shortcut menu.

3.   Click on the **OK** button on the Delete Database dialog box. SQL Server will drop the database, all of its objects and all references to it in the master database.

Note

Before dropping a database, it is always a good idea to do a complete dump of the entire database, both data and logs. This will ensure that you can recover the information, if for some reason you later decide that the database should not have been dropped.

Summary

In this chapter, you have learned to manage the space available to you on your disk drives and on your database devices. Specifically, you have learned:

- How Windows NT and SQL Server allocate memory resources between them.

- How to change SQL Server's memory configuration, including the total memory it allocates and the distribution of buffer and procedure cache.

- Learned what stripe sets are and how they can be used to optimize disk performance.

- How to set and use thread affinity masks for a multiprocessor system.

- How the query optimizer uses indexes to increase the speed of returning a results set.

- What index statistics are, how to read them, and how to update them.

- How to use the Performance Monitor to observe system and SQL Server's current performance.

Chapter 10

Security

IN THIS CHAPTER

- Identification and Authentication
- The Role of the System Administrator

Another of the many important jobs of the system administrator is managing the security requirements of SQL Server. In the world of the client/server, controlling who has access to what resources is a very important requirement. Simply controlling who has access to read and write in the database and its tables is only the beginning of controlling the security.

Using SQL Server to manage security is not a difficult task, but is one that should be taken seriously. Having an unauthorized person hacking into your system can be a formula for a great many problems, especially if they gain access to sensitive information.

Identification and Authentication

The key to any security system is to identify and to control. SQL Server can take this task onto itself, use Windows NT's security features, or can mix the two together. In order to use an object contained in an SQL Server database, a user must pass through four levels of security.

- The Windows NT operating system

- SQL Server application running on Windows NT

- The SQL Server database

- The SQL Server database object

Each of these is a security hurdle, or door, through which a user must pass before being able to gain access to the resources available at that level.

The central theme in using a secure client/server system is the identity of the user. This identity must be maintained throughout a session, regardless of the work they are currently doing. As with any security system, whether it is a computer system, a bank vault, or a store's front door, the security system is only as good as the people who use it. If a trusted individual gives their keys to the front door and their code to the alarm system to another person, they have created a very real breach in the security of that front door. This breach gives the second person access to everything in the store. SQL Server and Windows NT uses a system of usernames as a means of identifying a specific individual. A username is a partial set of keys to the front door; more is required.

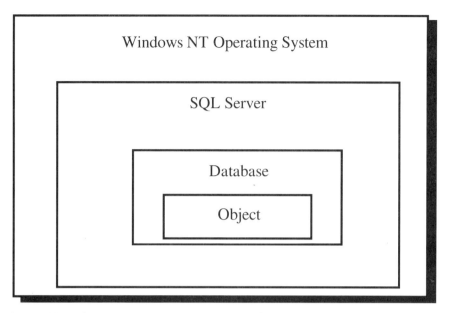

Figure 10.1: A user must pass through all four levels of security to use an SQL Server database object.

Usernames are just the first half of the key. Since the username is simply typed in through a keyboard, how does the computer know that this is really the person who should have access to the information and the applications authorized to the person with this username? The second half of the key is the authentication of the username through the use of passwords. The password is like the alarm code to the building. If the a person enters a correct username but an incorrect password, they will not be allowed access to the computer. Usernames must first be created by an individual who is authorized to do so. Depending upon the process in place in your company, and the level of access required, this may be the SQL Server system administrator, the Windows NT system administrator, or the network administrator. These are the people most often charged with this task. Usernames and passwords may also be called logins.

In addition to controlling access, the username can be used for audit purposes. With most network systems, you can view an audit log showing what actions were performed, and what files were accessed by an individual username. This can be especially helpful when tracking down unauthorized accesses to a database. Security audits can be logged by turning this feature on during the SQL Server setup procedures; it is one of the options in the "Set Security Options" dialog box. The audit log can then be viewed either in SQL Server's error log, or in the Security section of the Windows NT Event Log.

You can create many more levels of security, if your specific application needs a very high level of security. In the next several sections, you will become familiar with the various levels of security.

Windows NT Security

The typical client/server system may require that a user have to access more than one operating system in order to run a typical application. For example, a user who is running a client application on their own computer will access the operating system of the computer they are using. The client application may have another security door which must be passed through before gaining access to the client application. Then the user will also have to login to the Windows NT operating system, or other network operating system to gain access to the server on which SQL Server resides. This simple system requires the use and access of at least three security systems, each with their own requirements and uses. In most business systems, each of these processes will be running on their own individual systems. Few, if any, client/server systems run with both the client application and the SQL Server database engine running on the same computer.

An individual user does not require a Windows NT login on the host machine where SQL Server resides, unless SQL Server is running on their local computer. The exception to this is that the system administrator, who does need to have access to the Windows NT operating system, also needs to have a valid Windows NT login.

Windows NT's security requires a valid username and password to be entered before access is given to any of the system resources. The Windows NT system administrator will set up individual user accounts and logins, at the same time determining the level of access to various system resources.

SQL Server Security

SQL Server can also be used to create an additional level of security by requiring another set of logins. In systems that require a high level of controlled access, this additional layer can help to avoid potential hacking problems. SQL Server supports both standard logins and integrated logins.

Whichever type is used, both grant access to the SQL Server processes. Once in, a wide variety of additional doors can be made available to the user. These doors lead to the databases which have been created. The first door is to the master database, and this is where everyone will go unless a different default database is specified when the login is created, or if the user's default database becomes unavailable due to damage or has been closed for other system processes.

Database Security

Once a user login has been created, a certain level of access is granted to it. This database security level can take several forms.

- Giving that login ownership of the database. This grants the login all rights to the database.
- Creating the login as a guest user. This is the most restrictive level of access.
- Creating an alias. Tells the database to regard the user as a different user login, and subsequently granting all of the same rights and privileges as that granted to the owner of the aliased login.
- Adding the login as a new user to the database.

Even though a user has been granted login access to the database, the user still must be granted permission to access each database object. This is the final level of security. To see how permissions are controlled, read the section "Setting Permissions," later in this chapter.

The Role of the System Administrator

In the context of this book the system administrator refers to the SQL Server system administrator. The system administrator must work closely with the network system administrator in order to make the sure that the security of SQL Server is maintained. The first level of security is the responsibility of the network system administrator and he or she will be responsible for creating the initial user accounts and passwords.

The system administrator will then be responsible for ensuring that proper logins receive appropriate access to the correct databases and objects within each database.

There are several types of security that can be implemented with Windows NT and SQL Server. Each of these will be discussed through the next several sections with some of the pros an cons of each listed.

Selecting the Type of Security

How security is implemented is a basic determination that will be decided based on the business needs and security requirements of the database owner and the information the database contains. Security of information contained in a SQL Server database depends not only on a system of user logins and passwords, but also in the physical security of the network, and especially the server where SQL Server resides. A computer system where the server is located in a secure room is safer than one which is placed in an out of the way closet. The same can be said of the network itself. If there is no access to the network from the outside, for example, a modem connection, then it is relatively safe from outside hacking. The physical security of your server and network must be taken into consideration when designing your overall security policies and procedures.

There are three security modes from which you can choose from—integrated, standard, and mixed. Each have their own advantages and disadvantages.

Integrated Security

The integrated security option allows you to use the Windows NT security logins and authentication systems for all SQL Server connections. This mode allows only trusted multiprotocol and named pipe's connections to have access to SQL Server.

This method of security allows your users to connect to SQL Server without having to supply a separate login name and password. This can be an especially helpful for those users who have a hard time remembering one login name and password, let alone several.

By using integrated security, SQL Server applications can take full advantage of the security features available from Windows NT. These features include:

- The ability to pass encrypted passwords through the network. Many networks store passwords in an encrypted form at the users workstation, but send the password to the server in a clear text format. This has the potential of allowing someone to capture a password, and to later login as an authorized user.

- Using password aging. Requires a user to change a password once it has becomes more than a specified number of days old. The number of days is entered as part of Windows NT's User Manager Domains application, as an Account Policy option. The maximum number of days that can be set is 999, or you can set a password to never expire.

Integrated security can be used with any trusted connection. Trusted connections can be multiprotocol or named pipes from other Windows NT workstations, Windows for Workgroups, Windows 95, and Microsoft LAN Manager running under either MS-DOS or Microsoft Window's clients. By using the multiprotocol Net-Library, you can also create trusted connections with Microsoft Windows clients using Novell Netware and running the IPX/SPX protocol. This user will be prompted for a login when connecting to SQL Server. Clients using other network protocols are not supported as Windows NT trusted connections, and so must be handled using SQL Server standard security.

When integrated security is in force, a user is mapped from their trusted connection to a valid SQL Server login that has been setup for them, to a default login—usually the *guest* login, or to the system administrator login if the user has administrator privileges. Once the user has gained access to SQL Server, all additional security is handled by SQL Server itself. This will include user access to a database, and to any of the resources or information available in that database.

The most widely recommended way to use SQL Server integrated security is to create at least two security groups within Windows NT and to provide each with the appropriate access to SQL Server. These groups are often named:

- SQLUsers, and are assigned all user privileges. Assign anyone who needs to have access as a user to this group. They will be able to perform normal UPDATE, SELECT, DELETE, and INSERT functions necessary to their particular job.

- SQLAdmin, are assigned administrator duties and use the system administrator login. The individuals assigned to this group will have all of the privileges and responsibilities of system administrator, and will be able to use the CREATE DATABASES command, add new users, and other such duties.

When using integrated security, users and user groups must first be set up within the Windows NT security system. Depending upon your own business situation, this responsibility may belong to another person within your organization. If so, contact them about setting up the necessary accounts for users who need access to SQL Server. Otherwise, set up the accounts by following these next few steps:

1.   From Windows NT's Administrative Tools program group, open the User Manager Domains application. The User Manager dialog box will be displayed. This is where you create user accounts, set permissions to access SQL Server, access to other Windows NT system resources.

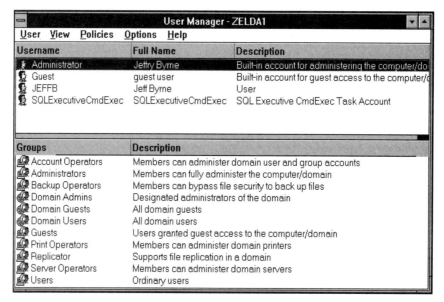

Figure 10.2: The User Manager dialog box is used to enter account and user profile information.

2.   Select User, New Local Group from the menu, displaying the New Local Group dialog box. In the Group Name text box type **SQLUsers**. Move down to the

Description text box and type **SQL Server User Group**. Click the OK button to save the new group. You are returned to the User Manager dialog box, where you will see your new group has been added to the group list.

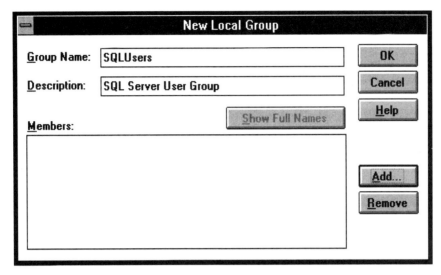

Figure 10.3. A new user group has been created for those people who will be assigned as SQL Server users.

3.   Select User, New User from the menu, displaying the New User dialog box. From here you can add the user accounts for everyone who will be working within the SQL Server User Group you just created.

4.   This dialog box is used to enter new users into the Windows NT security system. Below is a sample of the information which must be supplied:

Username:	egermesin
Full Name:	Eric Germesin
Description:	Member SQLUser group
Password:	(type a password - only asterisks '*' are displayed in the text box)
Confirm Password:	(retype the password for confirmation, exactly as entered in the Password text box)

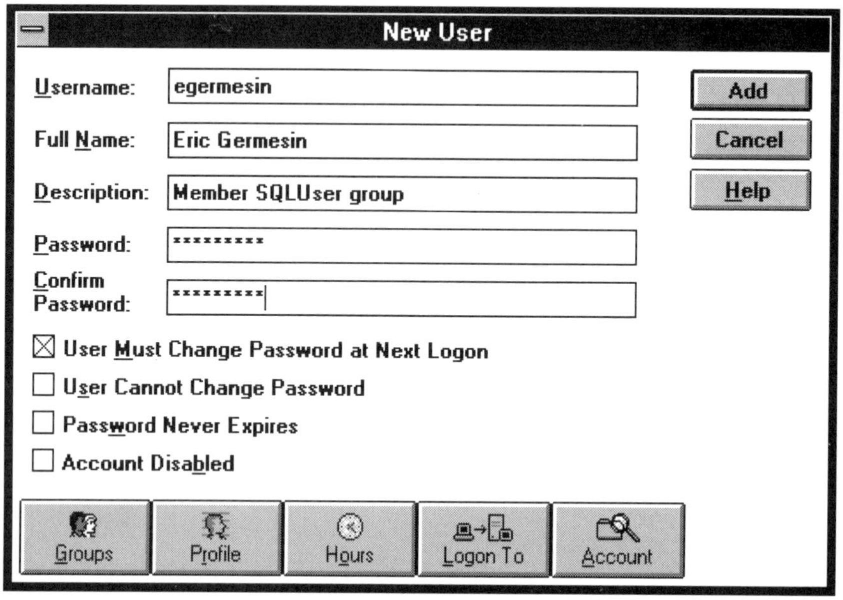

Figure 10.4: This basic information is required for a new user account.

When entering the initial password you have several options. The default setting User Must Change Password at Next Logon allows you as system administrator to enter a default password for each user, and requires them to change it when they next login, or for the first time they use it. You can also select one of the other three options by clicking its checkbox:

- User Cannot Change Password. As it states, a user can not change this password.

- Password Never Expires. This password will not expire without manually changing this option.

- Account Disabled. Disables the account. This option is often used if you are using the account as a template when creating a number of similar accounts. You may also want to disable an account when a user goes on vacation or on a leave of absence.

5.   Click the Groups button. You will now see a new dialog box, Group Memberships. Scroll through the Not member of combo box until you find the group you just created, SQLUsers, and select it. Click the Add button, adding the group to the Member of combo box.

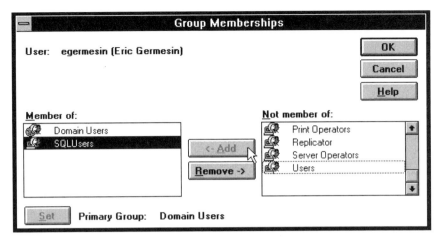

Figure 10.5: The new user has been added to the SQLUsers group.

6.   If this is the only group that this user is to be added to, then click the OK button, returning to the New User dialog box. If you are done, click the OK button to return to the User Manager window. You will see the new user listed in the upper half of the window. Close this application window unless you plan to add additional groups or users.

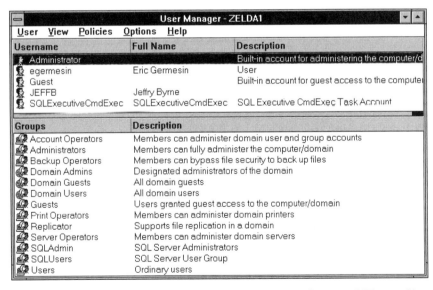

Figure 10.6: The new user has been added to the Windows NT user list.

Create the SQLAdmin group in the same way you just created the SQLUsers group. If necessary, create logins for any users who have not yet been added to the Windows NT user list, and then add only those users who will have system administrator privileges to this new group.

In the New User dialog box there are several additional buttons. Each of these displays another dialog box, allowing you to exercise additional control over the user account:

- Profile: This option is used to set additional user environment profile options. You must create a profile file for the user and then enter the required information into this dialog box. A profile can be used to give each user a customized Windows NT desktop and access to selected resources, including network connections.

- Hours: This option is used to select specific days and hours of the day that this user can log on to the system. This does not restrict them from using their own workstation, but does restrict them from logging on to the server outside of the specified hours. The default setting allows access 7 days per week, 24 hours per day.

- Logon To: Here you can choose to allow a user to log on to the server from any workstation, or from a selected workstation. If you choose to allow access from a specific workstation, you can allow the user to log on to the server from any one of eight different workstations. Once you have selected the workstation from which the user can log on, they will not be able to use another person's station to log on to the server.

- Account: Allows you to set an expiration date for the account and determine if the account is a regular user of the domain or a user from an untrusted domain.

Once you, or the Windows NT system administrator, have created and set up all of the necessary groups and user accounts, you have completed the first half of setting up the requisite security processes for SQL Server. Setting up the next half will be discussed later in this chapter in the section "Setting Security Modes."

Standard Security

The standard security mode is the default option when you first setup SQL Server. Under this security mode, SQL Server manages its own login authentication process for all users attempting to connect to the server. The only exception is for client applications that explicitly request integrated security connections from a trusted connection.

> **Note**
>
> You can force the server to deny all trusted client connections, but this will also restrict the use of applications and features that use forced trusted connections such as SQL Enterprise Manager, and SQL Server's replication features.

When you select standard security mode, SQL Server uses the *syslogins* table to store a user's login ID and password. When the user attempts to log in to the server, SQL Server looks for a valid login ID and password. If one is found, the user is granted access to SQL Server.

Mixed Security

This final security mode, mixed, allows the use of both standard and integrated security modes, depending upon the type of connection requested by the client application. Under the mixed security mode, SQL Server will use integrated security for all trusted connections. If the connection fails the integrated test by not being a valid login, standard security mode will used, requiring the entry of a valid SQL Server login.

If the user attempts to log on through any connections other than a trusted one, the user is required to supply a login ID and password. SQL Server will then use the standard security mode, checking the login attempt against the valid entries in the *syslogins* table for authentication.

Trusted Connections

Both ODBC and DB-Library clients can be configured so that they always request a trusted connection and integrated security from the server. This enables SQL Executive to connect to remote servers as long as it is running on a properly configured Windows NT account that has been granted system administrator privileges.

Setting Security Modes

The various security modes are set from within SQL Enterprise Manager. By using SQL Enterprise Manager you can choose the security mode that you will use with SQL Server. Additionally, if you have selected standard or mixed security, you will need to set up users and user groups. Use these next steps to set a security mode, and then additional users and groups for standard and mixed security modes:

1.   Open SQL Enterprise Manager and select **S**erver, **SQL** Server, **C**onfigure from the menu, or right-click the server folder and select **C**onfigure from the shortcut menu. The Server Configuration/Options dialog box is now displayed. Click on the Security Options tab. From here, you can set the security mode that will be used by SQL Server, and some additional features.

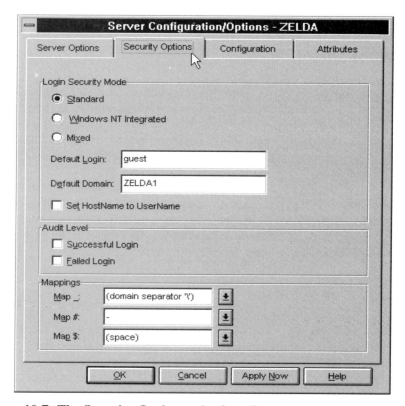

Figure 10.7: The Security Options tab of the Server Configuration/Options dialog box is used to set the security mode that SQL Server will use for all user logins.

You can now choose which security mode you will use with SQL Server.

2.   Click on the **Mix**ed option button. Earlier in this chapter you have already created Windows NT security groups for integrated security—and you will also create some user logins and passwords within SQL Server's standard security mode.

3.   (Optional) In the Default **L**ogin text box, enter a default login name, if necessary for your system. Adding a value here does not create the login ID; this is a separate step that the system administrator will have to do. The default login name is used for any user from a trusted connection whose name does not appear in the *syslogins* table. If you leave this box blank, any such user will be denied access to SQL Server.

4.   (Optional) Enter a default Windows NT domain name in the D**e**fault Domain text box.

This entry is especially needed in networks where there is more than one Windows NT domain setup, allowing SQL Server to distinguish between two users who belong to different domains. For example, you have two domains in your company; SALES and ACCOUNTING. This server belongs to the ACCOUNTING domain. Both SALES and ACCOUNTING each have a separate user with username *marisa*. Marisa in the accounting department will be known to the SQL Server ACCOUNTING simply as *marisa*, while the Marisa in sales will be known to the accounting server as SALES_marisa. If most of SQL Server's users belong to one domain, set this as the default domain.

Note

The default domain parameter is not used in the standard security mode, with the exception of client applications that expressly request a trusted connection.

5.   (Optional) The Se**t** HostName to UserName is unselected by default. Selecting this option allows SQL Server to override a hostname with the actual Windows NT username. This enables you to see the actual username when using the stored procedure sp_who, instead of simply the hostname. This option can be effectively used to help you identify a specific login ID to a specific computer or network ID.

6.   (Optional) There are two choices available in the Audit Level. When selected, these options will make an entry into either the SQL Server error log or the

Windows NT event log, or both, depending on how you have set up logging for SQL Server. SQL Server can log either or both successful or failed log in attempts, in any of the three security modes and from both trusted and untrusted connections. This option can be very useful, and required, in a high security database operation. These settings are both unselected by default and are turned on by clicking the checkboxes.

7.   (Optional) Windows NT and SQL Server are not in complete agreement in how usernames should be created. Windows NT allows additional characters to be used, that SQL Server does not. The Mappings section allows you to tell SQL Server how convert, or map, some of the characters that Windows NT allows. In most cases the default values will work, but talk with your network administrator if you are not sure how the network logins are defined.

Creating Users

You have already learned to create a user and a group under Windows NT. You also still need to know how to create users and groups within SQL Server. This is necessary if you are using untrusted connections, mixed security mode, or if you are using standard security mode.

All users who do not come from a trusted Windows NT system, and so have already had user accounts created in the User Manager application, have to have usernames registered with SQL Server. This is accomplished by using SQL Server Enterprise Manager. In the next several sections of this chapter, you will become familiar with adding user accounts and working with groups.

Devising Usernames

The username is the point of entry for all people who want to gain access to SQL Server. When you have decided to use either standard or mixed security, you will have to add at least some, if not all, of the usernames so that SQL Server will recognize the user as being a person authorized to have access to information contained in a database.

When setting up user accounts you must supply SQL Server with several pieces of information, the first being a username. It is highly recommended that you work with your users when devising their usernames. While you must be concerned with the security of your data, you must also ensure that your users can access the databases which they must use for their own work. A complex username and password system, while secure, is also prone to human error. Many people have a hard time remembering complex security schemes. They then end up forgetting their password or username and require you to rebuild it for them, or they write them down where they can easily prompt themselves—like underneath their keyboard.

<table><tr><td>**Note**</td></tr><tr><td>This warning is included for those of you who are either Windows NT or SQL Server administrators. If you forget your username or password, it is not as simple as rebuilding an account and/or password. Unless there is a backup administrator who still can access the proper applications, recreating your user account will require reinstalling either Windows NT or SQL Server. Be careful.</td></tr></table>

Creating user accounts within SQL Server Enterprise Manager takes just a few simple steps:

1.   Open SQL Server Enterprise Manager. Click the server folder to open it, and then right-click on the Logins folder and select **N**ew Login from the shortcut menu. Remember, you can also select **M**anage, **L**ogins from the menu without opening the server folder. You will see the Manage Logins dialog box displayed.

2.   Enter a name for the user in the **L**ogin Name list box, and then enter a password in the **P**assword text box. The password will be echoed back as a series of asterisks. You are not required to confirm the password until you are ready to add this login, so please be sure you know what it is.

3.   Now choose the databases that this user will have access to and set one of them to be their default database. Click in the first column box beside those databases to which this user should have access. Click the box beside the pubs database. SQL Server will add the additional information into the necessary boxes for this user, including making this the default database for this user. If you are allowing the user to access more than one database, you must be sure to check the Default box beside the database that will be their default database.

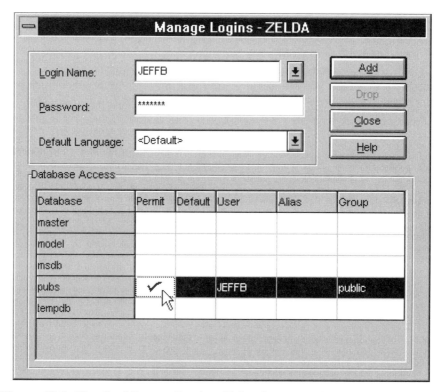

Figure 10.8: Use the Manage Logins dialog box to add new users to SQL Server. You can also assign a default database and select an alias login.

Note
If you have already created user groups within a specific database, and want this new user to be assigned to it, then select it from the drop-down list available in the Group box for the database. This will change the group from the default setting of *public* to the group you select. This can also be done in a later step if you are not sure to which group the user should be assigned.

4.   Click the **Add** button to add this new user to the logins folder. Another dialog box, Confirm Password, is displayed. Reenter the password you entered above in step 2. You must use exact same password, including the case of the letters and any additional symbols. If you do not, an error box will be displayed.

5.   Click the Close button to return to the SQL Server Enterprise Manager window, unless you have additional users to add at this time.

6.   Click the Logins folder. You should be able to see the new user in the Logins listing.

You can drop a user by selecting the user name from the Login folder and pressing the delete key on your keyboard, or selecting the login in the Manage Logins dialog box and clicking the Drop button. You can remove a user from an individual database by selecting their login from the Group/User folder under the specific database and pressing the delete key. This action will not remove the user from any other database.

> **Note**
>
> After dropping a login you may still find that particular login under other databases. By right-clicking the Login folder, or a Group/User folder and selecting Refresh from the shortcut menu, SQL Server will redisplay the list, showing only currently valid logins.

Guest User

The guest user is a special login that can be created. It will allow anyone access to a database on the server if they do not have an otherwise valid login. You must expressly create the guest login if you want it to exist on your server. The purpose behind the guest user is to allow someone who has proper access to SQL Server databases to work within the database before their own login is created. The guest login permissions default to the values given to the public group, unless you place additional specific restrictions. The guest user is installed and placed in both the master and pubs databases when you install SQL Server. The other databases that are also installed, including model, do not have a guest login.

When a guest login is created, any user who can login to SQL Server can also gain access to any database the guest user has been given access to. This login is added in the same way that you added a user in the previous section. You should be cautious in adding the guest login to the model database. This would allow almost anyone access to all databases subsequently added. This can create a potential hole in your security system.

Building Groups

Groups in SQL Server are used in the same way that groups are used in Windows NT. It allows you to set permissions for several users only once, by assigning them all to the same group. Groups are an easier way to manage the security burden placed on the system administrator. Create the necessary groups and then add users to the group. Each user will then automatically inherit the permissions and access to the various databases that are assigned to the group. This can greatly simplify an otherwise potentially arduous task, especially when you are working with many users.

When you create a database, there is one group that is automatically created—the *public* group. Every user who is given access to a database is added to the public group. A user can belong to only one group at a time. If you drop a group, all of the users contained in the group are removed and moved to the public group. This does not drop the users, as they are still valid members of the database and members of the public group by default.

Any group that has been created under Windows NT for use with an integrated security mode is not automatically tied to a SQL Server group. The simplest method of making a Windows NT group a valid SQL Server group is to use the SQL Server Security Manager application. This is discussed in a later section of this chapter, "Using SQL Server Security Manager." Unlike a SQL Server security group, a member of a Windows NT security group can be a member of many Windows NT security groups.

In most production database environments, the group is a natural way to classify categories of users. For example, you have an inventory database that tracks information about products, sales, customers, and purchases. Your users can be divided into groups; sales, purchasing, and customer service. While each of these groups of people need access to some of the information available in your database, only the members of the purchasing group really requires access to all of it. So it would be easy to create three groups of users for security purposes: SALES, PURCHASING, and CUSTOMER-SERVICE. A new user group can be added like this:

1.   Open the database folder of the database that you want to add a new group. Select the pubs database. Right-click the Groups/Users folder and select New **G**roup from the shortcut menu. You will now see the Manage Groups dialog box. You can also reach this same dialog box by selecting the pubs database and then selecting **M**anage, Groups from the menu.

2.   Type **Purchasing** in the **G**roup combo box as the name of the new group to be added to the pubs database. In the **U**sers list box is the list of all currently valid users of the pubs database. The users' current group affiliation is noted beside their usernames.

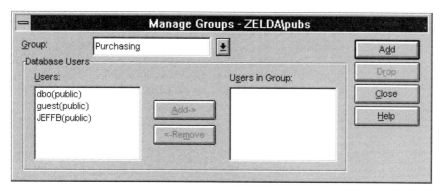

Figure 10.9: Use the Manage Groups dialog box to add new user groups.

3.   Select the username to be added to this group. Click the **A**dd button and you will see the name moved from the **U**sers list to the Users in Group list box.

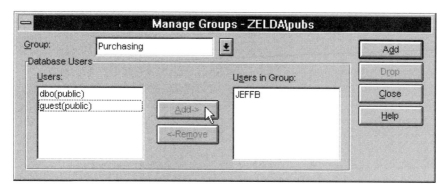

Figure 10.10: Select a username from the Users list box and transfer it to the Users in Group list box to add a user to a different group.

4.   Once you have added all of the necessary users to the group, click the **A**dd button. The new group, along with its users, will be added to the pubs Groups/Users folder. Click on the **C**lose button to close this dialog box.

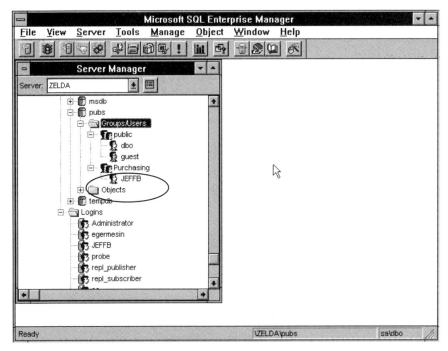

Figure 10.11: The new group has been added to the pubs Groups/Users folder, and a user has been placed in the group.

In some circumstances, you will find it easier to create your groups first, and then assign your users to the necessary groups as you create their logins.

An Owner

Every database and database object has an owner, the user who created it. Some permissions are granted only to an object's owner, while others can be granted by them to another user. An owner must give permission to another user to use their object.

The system administrator can grant the use of the CREATE DATABASE statement to another user, but great care should be taken in granting this capability. In most normal production environment, the ability to use the CREATE DATABASE statement should remain only with those users who are acting as system administrators. Anyone who is given this permission can create a new database, which they are then the default owner of. The ability to create a database also gives the power to use system resources. Ownership of a database can be transferred to another user.

When SQL Server is installed, the system administrator login is the default owner of all database objects, and remains the owner of the master database. SQL Server will also treat the system administrator as the database owner of any databases he or she uses, regardless of who actually created it.

A database owner, is the creator of that database and has full authority to:

- Give access to the database.

- Grant other users permission to create objects.

- Grant others to execute commands and statements on objects.

- Revoke any permissions granted.

- Set up and manage groups.

- Assign users to specific groups.

Database ownership can be transferred to another user. This often occurs when a database passes from a developmental stage to a production stage. Database ownership may also be transferred so that some of the responsibilities for day-to-day management of the database can be carried on by someone other than the system administrator. Only the ownership of a database can be transferred from one user to another: ownership of tables, views, and other objects can not be transferred.

Neither the granting of the CREATE DATABASE statement, or changing ownership of a database can be accomplished from the SQL Server Enterprise Manager. Changing the ownership of a database is accomplished with the stored procedure sp_changedbowner. The ownership of the master database can not be transferred.

Use the ISQL/w application and the stored procedure to change the ownership of a database like this:

> sp_changedbowner *login*, true

You must be sure that the database whose ownership is to be changed is the current database by selecting it in the **DB** list box. The new owners *login* can not be known as either a user or an alias. If the new owner is listed in either the *sysusers* or *sysalternates* system table for that database, they must be dropped before running sp_changedbowner. The *true* parameter transfers all aliases and their permissions to the new database owner. Only the system administrator system administrator login can use the sp_changedbowner stored procedure.

Only the system administrator can grant the privilege of creating a database to another user. Again, this ability should only be given to a user who is not a system administrator when absolutely necessary. The user must already exist, and you must be using the master database to grant this permission. It is granted like this:

> GRANT CREATE DATABASE TO *username*

Substitute the name of the user to whom you want to grant the CREATE DATABASE permission to in place of *username*.

Using Aliases

Often in a developmental environment, several people will share the responsibility for developing particular pieces of the database. In this environment, each user requires ownership rights on the database. In a production environment you may want to allow another login to be able perform the duties of the database owner. Since only one login can be database owner, SQL Server provides the ability to allow you to relate logins to each other, through *aliases*.

When an alias is be created using the stored procedure sp_addalias or from the SQL Server Enterprise Manager, an entry is placed in the system table *sysalternates*. SQL Server uses this table to map users and aliases. When a user attempts to log on to SQL Server, their login is checked against the values found in the system table *syslogins*. If found, then SQL Server matches the login with the value found in the suid column. The value in this column is taken and SQL Server tries to make a match in the *sysusers* system table. If one is found, then the user is logged in to the database. If no match is found, then SQL Server goes and looks at the *sysalternates* system table and tries to find a match for suid there. If a match is found, then SQL Server looks at the altsuid column, and once again goes back to the *sysusers* table and matches the altsuid to a valid suid in the *sysusers* table. The relationships between each of these tables is shown in figure 10.12.

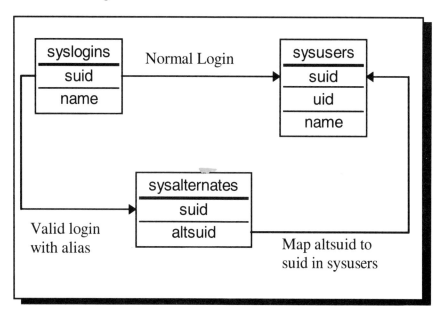

Figure 10.12: The relationships created between the login, the user, and the alias depicted here.

Create an alias for a user by following these steps:

1.   Open SQL Server Enterprise Manager and then the Logins folder. Select the user login that you want to alias to another login, in this case the pubs database owner.

2.   Right-click on the login and select Edit from the shortcut menu to display the Manage Logins dialog box.

3.   Click in the box belonging to the Aliases column and the pubs row and click the down arrow to display the list box

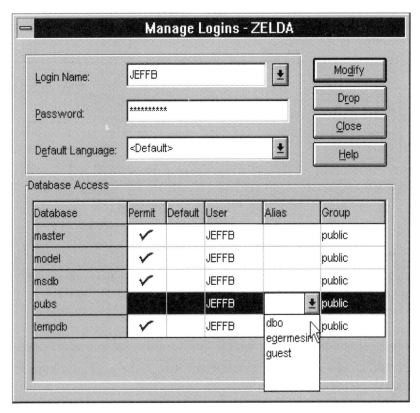

Figure 10.13: Select the login you want the user, JEFFB, to be aliased to in the Alias column.

4.   Select the dbo login from this list. Notice how the login name disappears from the User column.

5.   Click the Modify button to complete the alias process. SQL Server will now add the appropriate entries in the *sysalternates* table.

240

Figure 10.14: The Manage Logins dialog box is easily used to create an alias. The user JEFFB now will log in to the pubs table under the alias dbo.

Passwords

Passwords are used to authenticate a login. Without a password, anyone who manages to get access to a valid login can gain access to SQL Server. SQL Server has no minimum requirements for a password, but does have an upper limit of 30 characters. When creating a password, you can use any printable character, including A–Z, a–z, 1–0. When adding a password, either by using the stored procedure sp_password, or

241

in the Manage Logins dialog box, the password must be enclosed within quotes if it uses any character other than A–Z, a–z, 1–0, or begins with a number.

Just like login IDs, a password should be something that a hacker will not immediately guess, but not so difficult that the user will forget it. Hackers will generally tell you that their first guess on a password is the login name.

Granting and Revoking Permissions

Permissions is a system whereby the system administrator, or an owner of a database or object give their permission to use objects, to use commands. Simply put, permissions are the final system of controls over who can use the objects within a database, or select, insert, or delete any of the information contained in the tables. Some permissions cannot be granted, but belong exclusively to the system administrator.

The permissions which you can be granted, or given, and those which you can grant depends on your status as a user. As a system administrator you can grant the widest range of permissions, while as a user without ownership of any objects, you will probably not be able to grant any permissions to another user. Permissions are granted and revoked to users and groups, not to login IDs.

When a permission is granted to a user any entry is placed in the *sysprotects* system table, a copy of which is maintained in each database. For most users and groups, permissions for the most commonly used commands and stored procedures can be granted from within SQL Server Enterprise Manager. Permissions for the higher level commands, such as CREATE DATABASE, are granted by using the GRANT statement. When a user is granted permission to use an object or command, they do not have the ability to pass it to another user, unless they have been given explicit permission through the use of the WITH GRANT option.

Permissions can be granted or revoked using these T-SQL statements:

```
GRANT {ALL [PRIVILEGES][column_list] | permission_list
    [column_list]}
ON {table_name [(column_list)]
| view_name [(column_list)]
| stored_procedure_name}
TO {PUBLIC | name_list }
[WITH GRANT OPTION]
```

The GRANT statement can be a complex command to use, and should be used with great care. Whenever possible, use the simpler format in SQL Server Enterprise Manager. Within the GRANT statement, everything inside of { } is either optional, or one of the options is used. The statement can broken down like this:

One of these options can be used.

ALL: Grants all permissions available on the object(s) listed in the ON clause. When ALL is used in reference to T-SQL statements, only the system administrator can use it, since only the system administrator can grant the CREATE DATABASE statement.

PRIVILEGES[column_list]: Use this option to grant only system administrator or user privileges to Windows NT users or groups. The column_list option allows you to specify which column(s) these users will have access to.

permission_list [*column_list*]: Substitute a list of specific permissions that you want to grant, and if necessary the column(s) over which these permissions will be effective. This option is often used when you want to grant several very specific permissions, such as SELECT, INSERT, UPDATE.

This clause is required:

ON: This clause is used to specify the object over which the permissions to be granted will be effective. You can grant permissions to tables, views, stored procedures, or any other object. The column_list option again allows you to specify a column(s) over which the permission is granted.

This clause is required:

TO: This clause specifies to whom the permissions are to be granted. You can grant permissions to a group, such as PUBLIC, or to a specified list of usernames.

This clause is optional and should be used with caution:

WITH GRANT OPTION: Allows the user granted this permission, or permissions, to grant them to another user. This clause can not be used with the CREATE DATABASE statement.

Revoking a permission takes away a previously granted permission to a statement or object. You can revoke permissions from a group or a single user. Like the grant statement, REVOKE also can be complex. Many revoke permissions can be accomplished from SQL Server Enterprise Manager. The REVOKE statement is used like this:

```
REVOKE [GRANT OPTION FOR]
{ALL [PRIVILEGES] | permission_list } [(column_list)]
ON { table_name [(column_list)]
| view_name [(column_list)]
| stored_procedure_name | extended_stored_procedure_name}
FROM {PUBLIC | name_list}
[CASCADE]
```

The REVOKE statements options are very similar to the GRANT statement, with the exception of the last option:

CASCADE: This option allows you to revoke a permission granted with the WITH GRANT OPTION, and cascades the revoke statement down through all users who have been subsequently granted permissions from the user or group whose permissions are now being revoked.

Note

Be sure that you use the grant and revoke statements so that they work the way you intend them. There is no hierarchy for grant and revoke statements other than one— *the last statement committed is the one that will take effect.* If you revoke permissions to the guest user and then grant them to the public group, the guest user will also get the permissions since they are a member of the public group. If you are restricting access to specific users, grant all of the required permissions to the group, and then revoke any specific permissions from the single user.

Permissions By Object

Permissions can also be granted and revoked from within the SQL Server Enterprise Manager application. The number and types of permissions is more limited than with the GRANT/REVOKE statements, but covers most objects and commands users need access to. Use these steps to grant and revoke permissions with SQL Server Enterprise Manager:

1.   Open the SQL Server Enterprise Manager window, and then the Database folder. Click on the specific database to which permissions are to be granted or revoked, in this case pubs, and then select Object, Permissions from the menu to display the Object Permissions dialog box. Be sure that the By Object tab is selected.

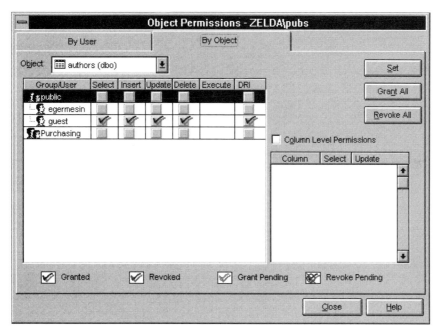

Figure 10.15: The Object Permissions dialog box is used to grant and revoke permissions.

Permissions can be granted or revoked in two ways—by object or by user. There is a tab on the Object Permissions dialog box for each option. Select the specific object that you want to work with in the Object combo box.

2.   Revoke all permissions from the guest user except for SELECT permissions. Click on the checkmarks in each column except for the Select column in the guest row. This will change the mark from a Granted checkmark to a Revoke Pending checkmark. The guest user will be allowed to use the SELECT statement within the pubs database, but none of other statements.

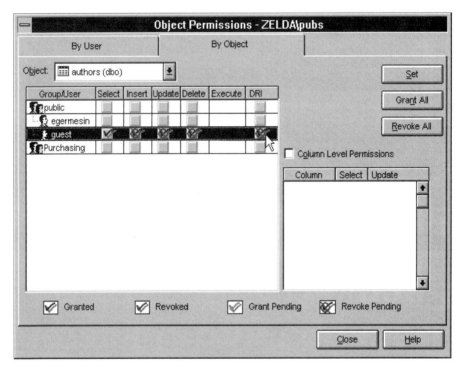

Figure 10.16: Permission to actively alter information in the authors table is pending revocation for the guest user.

3.   Now select all of the boxes in the public group login.

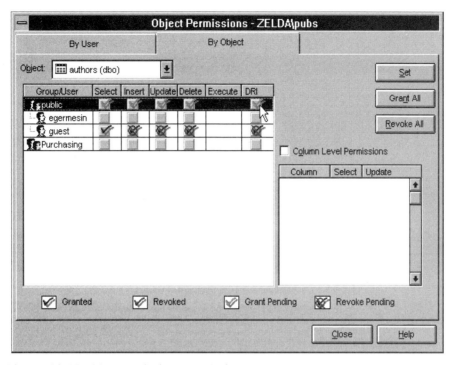

Figure 10.17: All permissions are being granted to other users of the public group in the authors table.

4.   Click the Set button to perform the actions you have specified—granting the checked permissions to the public group and revoking several permissions to the guest user. Remember, these permissions have been set only on the selected object—in this case, the authors table. To set other permissions using this tab, you must select each object, one by one, granting or revoking the necessary permissions.

Column-level permissions can also be specified by clicking the Column Level Permissions box, selecting the necessary columns and then selecting or unselecting the boxes in the Select or Update column. This allows you to restrict either or both SELECT and UPDATE statements on specific columns of the selected object.

Permissions By User

In addition to granting or revoking permissions by a specific object, you can also do the same by user or group. Often these options are used together in tandem. Grant a wide range of permissions for a group of users, and then revoke some or all permissions for a specific user.

1.   Click the By User tab button.

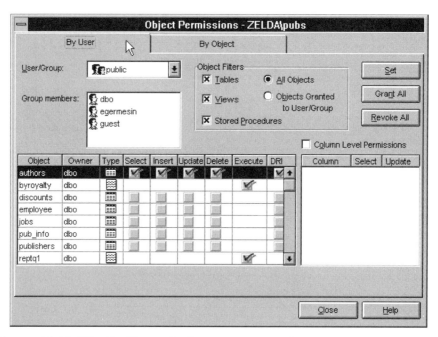

Figure 10.18: The By User tab gives you a way of granting and revoking permissions by user instead of by objects.

2.   Select the guest user in the User/Group combo box. You will see the objects list change to show the permissions now granted to the guest user. See how the authors table only has SELECT permission granted. This is because you revoked the other permissions in the previous section.

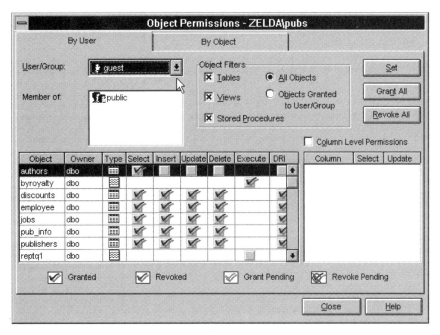

Figure 10.19: The permissions available to the guest user are shown.

Permissions can be granted or revoked by clicking on the various boxes in the permissions columns beside the different objects. Notice that the Object Filter box has been set to display **All** Objects that are available in the pubs database. You can restrict the display by setting the filter to show only those objects to which the user has been granted by clicking the **Ob**jects Granted to User/Group option button. You can also display fewer objects by unselecting **T**ables, **V**iews, or Stored **P**rocedure. Only those objects selected will be displayed.

Just like when using the GRANT or REVOKE statement, be sure that you work from the group level down to the individual user. This will ensure that you do not inadvertently grant permissions you had previously revoked.

Using SQL Security Manager

When using integrated or mixed security, your Windows NT users and user groups are not automatically mapped to SQL Server login IDs. SQL Server provides the SQL

Security Manager application for this job. When you are using standard security, you can use SQL Security Manager to create login IDs.

When you first login to the SQL Security Manager, it will be blank except for the system administrator information. There is a pair of buttons on the toolbar, one shows logins with user privileges and the other shows system administrator privileges. Click the system administrator button and you will see a window something like figure 10.20.

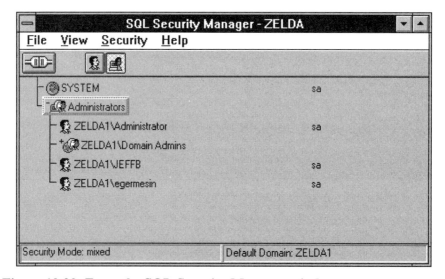

Figure 10.20: From the SQL Security Manager window you can manage login mapping from Windows NT security groups for integrated security and login IDs for standard security.

Adding users or administrators is basically the same process and is done like this:

1.   Click the User button. You will either see a grouping similar to that in figure 10.20 or a blank window.

1.   Select Security, Grant New from the menu. You will see a new dialog box, Grant User Privilege.

2.   Select the group you created earlier for users, SQLUsers, from the Grant
privilege list box, and then click the Add Users to Database checkbox. Finally, select
the database they are to be added to as users by selecting pubs from the combo box.
This will become their default database when they log in to SQL Server.

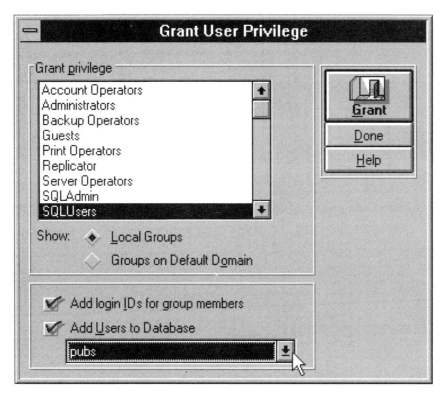

**Figure 10.21: By using the Grant User Privilege dialog box you can select
groups, automatically create login IDs and specify the database they are
to be added to.**

3.   Click the Grant button to add the members of this group to SQL Security
Manager and have SQL Server create login IDs for each.

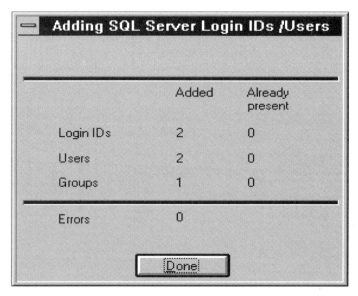

Figure 10.22: The Adding SQL Server Login Ids/Users dialog box shows how many users are added, how many login IDs are created and how many groups are created.

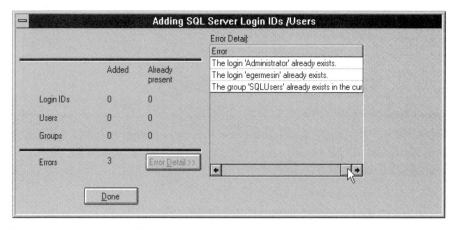

Figure 10.23: This dialog box shows what errors were encountered when trying to add a user or a group.

If any errors were encountered, click on the Error **D**etail to view the errors. Figure 10.23 shows examples of errors that may be encountered. By scrolling the Error Detail box you can see the operation, the item (user or group name), and a description of the error encountered.

4.   Click the **D**one button in both of the dialog boxes to return to the SQL Security Manager window. You should now see the SQLUsers group displayed. Double-click on the group button to see the users who belong to the group.

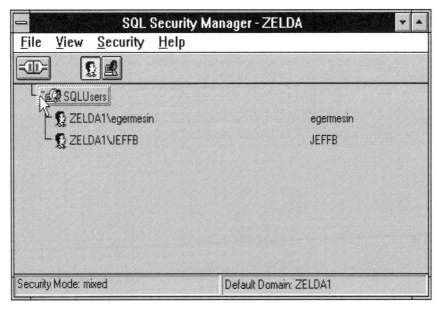

Figure 10.24: You can now see the users who belong to the SQLUsers group.

Notice that SQL Server has added the users to the database, and given each user their own individual login name. Back in figure 10.19 when you looked at the system administrator logins, all of the users their had a login of sa and did not have an individual login name.

Summary

In this chapter, you have learned to work with Windows NT's and SQL Server's security systems. Specifically, you have learned:

- How Windows NT and SQL Server identify and authenticate a user login through the use of usernames and passwords.

- How to choose between integrated, standard, and mixed security modes.

- How to create both a user group and a user login for Windows NT.

- To create both user groups and user logins for SQL Server.

- To use an alias for another user.

- How to grant and revoke permissions.

- And, finally, to use SQL Security Manager with integrated and mixed security.

Chapter 11

Backups and Disaster Recovery

IN THIS CHAPTER

- Types of Failures
- Backup and Recovery
- Restoring a Database
- Rebuilding a Lost Device
- Heavy Duty Protection—Mirrors and RAID
- Using Removable Media

Disaster recovery and the preparations for it, are a form of insurance that a simple policy cannot make up for. While an insurance policy may be able to replace your physical equipment that has been damaged, there is no way for it to replace the far more valuable asset—your data. Your data and your system have several forms of protection, each with a different level of effectiveness.

The fastest, and most costly in hardware dollar terms, is to have a complete backup server ready to take over for the primary server. A backup server must have SQL Server running, and complete copies of all databases and system and user accounts. As dumps of both the transaction logs and databases are created from the primary server, they should be immediately loaded onto the backup server. If the primary server has to be taken offline for an extended period of time, you simply have to bring the backup server online and rename it as the primary. It will then take over as of the last transaction log dump as if nothing had ever happened.

Next in effectiveness is the use of a Redundant Array of Inexpensive Disks (RAID) subsystem. A RAID system can be of several levels—0 through 5—each offering different levels of performance and recovery abilities.

The third level of disaster preparedness is through the use of backups. Backups are usually dumps of the transaction log and/or the database to a tape device.

The final level of protection is that of power protection. Many failures of computer hardware, and the resulting loss of data contained on that hardware, stem from the power supplied to the equipment. Be sure that your computer and all peripheral devices are properly protected with both surge/spike suppressers and uninterruptable power supply (UPS)/battery backup. Do not buy the inexpensive surge/spike bars you can buy at your local hardware or department store. These are not adequate for computer protection and should not be used. Expect a four-outlet computer-grade surge suppresser to start at about $50.00. A good UPS for a server should not only give you enough battery time to shut down the server, but should have a serial port and software that will shut an unattended server down in the event of a power failure.

Types of Failures

Computer systems fail in many ways. A system can fail due to mechanical breakdown, power failure, natural disaster, user error, or malicious tampering. There are many more individual types of failures, but most are variations of one of these themes.

Mechanical failures of components other than disk drives are usually an inconvenience, and can be easily remedied. Your server may be down until a technician can replace a part, but you will probably not lose any data if a video adapter, or even a motherboard, fails. Short of having a backup server ready to take the primary server's place, there is little to do but quickly replace the necessary parts.

Power failures can be partially alleviated with UPSs, and, in mission critical situations, emergency electric generators. Otherwise, have good protection against the inevitable power surge and spikes that come with the restoration of electrical services, and wait the problem out. Most types of natural disasters fall into the power failure category. Depending upon their severity, hardware may or may not be lost.

A comprehensive disaster preparedness plan is beyond the scope of this book, but if you want more information read Patrick H. Corrigan's book "LAN Disaster Prevention and Recovery" published by Prentice Hall PTR. For what could easily be a very dry subject, he has written a very readable, and complete book on a very important subject.

There are three major categories of failures for which you can prepare. Each entail different recovery issues, and they will be discussed in this chapter.

Client Application Failure

For some reason a client application fails, leaving uncommitted transactions in process. This can happen for a variety of reasons. The user may exit their application improperly, leaving the uncommitted transactions. A network connection may fail between the client workstation and the server, or a power failure may be localized to the client workstation. Whatever the reason, each of these failures has a common thread—a client application has unexpectedly terminated and left transactions that have not been committed or rolled back.

SQL Server uses the system of *checkpoints* and the *recovery* process to ensure that all committed transactions are written to disk, and that uncommitted transactions are rolled back. Checkpoints occur under three circumstances:

- When explicitly issued by the database owner.
- As additional cache space is needed by the server.
- The specified recovery interval has been exceeded.

When a checkpoint is issued, all dirty pages in the database are written to the disk and then a checkpoint marker is placed in the log. SQL Server then assumes at the next checkpoint that any data prior to the checkpoint marker has already been written to the disk.

When SQL Server is next restarted, the automatic recovery is started. This procedure automatically checks the logs for uncommitted transactions and rolls them back. Recovery also checks for committed transactions were not written to the data files. These transactions are rolled forward into the data file, completing SQL Server's guarantee that a transaction that has been committed will exist in the data files, even in the event of a failure. By mirroring the transaction logs, you can help to ensure that recovery can take place even if you have a disk failure.

Program Failure

A very similar process occurs in the event of a server program failure. The same things that can affect a client machine can also happen to the server. While the server is often better protected, with a larger battery system, tape devices, and other protections, there will be times when the server fails, leaving the potential for many committed transactions not yet written to disk and uncommitted transactions littering the transaction logs.

The same automatic recovery process takes care of this problem also. The time to recover may take a little longer than if a single client fails, but the server will recover nonetheless. The only thing that the system administrator will have to do is to notify the users that the server is up and running again, and that they may need to check that all of their last running transactions were properly committed.

Disk or Media Failures

Disks and media—what is meant by these two terms? Media is an all encompassing term, which, in the computer world, refers to any form of magnetic storage. Disks can mean a floppy disk, a CD-ROM disc, a magneto-optical disk, or most often—a hard disk drive.

Disk drives, being mechanical in nature, are subject to failure over time. They may develop bad spots that can corrupt data stored there, or they can suffer catastrophic failure—a head crash. Today's hard disk drives are much more reliable than they were just a few years ago, with mean-time-before failure rates ranging into the tens of thousands of hours. If a disk fails, the system administrator will have much work to do to recover. SQL Server cannot automatically recover from this failure. How much work, will depend on how much, if any, of the data is recoverable, when the last backup was performed, and whether the disk that failed contained program files, data files, transaction log files, or some combination of all of these. Whenever possible, try to separate data files and transaction logs onto different disks.

Media, often referring to tape, can also fail. A tape can be damaged by the drive mechanism, not be written to properly–(and so not be able to be read)–or damaged due to improper storage. Be sure that you test-load your backups from time to time. Loading a backup from a bad tape is doomed to fail. Be sure that you have a good backup before you really need it—testing a backup may not only save your data, but may save your job.

Backup and Recovery

Making regular backups of your database is one of the surest ways to recover in the event of a disk failure. It is a relatively cheap form of insurance for your businesses data, and the most foolproof way to guarantee that you can restore most, if not all, of the information.

Without a backup it can be nearly impossible to recover information lost through disk failure. You would have to go back to the physical files, if any, and reenter all of the data again. Think of how many hours and days it took to enter the information in the first place. And at the same time you are trying to reenter old data, new data is coming in. There is no excuse for not having a good tape backup device for a server. The relatively small cost more than outweighs the potential in irrecoverable business information and people-hours.

SQL Server assigns backup responsibility to the database owner by default. The database owner, and of course the system administrator, is given the capability to use the dump and load statements. Depending upon the size of your organization, and the number of servers and disks, you may want to assign one or two people to perform backups, granting to them the use of the dump database, load database, and dump transactions statements. The database owner and system administrator still can perform backups and restore operations.

Forms of Backups

There are three types of backups that can be performed: the *full* backup, the *incremental* backup, and the *table* backup. A full backup is a complete copy of all allocated pages in the database, and includes all system tables. This includes the system table, *syslogs*, which is normally referred to as the transaction log.

> **Note**
>
> A full backup does not truncate the transaction log. Remember, if the transaction log is not truncated, it will continue to fill up with transactions, and once the transaction log is full all further transactions will be stopped.

The incremental backup copies only the transaction logs, which contain all transactions that have occurred since the last dump transaction statement. This ensures that all transactions that would have made changes to the data files have been saved. Unless otherwise specified, when the transaction log is dumped, it is also truncated, making the space available once again.

The table backup is new to SQL Server 6.5, and allows you to recover single tables without having to restore the entire database. This can be especially helpful if you have a single corrupt table, that does not have any foreign key columns or columns based on columns in another table. You cannot use a table backup if the table contains image or text columns, or if the table has been published for replication.

> **Note**
>
> Once you have performed a table restore, the DUMP TRANSACTION statement is disabled by SQL Server until you perform a full backup.

While there are three types of backups you can perform, these backups can be accomplished on live data that is being accessed while the backup is working, or on data that is not currently in use.

Files created with the dump statement are not readable by other applications. You must use the load statement when working with any SQL Server backup file.

Offline, or Static, Backups

An offline backup is the preferred method of backing up. This means that there are no transactions being processed through the database while the backup is being processed. A static backup is most often done by stopping SQL Server and then restarting the server in a single-user mode. The backup is created, and then SQL Server is restarted in normal mode. This process ensures that you have a complete backup of all data and system tables and transactions logs as of a single point in time.

Online, or Dynamic, Backups

Online, or dynamic, backups are done while live transactions are ongoing through the database. This method, while it does provide you with a backup of all of your data, also has some disadvantages. SQL Server will suffer some performance degradation during the backup. When the **dump database** statement is used, it automatically issues a checkpoint to all transaction logs that belong to those databases that will be backed up. This forces all transactions that have been committed to be written to the database. An image of the database is then created as of that point in time, and then the backup proceeds.

As the dump proceeds, a transaction log page becomes available to users once it has been dumped. If a user tries to update a page that has not yet been dumped, SQL Server will immediately dump that page and then allow the update. The client application must wait for the page to become available before users can continue with their work. Remember, any transaction that was not committed before the dump begins will not be reflected in the database. These transactions will be captured when you do the next transaction log dump.

Creating Your Backup Strategy

A complete backup strategy takes into account many factors. How these factors are weighed will be unique to the needs of your own business. Some of these factors include:

- How often should you backup?
- Should you use a static backup or a dynamic backup?

- Should only full backups be done, or can you use full and incremental backups?

- What media will be used, tape or disk?

- Should backups be done manually, or can you use an automatic scheduling program?

- How often should you verify that a backup was properly completed?

- How long should backups be kept before reusing the media?

- Is the storage place for your backups secure from theft? From magnetic disturbances? From fire? Do you have on-site or off-site storage?

- Has someone been assigned to perform backups? Do they have the necessary login and passwords to perform the job?

- Do you have a backup person who has the authorization and know-how to perform backups and restores in the event the primary person is not available?

This is a short list of some of the questions every system administrator or database owner will need to consider when deciding how backups are to be done. These decisions must be made before you actually need a backup to recover from a disk failure. Not all of these questions will be answered here, but use your own answers to them as a guide.

How often a backup should be performed can be answered with the help from the answers to several questions:

- How long can you afford to be without the database and its information? If the database and its data is critical to the day-to-day operation of your business, then backups should be frequent. Historical data THAT does not change can be backed up once. Making several copies of this backup should ensure that the data can be recovered even if one tape was bad.

- How long do you want a recovery to take? Full backups take less time to recover from than do full backups with incremental backups, but take longer to create than does an incremental backup. Depending on your needs you may decide to do weekly full backups and daily incremental backups. A heavily used database may require several incremental dumps during the day.

- How frequently is data in the database updated? If a database is part of a heavily used online transaction processing system, it may require several log dumps during the day, with full dumps once a day. Conversely, a database with infrequent updates may only need to be dumped once a week or once a month.

The type of media to be used for backups is also very important. The fastest form of backup is to dump to a local hard disk dump device. But this affords you with the least security. Be sure that such backups are immediately copied to a tape device, or at the very least to another disk on a separate machine. Often backups are kept conveniently at hand so that they can be used when necessary—but this is not the safest course. If you keep backup tapes stored near the server, be sure that a copy of the backup is kept in a secure place in a different building, or even better in a secure, fireproof storage facility (bank safety deposit boxes are often used). This ensures that your data is still available to you in the unhappy event of damage to the building that houses your server.

Finally, be sure that you test your backup strategy. Does it meet the needs of your business? Is the recovery time acceptable? Are the backups themselves actually working? Test your backup devices, both logical and physical, several times before relying on them, and then test them periodically.

Creating a Backup

Backups are created by using the **dump database** or **dump transaction** statements, and are placed onto a backup device you have already created. You can use the dump statement whenever necessary to create a backup, or SQL Server can schedule the backup to run at a convenient time. From SQL Server Enterprise Manager you can backup selected databases, or tables within the database, like this:

1.   Open SQL Server Enterprise Manager and select **T**ools, **D**atabase Backup/Restore from the menu to display the dialog box you will use to control both backup and restore operations. Be sure to click the Backup tab.

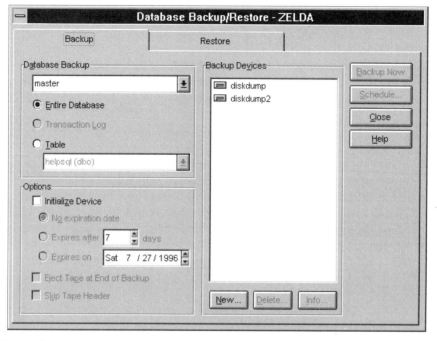

Figure 11.1: Use the Database Backup/Restore dialog box to control what databases will be backed up and where a backup will be placed.

2.   Select the database you want to backup from the **D**atabase Backup combo box. For this example, choose the pubs database.

3.   Click the option button for the entire database in the **D**atabase Backup options box. You can now choose to backup the entire database, its transaction logs, or a single table.

- **E**ntire Database: This option allows you to backup the entire database selected in the above combo box.

- Transaction **L**og: This option is available only if the database's transaction log is contained on a separate database device.

- **T**able: This option allows you to select a specific table from the selected database. Select the table in the combo box below the option button.

4.   Now make the appropriate selections in the Options section. Check the Initialize Device, and the Expires after days options, and type 30 into the text box as the number of days that must elapse before the file can be overwritten. The options available here include:

- Initialize Device: check this option to allow backups to be appended to an existing tape. This allows you to keep multiple backups in the same physical location or on the same tape. If a tape has already been used by another application and contains an unfamiliar format, you must uncheck this box, allowing the tape to overwrite the existing information, or SQL Server will reject the tape. If this is the first backup to a device, you must check this box so that a label will be written to the device.

   - No expiration date: this option creates a tape without an expiration date. The data on this tape can be overwritten at any time, without any warning.

   - Expires after # days: this option allows you to enter a specific number of days that must elapse before the backup can be overwritten by a new backup.

   - Expires on *date*: this option allows you to enter a specific date that must pass before the backup can be overwritten.

- Eject Tape at End of Backup: this option is used if you do not plan to place any further backups onto the tape, or if this is the last backup to be placed on the tape. When selected, the tape will be rewound and then ejected from the tape device. Otherwise, the tape is not rewound, allowing another backup to be placed sequentially on the tape.

- Skip Tape Header: when selected, this option allows SQL Server to not read any ANSI header information that has been placed on the tape. The ANSI header is where backup places information such as a file's expiration date. When selected SQL Server will not attempt to read any headers and will overwrite an existing file. Select this option when you are using a new tape, otherwise backup will attempt to read a nonexistent header several times.

5.   From the Backup Devices list, select which device(s) will be used to save the backup by clicking it. The backup in figure 11.2 will be striped on the devices diskdump and diskdump3. A backup can be placed on single or multiple devices.

When you select multiple devices, the backup will be striped across them. This will allow for faster backups and restores.

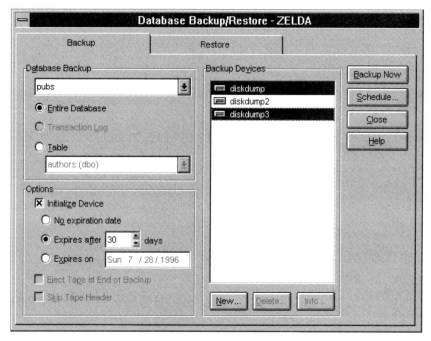

Figure 11.2: Ready to start the backup procedure.

When you have multiple backup devices to choose from, you can place your backup on a single device by simply clicking it. To stripe the backup across multiple devices, you can select the first device and then drag the mouse across the group of devices you want to include as members of this particular stripe set. You can choose specific devices by pressing and holding the Ctrl key while clicking the specific devices you want to include. A stripe set can include a maximum of 32 devices.

You can also do some device management from here. You can create a new device by clicking the **N**ew button and providing the necessary information in the New Backup Device dialog box; this requires you, enter a name for the device and a backup device. You can also delete a device listed here by clicking the **D**elete button. The

Info button provides such information about the selected device as what type of a
device it is, if there are any existing backups on the device and what they are, when it
is due to expire, if it is a member of a stripe set, and the names of the other members
of the set.

6.   Click the **B**ackup Now button to start the backup sequence. You will now
see the Backup Volume Label dialog box. A backup device is given a six character
ANSI label. You can override the default label, or simply accept it as SQL Server has
entered it.

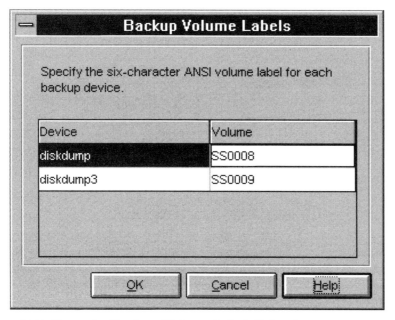

**Figure 11.3: From the Backup Volume Label dialog box you can enter
your own six character ANSI label for the backup.**

7.   Click the **OK** button to begin the backup. You will see a progress dialog box as the backup is proceeding, and then a status dialog box when the backup has been completed. Click the OK button to close this dialog box. You will be returned to the Database Backup/Restore dialog box, and then click the Close button to return to SQL Server Enterprise Manager.

If you want to schedule the backup to run at a time when there is less activity on the database, click the Schedule button in the Database Backup/Restore dialog box. You will again see the Backup Volume Label dialog box, but this time the volume label is blank. You can enter it now, or SQL Server will enter a volume label later when the backup is started. Clicking the **OK** button here moves you on to the Schedule Backup dialog box.

With the Schedule Backup dialog box you can name the task, and make any adjustments necessary to the SQL commands that make up the task. Do not make any changes here unless you are very familiar with T-SQL statements and commands. You can choose when this task will be run by clicking one of the appropriate option buttons:

- **Im**mediately: The task will run immediately after you click the **OK** button.

- **One T**ime: Allows you to run the task once. You must specify the date and time in the two text boxes that follow this option.

- **R**ecurring: This option allows you to specify how often, and when, a task will be run. This is an excellent way to create a backup procedure that will run unattended at a certain time. All you have to do is be certain a tape is ready, or that the disk dump device is available to SQL Server. If you want to change the default setting of once a week on Sundays at 12:00A.M. then click the Change button and use the Task Schedule dialog box to select a new schedule.

Finally, the Options button brings up the T-SQL Task Options dialog box. From this dialog box you can choose to have SQL Server notify someone of the tasks current operation. You can have SQL Server notify someone by e-mail or simply write a note in the Windows NT Application Event Log, either on success or failure.

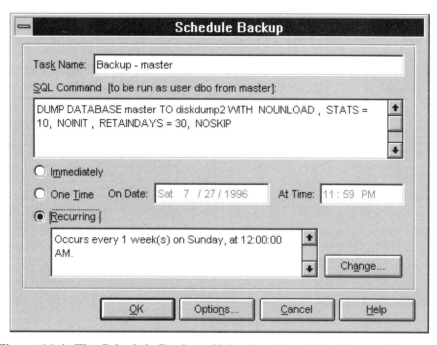

Figure 11.4: The Schedule Backup dialog box is used to choose when and how often a task will be run. This backup is scheduled to run once a week on Sundays at 12:00A.M.

Restoring a Database

Restoring, also sometimes referred to as loading, is the process you will take when a disk fails or a database becomes corrupt and you must reload it from a backup. This process involves determining which databases must be restored, which dumps are to be used, and whether they are full dumps, or incremental dumps as well.

When the load command is executing, no one, including the individual who executed the command, can use the database until the load is complete. Loading a database can

269

take considerably more time than the original dump did. The reason for this is that a dump only copies those pages that have been written to. Conversely, a load must read and then write all of these same pages, and then initialize all of the unused pages that belong in the database. While a dump may only take several minutes to a few hours, the subsequent load of the same information can take several hours to a few days, depending on the volume of information.

Reloading a Lost Database

There are two different events that may require you to reload a backup of a database: media failure and simple data corruption. The first event, that of a system failure, will require you to reload one or more databases—you must first drop the database. The second event, that of data corruption, may be able to be taken care of by simply reloading your last backup and any subsequent transaction log dumps.

Dropping a Defective Database

Dropping a database can be done from SQL Server Enterprise Manager by selecting the database and dropping it. You can also do the same thing using the command line options from ISQL/w. At times when a database has become corrupted, you may not be able use the DROP DATABASE command. When this happens, use the stored procedure sp_dbremove, like this:

sp_dbremove *database_name*, dropdev

This stored procedure is most often used with removable devices, but will also remove all references to the named database from both the *sysdatabases* and *sysusages* system tables. The keyword *dropdev* is used to drop a device which is being exclusively used by the named database. If the database does have exclusive use of the device, then all references to the device will be removed from the *sysdevices* table.

You can also use the dbcc statement dbcc dbrepair to remove a damaged database, like this:

dbcc dbrepair (*database_name*, dropdb)

This statement is provided to keep backward compatibility with earlier versions of SQL Server. Unless it does not work, use the stored procedure sp_dbremove.

270

Once the damaged database has been dropped, you can proceed with reloading and restoring your database and its data. The first order of business is to recreate the database's structure. If you are creating this database with the exclusive intent of reloading it, use the for load option with the CREATE DATABASE statement.

When the for load option is used the database is not accessible until the database is loaded from the backup and the DBO Use Only option is turned off. The for load option creates the database but does not initialize the pages. This is why this method can be much quicker than simply re-creating the database.

Note

The procedures for recovering the master database are more complex and are covered in a separate section of this chapter.

When rebuilding a database with the for load option, you must recreate the database as it was originally created. For example, you create a database that is 50MB in size, with a 10MB transaction log on two different devices, and then later alter the database, adding a 25MB data segment on a third device. Unfortunately, you can't simply create a database 85MB in size and expect to load the backup into it.

If you have kept a record of the original CREATE statements, so that you know how large the database segments were, you are in luck—simply reuse these. If you did not keep good records, all is not lost. You can still get the necessary information from the *sysusages* table. Run the following query to gather the necessary information:

```
SELECT segmap, "MB"=size/512
FROM sysusages
WHERE dbid=db_id("database_name")
```

This query takes the value in the *size* column and divides it by 512 so that you get an answer in megabytes instead of 2K pages, yielding results like this:

```
segmap          MB
----------------   ---------------
3               20
4               10

(2 row(s) affected)
```

With a little more deciphering, you will be able to rebuild the databases. The order in which the values are displayed is also the creation order. A segmap value of 3 is a data segment, while a value of 4 is a log segment. If the data and logs were placed on the same device the value would be 7. You now know that this database contains two segments, the first is 20MB and contains the data pages, while the second segment is 10MB in size and contains the transaction logs.

In this example, we are going to assume that the pubs database has been damaged, and that it was properly backed up earlier. To create a database on which to load the backup, follow these steps:

1.   Open SQL Server Enterprise Manager and open the Databases folder. Select the pubs database and drop it by pressing the Delete key. You can also right-click on it and select **D**elete from the shortcut menu. Either method will remove the pubs database from the Database folder list.

2.   Now right-click on the Databases folder and select **N**ew Database from the shortcut menu. You will now see the New Databases dialog box. Type pubs into the **N**ame text box.

3.   In the **D**ata Device combo box select master as the database device on which to create this database, and enter a size of 3 for this database. The pubs database has both data and log pages on the same device, so there is nothing to be added to the **L**og Device combo box.

If you were re-creating the database in the query example above, you would specify the log device and a size of 10MB.

4.   Click the Create **f**or Load checkbox so that the database will be set for a load only. Remember, SQL Server will not initialize all of the pages of this database, and it will not be available to any users except the owner until the load has been completed.

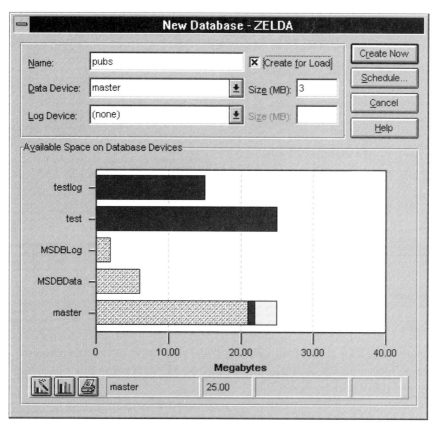

Figure 11.5: Use the New Database dialog box to enter the necessary information to create or re-create a database.

6.   Click the Create Now button so that the CREATE DATABASE statement with the selected parameters is run. If you wanted to run this later when there was less or no database traffic, and you did not need the database immediately, you could select Schedule and choose a time for this procedure to run.

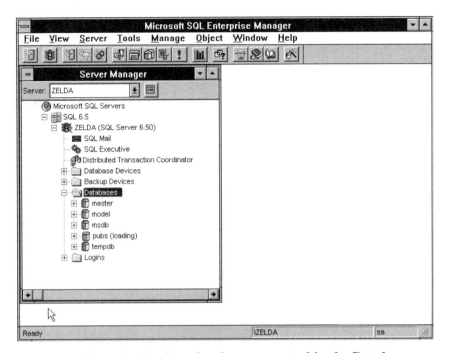

Figure 11.6: The pubs database has been recreated in the Databases folder. Notice the designation (loading) beside it. No one but the owner can use this database yet.

Restoring a Database Backup

Now that you have dropped the defective pubs database, or, alternatively, determined that you can simply load a backup over the existing data, it is time to take the step. This step requires loading the last full backup, and, of course, all transaction log dumps since this full backup. From the Database Backup/Restore dialog box, you can choose not only what you want to restore, but where to restore to. Follow these next steps to load a database:

1.   Right-click on the pubs icon and select Database/Restore from the shortcut menu. You will again see the Database Backup/Restore dialog box. Click the Restore tab. From this part of the dialog box, you can select the specific backup that you will use and which device to backup from.

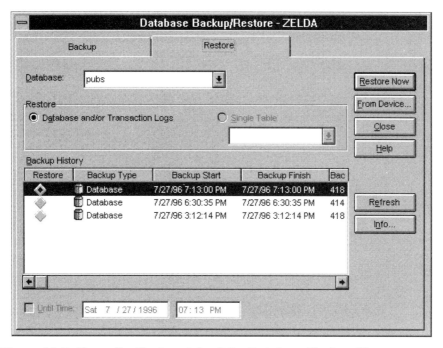

Figure 11.7: From the Restore tab of the Database Backup/Restore dialog box, you can select a backup and choose the device it will be restored to.

2.   From the **D**atabase combo box select the database that you want to restore, in this case pubs.

3.   The Restore section has two options: **D**atabase and Transaction Logs and **S**ingle Table. The **S**ingle Table option has combo box for you to choose the table that is to be restored. This option is not available for the pubs database until after you have completed the load process.

4.   In the **B**ackup History list, select the backup that you want to restore from. Most often you will select the backup with the one with the latest date/time stamp. If for some reason you choose an earlier backup, be sure that you restore the transaction logs that will restore the database from the selected full backup forward to the current time. This list box displays information about backups only for the database selected in the **D**atabase combo box.

The backup that has the blue diamond inside of the gray diamond button is the one that will be used when restoring, even if you move the selection bar to a different backup. The selected backup is the one with the diamond. In figure 11.7, this is the currently highlighted backup. The selection does not change by simply moving the selection bar. You must specifically click it.

5.   Click the **R**estore Now button to begin loading the database with the selected backup. Be sure that you have selected the correct backup from the **B**ackup History list. You are not given the option to cancel once this process has started.

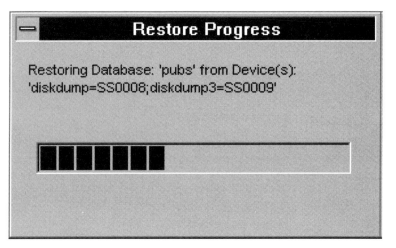

Figure 11.8: The progress bar information box shows you how far the load procedure has gone, and lists the devices from which the backup is being restored.

6.   Click the OK button in the next information box, which tells you that the dump has completed without any problems. If any problems did occur, you would see an error message informing you of such. Now click the **C**lose button on the Database Backup/Restore dialog box.

7.   Double-click the pubs database icon to bring up the Edit Database dialog box and click the Options tab. Click the **D**BO Use Only checkbox to remove the mark from this option and enable the database to be read by other users.

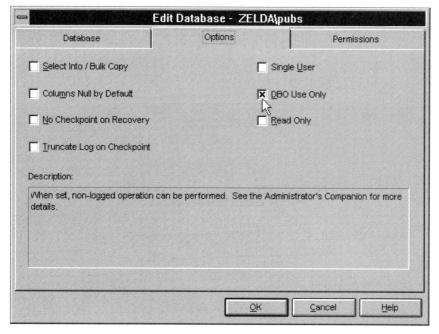

Figure 11.9: Use the Edit dialog boxes Options tab and turn off the DBO Use Only option by removing the X from the option box, so that others can once again access this database.

8.   Click the **OK** button to return to the SQL Server Enterprise Manager window.

9.   Finally, right-click on the database's icon and select Refresh from the shortcut menu. SQL Server will rewrite the screen and show the pubs database is no longer in the loading, single-user mode.

The pubs database has now been restored as of the last full backup. Since the pubs database incorporates its transaction logs on the same device, there are no transaction logs you must also load.

There was one button on the Database Backup/Restore dialog box which was not covered in the preceding discussion. It was the **F**rom Device button. This button displays the Restore From Device On Server dialog box, and is most often used to restore databases from earlier version of SQL Server, or to restore a database from a different device than was used to create the backup. For example, if you have two tape drives and create the backup on TAPE1 and want to use TAPE2 to restore from, you would select TAPE2 in the Devices and Files list box, as you see in figure 11.10.

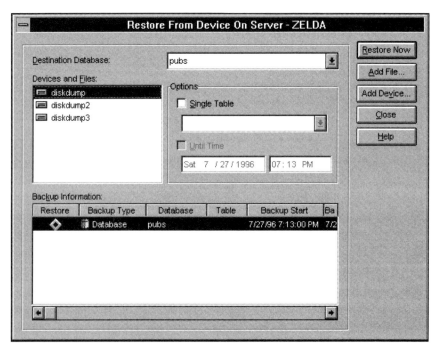

Figure 11.10: Use the Restore From Device On Server dialog box to select a device from which to restore a backup, and choose the database to restore the backup to if different from the original.

You can also select a new **D**estination Database from the combo box at the top of the dialog box. This enables you to load copy of the backup to a new database. If necessary, a new backup device can be created. This may be necessary when a backup was created on a device which has since been deleted. By re-creating the device, you can then restore from it.

Using Transaction Logs

Once you have loaded a database, you must next load all of the subsequent transaction logs. If a database has both data and log pages residing on the same device, you would not have to perform this separate procedure. When you do restore transaction log backups, you must restore them one by one, in the order that they were dumped. SQL Server will perform a recovery after each transaction log is restored, writing all of the committed transactions and rolling back all of the uncommitted ones. After you have loaded the last transaction log backup, your database will be fully recovered as of the time of the last transaction dump.

New to SQL Server 6.5 is the ability to restore a transaction log up to a specific date and time. Any transaction committed after the specified date and time will be rolled back. This option is only available when restoring a transaction log, not a full database, nor is this feature available with a database that combines both data pages and transaction logs on the same device. While this option is very simple to perform from the Restore tab of the Database Backup/Restore dialog box, it can also be accomplished using the T-SQL LOAD TRANSACTION statement with the STOPAT option.

This new point-in-time recovery option can be very helpful when you are recovering a database that may have become corrupted. For example, during the afternoon you begin to get calls from users complaining that they are getting inconsistent data from the server, and that the problem began sometime after the noon hour. Of course, since the noon hour you have had several client users continue to update data, and so you do not know exactly when the problem did begin, nor which transaction actually caused the problem. You can immediately dump the transaction log for the day's transactions. Then restore the database, and then the transaction logs up to a point-in-time such as 11:00A.M. Since your users complained that the problems appeared after 12:00P.M., you be fairly certain that your recovery will not include the transaction that caused the problem. If it does, then redo the recovery for an earlier time.

Remember, you must recover the database first, and then each of the transaction logs created subsequent to the full backup used to restore the database. Since you have just restored the database, it is assumed that the Database Backup/Restore dialog box is still open, if not open it. Restore a transaction log backup by following these steps:

1.   Select the first transaction log dump in the series to be restored.

In this example, there are two transaction log dumps. Notice the Backup Start date and time on both of them. Check the date and time for the full backup which you just loaded. The date and time for the first transaction log to be used will have the next sequential date and time stamp. SQL Server will not allow you to restore a transaction log with a date/time stamp earlier than the restored full backup.

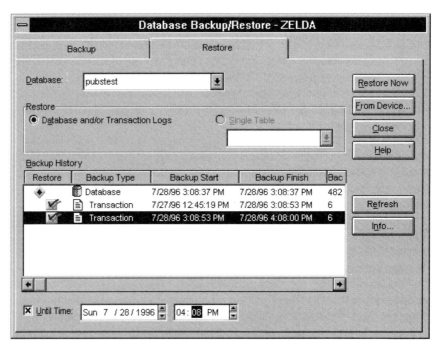

Figure 11.11: When restoring a databases transaction logs, you must include all logs created since the last full backup used in the restore procedure. Here, there are two.

2.   Click the Until Time checkbox to specify a point-in-time transaction recovery. Then specify the date and the time in the text boxes beside the checkbox.

3.   Click the Restore Now button.

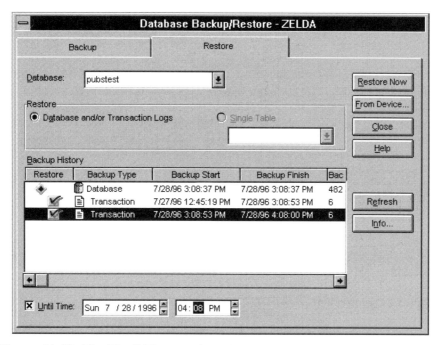

Figure 11.12: The Until Time option allows you to select a specific date and time through which you will recover transaction from the transactions log. Any transaction after the specified date and time will be rolled back.

If you inadvertently neglect to select a transaction log between the full backup and the transaction log selected, SQL Server will warn you that you have selected a transaction log that is out of sequence. SQL Server will not allow you to perform the restore procedure unless you do so with the transactions in the correct order. This is what would happen if you tried to restore the full backup displayed in figure 11.12, and then only the last transaction log. Even if you absolutely know that there were no transactions to recover on that transaction dump—for example, if you were closed that day—SQL Server will not allow you to skip it. If a transaction log dump was created, it must be restored and recovered.

Recovering the master Database

The recovery of the master database is a slightly different process from the procedure you use on a user database. It can not be emphasized enough: when you make changes to a user database that also makes changes to the system tables in the master database, dump the master database. This is the only way that you can be reasonably assured that all of the databases, tables, and users of your database system can be recovered in the event of a breakdown involving the master database. The most commonly performed actions that make changes to the master database are:

- Creating, expanding, or shrinking a user database.
- Creating, changing, or dropping a database device.
- Adding or dropping backup devices.
- Adding or dropping users and logins.
- Adding and dropping servers.

You may first notice that the master database has been damaged by an inability to start SQL Server, from segmentation errors, or I/O errors. Some of the dbcc commands can also report that an error has been found in the master database.

The master database must be recovered from its last backup. Any alterations made after this backup must be manually reapplied. This includes: adding new users and their security setups and re-creating databases built after this dump. Any database created after the last dump of the master database is lost, along with all of its data, if the master database is damaged or destroyed.

Re-creating the master database can be broken down into four primary steps: rebuild the master database, re-create a backup device, restore the latest backup of the master database, and, finally, restore the msdb database. Follow these steps:

1.   Select the SQL Setup icon in the Microsoft SQL Server 6.5 (Common) program group. Complete the information required in the dialog boxes, until you come to the Options dialog box. Select the Rebuild Master Database option button and click the Continue button. You will see a confirmation dialog box, warning that you will lose the information contained in your existing databases. This will be recovered when you load your master database backup. Click on Resume.

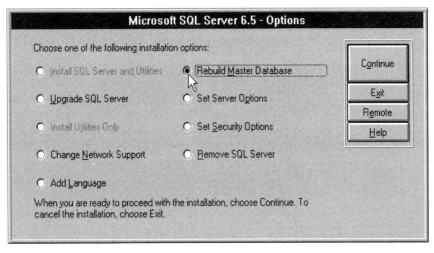

Figure 11.13: Select the Rebuild Master Database option button to rebuild only the master database.

2.   You must use the same character set and sort order from your previous install. Be sure that you know what this was before continuing. Make the appropriate selections in the Rebuild Options dialog box and click the Continue button again. If you originally selected the default settings, just click the Continue button now. SQL Server will not be able to restore use of the user databases if your choose a different character set and sort order.

3.   Use the SQL Server Installation Path dialog box to tell setup where to install the master database, and then click the Continue button. The original path and drive should be displayed.

4.   The final Rebuild MASTER Device dialog box is displayed. Unless you have expanded the master database device, the default settings should be correct. Click the Continue button again. SQL Setup will now rebuild the master database device and database. After a few moments you will see an information dialog box telling you that Setup has completed re-creating the master database.

5.   Start SQL Server normally, and then open SQL Server Enterprise Manager. Rebuild a dump device so that you can restore the last backup of your master database.

6.   Stop the SQL Server process by clicking the Stoplight button on the toolbar and then selecting **S**top from the dialog box. Open the command line window and type:

    sqlservr /c /d*path_master_dev* /m

This statement starts SQL Server independent of the Windows NT Service Control Manager and in a single-user mode. Substitute the drive, path, and file name for the master database into this statement.

7.   Open SQL Server Enterprise Manager and select **T**ools, **D**atabase Backup/Restore from the menu. Click the Restore tab and then the **F**rom Device button. Select the device you created where the last backup of the master database was placed, and then select the master database in the Bac**k**up Information list box. Click **R**estore Now button to start restoring your master database.

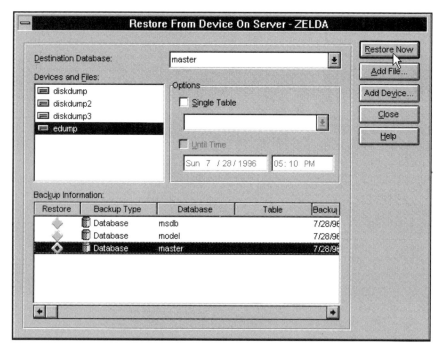

Figure 11.14: The master database is ready to be restored.

8.   Restart SQL Server Enterprise Manager.

Again, be sure to backup the master database whenever you make any changes to your databases that are reflected in the master database. You may save yourself a tremendous amount of work trying to reconstruct it by hand.

Rebuilding a Lost Device

At times you may loose the information about a specific device. This can often occur when you have to restore a backup of the master database created prior to the creation of a new device. Consequently, the information about the device is not located in the restored master database. In order to recover a lost device you must use two statements: DISK REINIT and DISK REFIT.

In order to recover a lost device, you must know some information about the device: the physical file name of the device and its size in 2K blocks. This is the minimum information required to recover a device. You can use the File Manager application to get the device's physical name and size in bytes. Follow these steps to restore a device:

1.   Using File Manager you have recovered the physical file name and path, e:\mssql\data\testdb.dat, with a size of 52,428,800 bytes. Convert this to 2K pages by dividing the size of the file by 2048 (number of bytes in a 2K page), resulting in 25,600–2K pages.

2.   Open the ISQL/w application, being sure to select the master database in the **D**B combo box, and enter this statement:

```
DISK REINIT
NAME = 'testdb',
PHYSNAME = 'e:\mssql\data\testdb.dat',
VDEVNO = virtual_device_number, (must be between 1-255 and
unique)
SIZE = 25600,
VSTART = virtual_address (optional, 0 is default, do not change
unless told to)
```

3.   Execute the above statement. ISQL/w will report any problems and indicate that the procedure was run in the Results tab.

4.   If DISK REINIT was successful, then it is time to run DISK REFIT. Click the Query tab, type **DISK REFIT**, and click the Execute button.

5.   Shut down, and then restart, the server so that the changes will take effect.

This is the technique to recover a damage or lost device, and it is not necessarily a very pretty process. You may still have more manual changes to make to the system tables *sysusages, sysdatabases,* and *syslogins.*

Save yourself a great many headaches by dumping the master database if you make any changes to a database, a device, or a login that are reflected in the master database's system tables. It only takes a few moments to backup the master database, and it can easily take you many hours of sweat and tears to rebuild it—if you can.

Heavy Duty Protection—Mirrors and RAID

This section describes additional types of disk devices, both hardware and software, that you can use to give an added dimension of protection to your data. Up to now, it has been assumed that your data and all SQL Server's devices have resided on a single disk drive. This is often true for a standalone PC, a small server, or a database in a developmental environment.

In a true production environment, having a single disk drive for all of your database functions is usually not seen, not to mention foolhardy. Often a single disk system is too slow in a multiple user environment, and too dangerous, with the potential of losing the one drive to a failure.

There are several forms of additional security and protection that you can incorporate into your system, including:

- Software disk mirroring
- Hardware disk mirroring
- Duplexed controllers
- RAID (levels 0 through 5)

SQL Server has the ability to manage disk mirroring, while Windows NT can handle disk striping and striping with parity, in addition to disk mirroring and duplexing controllers. Within Windows NT, duplexing and mirroring are often used to mean the same thing.

Generally, the difference is that duplexing refers to having two different disk controllers—one controlling the primary disks and the other controlling the mirrored disks. This ensures that a failure of one controller will not bring your server down. You can also use duplexed controllers to share I/O load between them.

Mirroring, on the other hand, refers to the technique of keeping an entire duplicate of your database on a separate disk. As an update is performed, it is immediately copied to the mirror. You can think of mirroring as a form of continuous backup. It is highly recommended that you mirror at least your transaction logs and the master database. This can help to ensure a quick recovery time.

Mirroring a Device

SQL Server and Windows NT mirror in different ways. If you have the option, use Windows NT mirroring over SQL Server's mirroring. Windows NT mirrors at the partition level, while SQL Server mirrors at the device level. If you have a database that spans more than one device, be sure that you mirror all of the devices the database uses.

For mirroring to work as it is meant to, you need a minimum of two disk drives. The mirror drive should be of a size equal to or larger than the primary drive. Normally it will be equal in size. If you use Windows NT mirroring, you must create partitions that are equal size. Be careful when selecting a drive to be mirrored and the drive where it will be mirrored to. Windows NT and SQL Server both allow you to select any disk device that can be accessed. Remember, a single disk can be partitioned into several drive letter designations. You would not want to place the mirror on a partition located on the same physical drive.

If you decide to use Windows NT mirroring, be sure to check the documentation on the subject. If you decide to use SQL Server's mirroring function, then use these steps:

1.   Open SQL Server Enterprise Manager and then open the server folder, and the Database Devices folder. Right-click on the master database device icon and select **E**dit from the shortcut menu. You will now see the Edit Database Device dialog box.

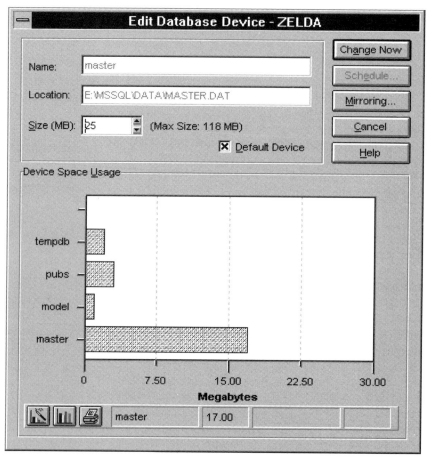

Figure 11.15: From the Edit Database Device dialog box you can begin the mirroring process.

2.   Click the Mirroring button, displaying the Mirror Database Device dialog box.

3.   Type the path and name of the mirror device into the text box. SQL Server places the mirror in the same path as the master device, and uses the primary device's name, appending mir as the filename extension.

It is recommended that you create a new directory for your mirror devices on a separate disk. SQL Server does not create a directory for you—it must already exist on the disk where you want the mirror to be placed.

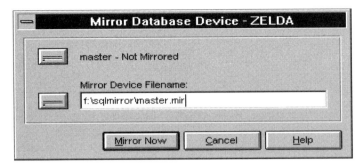

Figure 11.16: The Mirror Database Device dialog box is ready to complete the mirroring procedure.

4.   Click the Mirror Now button. SQL Server will immediately copy all of the pages from the master database device to the mirror device. This may take some time, especially if you are mirroring a very large database. Once the mirror has been created, you will see a final dialog box telling you so. Click its OK button to close it.

To later unmirror the two devices, or to switch to using the mirror device, click the Mirroring button on the Edit Database Device dialog box. Notice that the name of this button has changed from Mirror Now to Mirroring. This is one indication to you that a device has been mirrored. The dialog box Unmirror Device is displayed.

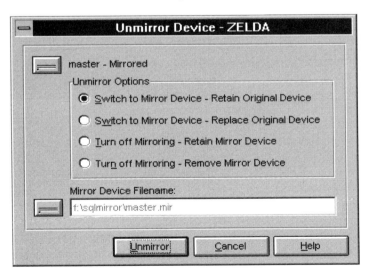

Figure 11.17: Use the Unmirror Device dialog box to change mirror settings, or to remove a mirror.

From within this dialog box you can choose four options:

- Switch to Mirror Device - Retain Original Device: This option causes the mirror to take over as the active database. The old primary database is retained.
- Switch to Mirror Device - Replace Original Device: This option causes the mirror to take over, and replaces the primary device.
- Turn off Mirroring - Retain Mirror Device: This option stops or pauses mirroring but retains the mirror so that it can be remirrored at a later time.
- Turn off Mirroring - Remove Mirror Device: This option stops mirroring and removes the mirror device.

Clicking the Unmirror button causes the option selected above to be activated. If you decide that you do not want to do any of these unmirroring actions, then click the Cancel button to return to the Edit Database Devices dialog box. The act of unmirroring, even if no transactions are processed, will force you to remirror the two devices again. Once unmirrored, the devices are considered to be out of sync.

RAID Disk Arrays

RAID devices and subsystems are the best protection you can have for your databases. But they come at a cost, as RAID systems are not just expensive, they are fantastically expensive. A good RAID system is a series of hot-swappable, redundant SCSI disk drives with duplexed controllers, and often redundant power supplies. This ensures that if a power supply fails, another takes over and you simply have to pull out the defective unit and replace it.

A RAID system takes care of all disk mirroring automatically for you. It is usually a system of five disks. Four are used for data, while the fifth is used for the parity information. If one of the disks fails, you simply plug in a replacement drive, and the other four bring the new one up to date. It is a great piece of technology, and if you can not afford to have a database go down, this is what you need.

RAID comes in different levels of protection, normally called RAID 0 through RAID 5. RAID 5 offers the highest level of protection, and if you are going to buy a RAID subsystem, this is what you want. Otherwise, Windows NT's mirroring and duplexing conform to RAID 1. Generally, you will see RAID levels 0, 1, and 5.

Using Removable Media

A last method of protecting your data is to use removable media. There are many forms of removable media that you can use, and not all require the very expensive drives and media that were required just a few years ago. Some of these include:

- CD-ROM
- WORM
- Rewriteable, or phase-change disks
- Magnetic disks

There are now several relatively inexpensive CD-ROM recorders available on the market. Several manufacturers make popular removable magnetic disks in the 100–300MB size range, some are even 1GB. WORM and rewriteable disks and drives still tend to be on the expensive side, but do provide excellent long-term archive storage.

There are several reasons that you may want to create a database and then place it on some form of removable media. A database could be marketed this way as a complete product, such as a phone listing. It can be used for long-term archiving of corporate information. A removable media database can be created for both read-only media, such as CD-ROM, or rewriteable media.

A database that will be later distributed on removable media should meet these guidelines:

- The database must be created on new devices.
- No other databases should be placed on these devices.
- The database should use three or more devices. One device for the system tables, another for the transaction log, and one or more for the data tables.
- Do not reference objects that are outside of the database since they will not be available once the database has been distributed.
- Do not add individual users to the database.
- You can add groups and grant permissions to the groups.
- Keep the system administrator login as the database owner.

There are two stored procedures that are used when creating and later, certifying a database for use with removable media. The first is **sp_create_removable** and the second is **sp_certify_removable**.

The stored procedure **sp_create_removable** creates three or more devices and places the necessary parts on each. The system tables are placed on one device, the transaction logs on another, while the remaining devices are used for the data tables. Once this stored procedure is run, complete the normal development of the database, being sure to keep all objects in these devices. The minimum size of a removable media database is 1MB, which allows it to fit on a floppy disk. Note that almost half of this space is taken up by system tables, allowing you only about 0.5MB for tables and data if this is your choice of removable media.

The stored procedure **sp_certify_removable** verifies that the database has been properly configured for distribution on removable media. Once the database passes the required tests, it is set offline. The stored procedure then truncates the transaction log and moves it to the system device and drops the transaction log device.

If you have met all of the necessary requirements, this database should now be ready to place on the removable media of your choice, and be ready for distribution.

Summary

In this chapter, you have learned the basics for developing and maintaining a backup and recovery plan for SQL Server. Specifically, you have learned:

- How to formulate a backup strategy.
- How to create a backup device.
- How to create a backup of a full database, its transaction logs, or of a single table.
- To use a backup and restore a database, transaction log, or a single table from it.
- How to use the FOR LOAD statement to load a copy of a backup on to a device without causing SQL Server to initialize every page of the database.
- How to determine the size of the various database segments, and how they were created.
- How to load a transaction log up to a selected point in time.
- How to rebuild and then recover the master database.
- How to rebuild a lost database device.
- How to determine what form of RAID protection you may require.
- How to mirror a selected device.
- How to create a database on some form of removable media.

Chapter 12

Distributed Transactions, Replication, Publishing and Subscribing

IN THIS CHAPTER

- Distributed Databases
- Two-phase Commit

By now you are familiar with how SQL Server works and interacts with its databases, their tables, and your users. But what about users who have their own server, or remote users? This chapter introduces the topics of using a distributed database, replication, publishing, and subscribing. You may already have a set of users who work from a suboffice in another part of the city, or even in another state, who need immediate access to information contained on the corporate SQL Server database.

With multiple servers, your remote users can maintain a copy of the data that they need to have access to. This database can be kept up to date using one of several methods, depending upon the needs of the remote users. Your final choice of distributing information will be dependent on several factors:

- What kind of access do the remote users need?

- Do they need to be able to update live information?

- Are they using information only for decision support?

- What kind of connection do they have to the current corporate server?

Answers to these and other questions will enable you to make decisions about what type of support do the remote users require. If they need to be able to access current information and update it from their remote location, then you can create a system using the Microsoft Distributed Transaction Coordinator (DTC), whereby transactions can be committed between the two databases. If they simply require information for decision support processes, then simply replicating the database, or portions of it, and providing it through the publish/subscription process will work quite well.

Distributed Databases

What is a distributed database? Any database that is involved in SQL Server's replication, publishing and subscribing process. Most often, a database is distributed for use within a corporate LAN or WAN for the internal use of the company.

Almost any information that exists on your server can be replicated and published. Some types of data that you may want to have distributed are:

- Customer data: updated names and addresses, current orders and their status, credit status.

- Product information: current inventory levels, pricing changes, cost changes, current orders.

- Company data: updated phone lists, e-mail lists, organizational reporting changes.

This is just a very short list of types of information that you may want to distribute to other users within your company. As you will learn through this chapter, SQL Server allows you to be very selective of the data that you actually distribute. Through the process of creating an article for replication you can filter data so that only selected rows and/or columns are replicated and then published.

There are three servers involved in this process of replication: Publishing Server, Distribution Server, and Subscribing Server. You can combine the publishing and distributing servers on a single machine. Either way, the Distribution Server requires a minimum of 32MB of RAM to be installed, with at least 16MB assigned to SQL Server's use.

A distribution server, or a publication/distribution server has a special database placed on it called the distribution database. The distribution server is the first to be installed, followed by the publishing and subscribing servers.

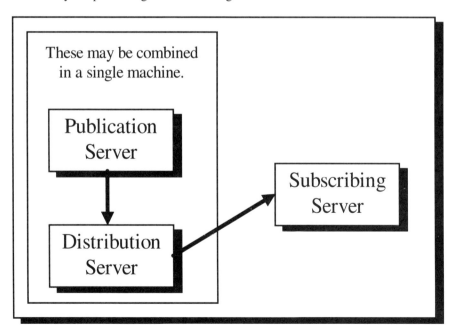

Figure 12.1: Publication and Distribution Servers can be one computer or two separate computers.

New to SQL Server 6.5 is the ability to support many additional databases as subscribers, rather than only Microsoft SQL Server databases. Those databases that are ODBC compliant subscribers are now supported, not simply SQL Server. In addition, replication also supports both text and image datatypes. This will be especially good news for those of you who have wanted to be able to publish catalogs, or product data sheets with extensive text and pictures.

Setting Up Your Servers

Before you can begin to publish databases, or to subscribe to a published database, you must first set up your distribution server. Once this has been accomplished you can set up the publishing and subscription servers. The first question you need to answer is about the distribution server. Will it be a separate computer or a combined publishing/distributing server? Unless you have the extra several thousand dollars to invest in a separate distribution server, you will probably create a combined server. You can always provide a separate server for the distribution function later. While not an easy task, it can be done.

If you decide to create a combined publishing/distribution server, the distribution database is also maintained on the local server. However you decide to build your publishing and distribution servers, the basic processes will be the same. The publishing server publishes and then sends to the distribution server an *article*. This article is composed of the databases or selected columns and rows of the databases that you want to publish to any subscribing servers. These articles are kept in the distribution database until either requested by or sent to the subscribing servers. The primary reasons to separate the publishing and distribution server tasks are for performance and space. If your server is heavily used for online transaction processing, publishing and distributing articles may take too many valuable resources from its primary task of processing the user transaction and updating tables.

Creating the Distribution Server

In this example, you will set up a combined publishing/distributing server. The process is similar for both a combined and a separate distribution server. There are a few things that you need to be sure of before beginning this section. Replication requires 32MB of RAM on the server, with a minimum of 16MB of memory allocated to SQL Server. Remember, this setting can be checked by selecting **S**erver, **S**QL Server, **C**onfigure from the menu, selecting the Configure tab on the Server Configuration/Options dialog box, and finally checking the memory setting—it should be a minimum of 8192–2K pages. If not, change the settings, stopping and starting SQL Server so that the new memory configuration takes effect. Now, follow these steps in setting up your publishing/distributing server:

1.   Click on the folder of the server that you want to use as the publication/distribution server in the Server Manager window, and then select **S**erver, **Rep**lication Configuration, **I**nstalling Publishing from the menu. You will now see the Install Replication Publishing dialog box.

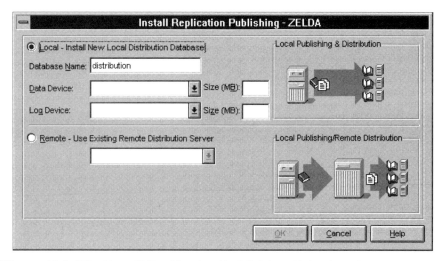

Figure 12.2: The Install Replication Publishing dialog box is used to begin the process of installing either a combined publication/distribution server or separate publishing and distributing servers.

2.   Select the **L**ocal-Install New Local Distribution Database option button. With this option you will create a new distribution database for use on the local server.

Selecting the **R**emote-Use Existing Remote Distribution Server option button allows you to choose a remote distribution server to connect to and place the distribution database on. The remote server must already exist, you can not create it from here.

You would then forward your published articles to this server for further distribution to the various subscribing servers.

3.   In the **D**ata Device combo box, select <new>. This will open the New Database Device dialog box. Create a new device named DistribPubs that is 50MB in size. This device should not be checked as a default device. Click the Create Now button.

4.   Do the same in the Lo**g** Device combo box. Select <new> and then create the device named DistribPubsLog, with a size of 20MB.

Be sure to make the log an adequate size. If you begin to publish many articles that require frequent updates, a small log may become full between publishing/subscribing cycles.

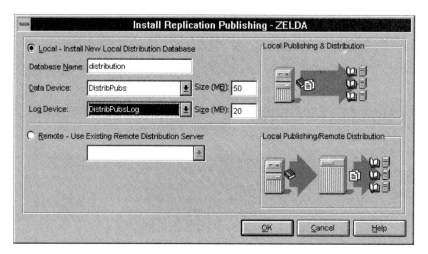

Figure 12.3: With both the Data Device and Log Device set up and selected, you are ready to continue creating your publication/distribution server.

5.   Click the **OK** button and SQL Server will create and install the distribution database on the devices you have specified. This may take a few minutes, depending on the size of the devices you have created and the overall speed of your system. If all goes well, you will see an informational dialog box telling you so.

You can quit the replication process at this point by clicking the **No** button on the dialog box. You can continue setting up your publishing and subscribing servers later without having to reset the distribution server. To finish creating the publishing and subscribing servers, and creating articles, continue on to the next section of this chapter.

Setting Up Publishing and Subscribing Servers

You can choose to continue and setup your publishing databases and subscribers now, or you can perform this procedure later. At this point you have created the distribution server, in this case using the local server, and are ready to authorize selected databases to be published and who—which other servers—will receive—subscribe to—them.

Before another server, and its group of users, can receive the information that you publish, you must specifically authorize them to be on your subscribers list. If you do not do this, or leave a server off, it and its users will not be able to receive the information which you publish. Follow these steps to setup publishing and subscribing servers:

1.   Click the **Yes** button on this dialog box to install publishing and add subscribing servers now.

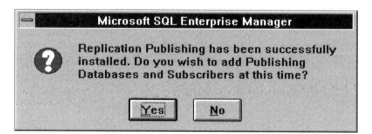

Figure 12.4: Your distribution database has been successfully installed on the devices you specified in the previous dialog box.

The Replication - Publishing dialog box in figure 12.5 allows you to select what and to whom you will publish. You will make several choices in the next several succeeding steps.

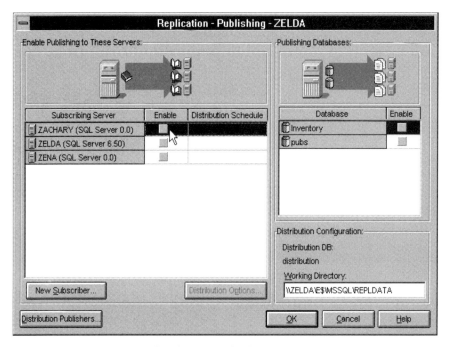

Figure 12.5: Use the Replication-Publishing dialog box to choose what databases are authorized to publish and what servers are authorized to subscribe to them.

2.   To allow a server to subscribe to your publications you must enable them by clicking the box in the Enable column beside their name. You do not have to enable the publishing server, ZELDA as a subscriber. You can also add an additional subscriber from this dialog box by clicking the New Subscriber button. You will see

the New Subscriber dialog box, which you can use to add either new SQL Server's or ODBC subscribers. Click the **OK** button to add the subscriber. You will now see them added to the list of available subscribers.

Figure 12.6: From the New Subscriber dialog box, you can add both new servers and register them, or ODBC subscribers.

3.   Select the first server in your subscription listing and click the Distribution Options button. From the Distribution Options dialog box you can choose how many transactions will be submitted to the subscriber as a single batch. The default is 100. You can also choose how often transactions will be distributed—continuously, or on a scheduled basis. You can create a customized schedule by clicking the Change button and using the Task Schedule dialog box. You also have the option to select a retention schedule. This is how long after transmitting an article to all subscribers, the distribution server will keep the information (see more about this in the section "Replication Cleanup" later in this chapter). Finally, you can set the necessary ODBC options for the selected subscriber. Click the **OK** button once you have made the necessary adjustments to the settings.

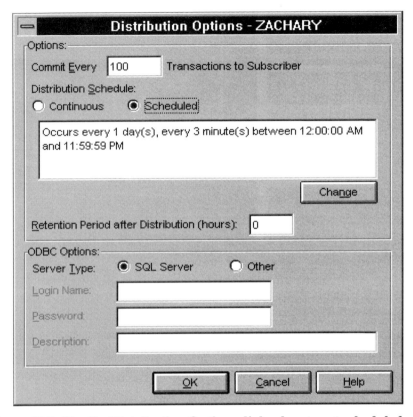

Figure 12.7: Use the Distribution Options dialog box to set scheduled releases of subscription articles and other choices.

4.   Make any necessary changes for each of your other subscribing servers.

5.   Select the databases that are authorized to be used in publishing by clicking the box in the Enable column beside the database name.

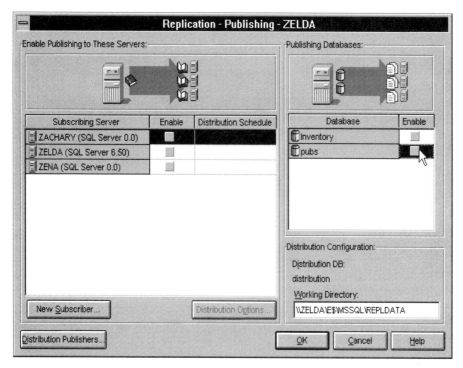

Figure 12.8: From the Replication-Publishing dialog box you will select those databases that can be used in publishing.

6.   Specify the distribution database's full path name in the **W**orking Directory text box, if not already displayed. This will enable SQL Server to speed up transaction processes if it does not have to look for the necessary information.

7.   Click the **D**istribution Publishers button to display the Replication-Distribution dialog box. By checking the box in the Enable column, beside the server's names, you can allow selected servers to use this distribution server to publish their own information. Once you have made any necessary changes, click the **O**K button to save them, or the **C**ancel button to return to the previous dialog box.

This option is especially helpful for those networks which have a dedicated distribution server. By allowing you to have many servers share resources already dedicated to the single purpose of handling the distribution of publications, you can save many hardware dollars.

Figure 12.9: The Replication-Distribution dialog box is used to select other subscribing servers that can also use the distribution server for their own publications.

8.   Now that you have made all of the required connections, click the **OK** button to complete the setup of your servers.

To view the topology of your publication/subscription network, select **S**erver, Re**p**lication Configuration, **T**opology from the menu. You will see the Replication Topology map. Many of the configuration options can be accomplished from here by right-clicking on a server icon.

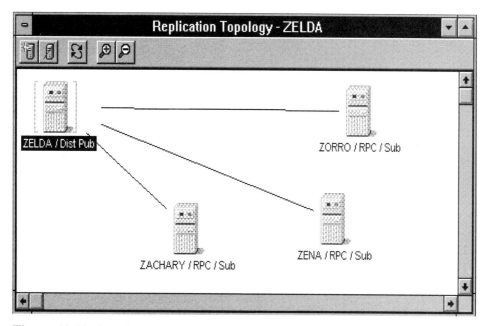

Figure 12.10: Here you can see the topology of your publication/distribution/subscription schema. The current server is indicated by the brackets surrounding it—in this case, ZELDA.

Replication

You have now successfully set up your publication/distribution/subscription network. Now for determining what specifically you will publish. Before you go any further, some definitions are in order. Several terms have been used without really defining them:

- *Replication*: This term has two general meanings. The first is that of the complete process of publishing, distributing, and subscribing to information. It also refers to the actual task of duplicating, or replicating, the published information and sending it to the distribution server. Replication provides read-only copies of the data selected for publication to the subscribing servers. The users on the subscribing end can use this data primarily for decision-making purposes, since they can not update the data themselves.

- *Article*: This is the smallest unit of a publication. An article consists of data from a table that has been marked for replication. A table can have many articles defined for it. An article will contain a defined group of data from the table. This data may be an entire table or a subsection of it. Articles can be defined such that only specific columns are included, provided one of them is the primary key column in a table with one. Articles can select specified rows, or range of rows. By combining both techniques you can publish very specific views of your data. This process of defining the data for an article is generally called filtering. Specifically, defining for rows is called horizontal partitioning, while defining for columns is called vertical partitioning.

- *Publication*: A publication is a collection of one or more articles that have been grouped together for replication. One publication may include many articles.

- *Distributing*: The act of moving publications from the distribution server to the subscribing servers.

- *Push Subscription*: A push subscription is configured from the publication server. This type of subscription allows you to define the publication and then who is to get it. This form of subscription ensures to the publisher that their information is getting to everyone they believe needs to have it.

- *Pull Subscription*: A pull subscription is configured from the subscriber server. Here you get to choose from among the publishing servers you are connected to and select the specific publications that you will receive. This format allows the subscribing server to not accept publications that they do not need.

- *Synchronization*: A process where the publication and destination tables are synchronized with the same table schema and data. This is normally a one-time process.

Before you can actually replicate information and send it on to the distribution database or the distribution server, you must decide what information is to be replicated. This decision will, of course, depend on who the information is for: a separate division of the same company, a branch office, or a customer. Each of these subscribing "customers" may have different information needs from your database, and you can easily customize the information contained in the articles which they receive. Articles for publication can be set up by following these steps:

1.   Open SQL Server Enterprise Manger and select the server that will be used as the publishing server. Select **M**anage, Replic**a**tion, **P**ublications to display the Manage Publications dialog box. From this dialog box, you can begin selecting the specific information you want to publish. The Manage Publications dialog box can also be opened by selecting a server and clicking the Replication-Manage Publications button on the toolbar.

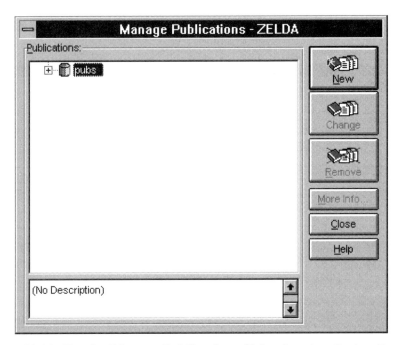

Figure 12.11: Use the Manage Publications dialog box to select and partition the information. Only the pubs database is listed here since it is the only database which has been selected for use in publication.

2.   Click the New button to create a new publication using the Edit Publications dialog box. If any publications have already been set up, expanding the databases folder would reveal them.

3.   Type authors_titles in the Publications Title text box as the title for the first publication. The name must be unique within the database it will be placed. In the Description box, type PUBS. Authors, titles, and titleauthor tables, including partitions. Use this box to be as descriptive of your publication as you need to be. You can use a maximum of 255 characters. Select between the two Replication Frequency option buttons to determine how often your publications will be updated:

- Transaction Based: All transactions that have been marked for replication will be read from the databases transaction log and applied to the destination databases.

- Scheduled table Refresh: All table data and possible table schemas will be replicated on a set schedule. At this time the replicated information will be applied to the destination tables. There are no updates between scheduled times, unless the publication is manually updated.

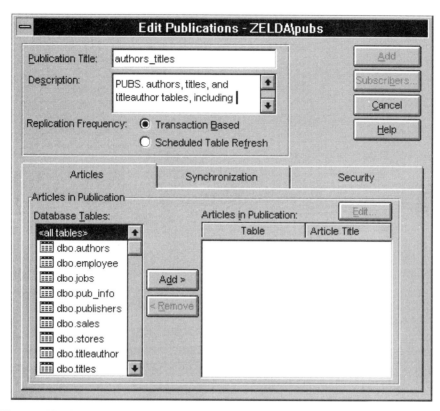

Figure 12.12: From the Edit Publications dialog box you can create or edit publications and select tables to be included.

4.   Now select the table(s) that will be included in this publication from the Database Tables list box, and click the Add button to move them to the Articles in Publication box. If you decide not to include a table in a publication, you can remove it by selecting it in the Articles in Publications box and clicking the Remove button, deleting it from the list.

5.   Select a table from the Articles in Publications list and then click the Edit button above the list. This will open the Manage Article dialog box. Within this dialog box, you can filter or partition your selected table so that only the data you choose to replicate will be published. Your options include:

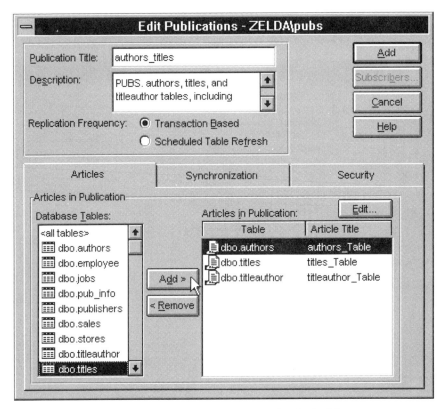

Figure 12.13: Select the tables you want to be included in your publication from the Database Tables list, and add them to the Articles in Publications list.

- Creating multiple articles within the publication by giving each a specific name in the Name text box. You can create many articles, but each must have a unique name within the publication. You can also place a description of this article within the **D**escription box. You are again limited to 255 characters. Use the Destination **T**able text box to place the name for the table that this article will be placed in. The default setting is the same name as the originating table. The upper section of this dialog box has two checkboxes:Owner-**Q**ualify Table Name: When selected, the ownership of the table remains the same, even when on a different server.

♦ Use Column Names in SQL Statements: Selecting this option ensures that replication INSERT statements will be able to execute correctly even when the subscribing server's columns are not in the same order. This is accomplished with the use of column lists with the replication INSERT statement.

There are two tabs available on this dialog box, Filters and Scripts:

- From the Filters tab, you can select specific columns to be included in your article. All columns are selected by default, as indicated by the checkmarks in the Replicate column. By clicking and removing the checkmark beside the name of a column, you will cause it to not be included in your article. Restricting articles by columns is called vertical partitioning. If you use vertical partitioning, you must include any columns that are primary key columns. These are indicated by the key icon displayed beside the column name in the Key column. You can further restrict the information that is published by horizontal partitioning. This is accomplished by using a WHERE clause in the Restriction Clause text box. For example, to find all authors who live in the state of California, type the following into the text box:

state = 'CA'

Figure 12.14: Using the options available on the Filters tab in the Manage Article dialog box can help you to restrict the data published, by using horizontal and vertical partitioning.

6.   Click the Scripts tab to view this set of options:

- Here you can tell SQL Server how to process **INSERT**, **UPDATE**, and **DELETE** queries when the log reader process finds a transaction marked for replication in the transaction log. You have the choice of using the default options, whereby the SQL Server statements for these transactions will be re-created and applied to the destination database.

- Alternatively, you can select the Custom option for any one or all of these types of transactions. You then have a choice in the text box of either:

    ♦ NONE: which means that transactions of this type will not be replicated.

♦ CALL *stored procedure*: enter the name of the stored procedure which you want called when this type of transaction is replicated. The stored procedure called must already exist in the destination database.

• Creation Script: This text box will display the full path and name of the schema script use to initially synchronize the databases. When you are creating a new article or publication this will be blank. The schema script is created when you first save the publication. You can edit an existing script by clicking the **E**dit button and making the necessary changes in the dialog box which is displayed. The **G**enerate button allows you to immediately create the schema script.

Click the **OK** button to complete and save your selections in the Manage Article dialog box, and return to the Edit Publications dialog box, or the **C**ancel button if you do not want to save any changes you may have made.

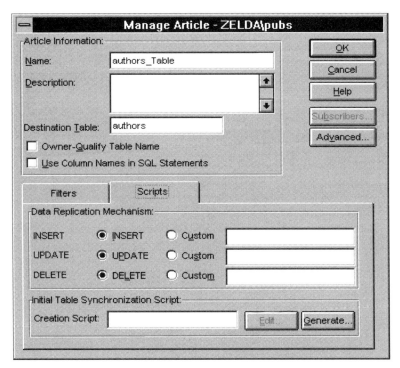

Figure 12.15: The Scripts tab in the Manage Article dialog box allows you to determine how the log reader will process certain queries.

7.   Click the Synchronization tab on the Edit Publications dialog box to view the options available to you. The first option allows you to choose between two bulk copy versions.

- Bulk Data Copy - Native Format: Allows build copy to subscribers who are also SQL Servers on the same type of architecture. This is the fastest format and the default option.

- Bulk Data Copy - Character Format: This option is available when your subscribers are ODBC compliant databases.

The synchronization process is a highly overhead-intensive procedure. This option allows you to schedule the database synchronization for a newly subscribing server. This way you can have this process occur during a lower-activity time frame. Click the Change button to open the Task Schedule dialog box and change the default schedule.

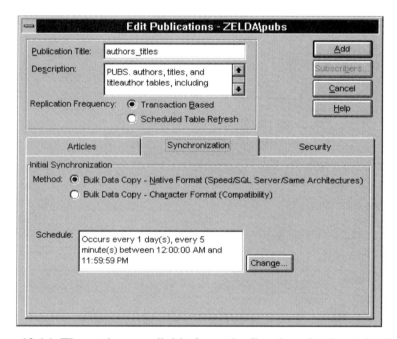

Figure 12.16: The options available from the Synchronization tab allow you to choose the method of bulk copy to be used and to schedule a time for the procedure to run.

8.   Now click the Security tab. From this tab you can make some additional choices about the security of the information you make available for publication.

- The default option is Unrestricted. This allows any subscribing server to see and receive a copy of this publication.

- The Restricted option allows you to choose the servers that will be able to see and subscribe to the publication. If you choose the Restricted option, you must also select those servers that can subscribe to the publication by clicking the box beside their names in the Allow Access column.

9.   Once you have created all of the necessary articles that belong to the publication, click the Add button to create it. You can now add additional publications, or change or remove existing publications. When you have created all of the publications that you now need, click the Close button.

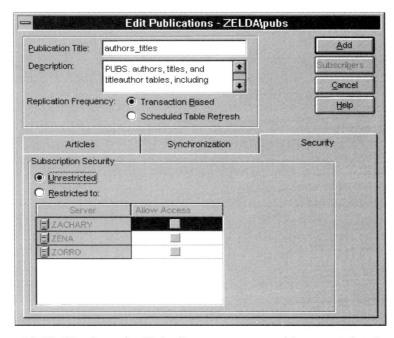

Figure 12.17: The Security Tab allows you to provide unrestricted access to your publication, or to select the servers which will be allowed to see and subscribe to your publication.

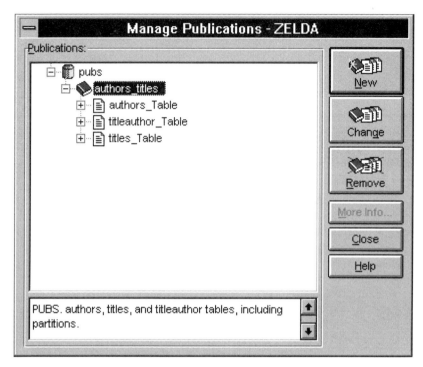

Figure 12.18: The Manage Publications dialog box now shows a publication and three articles.

You can now add additional publications and articles as necessary for the distribution of information to your subscribers. The idea behind a publication is not to overwhelm your subscribers with an overabundance of detail, but to provide them with the data they need to do their job.

Distributing

Once you have set up replication on your server, chosen what databases are available for distribution, created the necessary publications, and determined who can subscribe to them, you are ready to begin distributing them.

As you have already seen, SQL Server creates a publication and forwards it onto the distribution server where it is stored in the distribution database. At the scheduled time, the distribution server forwards the publication with the updated information onto the subscription server, where the local destination database is updated with the *current* information. Replication of this type is not an online transaction processing system among multiple servers.

There are several processes involved with the replication and distribution of information, each of which will be discussed in the next several sections of this chapter.

Synchronization Process

The first of these processes is the synchronization process. This process can be automatic or manually applied. The synchronization process takes a snapshot of the table data and the table schema, and then writes this information to the distribution database.

When publishing and subscribing are set up, an initial synchronization process is done. This process takes the data contained in tables to be published, and their table schema and writes both to a file. Table data can be found in the distribution databases path and are files with a .TMP extension, while the schema files are those with a .SCH extension. Each article in a publication must be synchronized.

Once the initial synchronization process has been completed, it does not have to done again. Subsequent changes to data in the published tables are automatically captured and applied to the destination databases. If new subscribers are added to a publication, a new synchronization set, data (.TMP) and schema (.SCH) files, are created. Only those new subscribers will be provided this information. Once the new subscriber has been synchronized, they will receive any updates that have occurred since the time the synchronization set was created and the current time.

Log Reader Process

Only committed transactions are written to the distribution server, and from there to the subscription servers. The second of these processes is the log reader process. The log reader is a process activated when you set up publishing, and it takes over once the synchronization process has been completed. This process continuously scans the transaction logs of the published table(s), looking for committed transactions to be written to disk. Once the transactions are flushed to the disk, the log reader scans the newly written pages and reconstructs the T-SQL statements involved in writing this data.

Once the T-SQL statement has been reconstructed, it is stored as a text string in a table in the distribution database. When the distribution database updates the subscription servers, the information contained in the stored text string is used to update the data contained in the subscription server's destination database. This ensures that the data contained in the destination table remains in sync with the publishing table.

You do not have to worry about a transaction being missed because a transaction log is truncated before the log reader has had time to read and copy it to the distribution database. When transactions are written to the transaction log they are marked at that time, if they are to be replicated. Transactions that have been marked for replication are copied along with other transactions when the log is dumped, but they are not truncated from the transaction log along with other transactions until after they have been read and moved to the distribution database by the log reader.

Distribution Server and Database

The distribution database is a special database created especially for the replication publishing/subscribing process. All transactions that are to be replicated are read by the log reader process and forwarded to the distribution database. They are stored in this database until the scheduled time to forward them on to the destination database in the subscribing server. The distribution database is also knows as a *store-and-forward* database.

The distribution database should be treated just as other databases as far as placing its transaction log on a separate device and being sure to back it up on a regular schedule. You can dump the distribution database's transaction log and the database itself just as any other database.

Automatic recovery is supported on the distribution database. If you must take the distribution server offline, all normal distribution processes will continue from the point of their last successful action. The replication log reader automatically brings all transactions forward to the distribution server. At the same time the distribution server checks for the last successful transfer to the subscription servers and starts forwarding information from that point.

Replication Cleanup

The final aspect of the replication process is its system of cleaning up after itself. When you set up replication, a cleanup task is also created for each publisher/subscribing pair. For example, if you have a single publishing server, a distribution server (or a combined publishing/distribution server), and three subscribing servers, you will have three cleanup tasks, one for each publisher/subscriber pair.

Replication cleanup is a very important task, helping to ensure that your system is maintained for the long term. Cleanup works with the retention parameter. The retention parameter determines for how long transactions are retained by the distribution database once they have been forwarded and applied to the subscribing server. It also determines for how long the initial .TMP files used in the initial synchronization event are retained.

You can use the retention period setting in conjunction with your backup procedures to ensure that the necessary transactions are always available if the need to recover from a failure occurs. For example: your subscription server ZACHARY's transaction log is dumped once every day. By setting the retention period to 48 hours for the ZELDA/ZACHARY cleanup task, you can be assured that all transactions would be recoverable if a failure occurred just before the next scheduled backup.

The retention period for a new publication is easily set using the Distribution Options dialog box. After selecting a subscription server, clicking the Distribution Options button will open the Distribution Options dialog box for you. Just type in the number of hours you want the distribution server to retain the transactions for into the text box.

If the publication/subscription process has already been created, you can change the retention period by following these steps:

1.   Open SQL Server Enterprise Manger and select the distribution server—in this example, ZELDA.

2.   Select Server, Scheduled Tasks to view the Manage Schedule Tasks window. Be sure to click the Task List tab if it is not already selected. All tasks scheduled for the selected server will be listed here. Notice that there is a cleanup task for each of the three publisher/subscriber pairs.

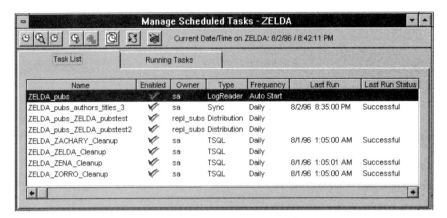

Figure 12.19: From the Manage Scheduled Tasks window, you can edit the retention period for a cleanup task.

3.   Select the cleanup task whose retention period you want to change. For example, select the ZELDA_ZENA_Cleanup task. Now click the Edit Task button on the toolbar.

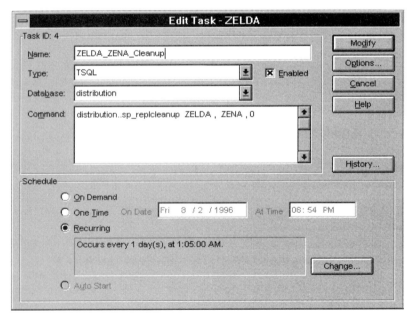

Figure 12.20: Use the Edit Task dialog box to change many of the settings on the selected task.

4.   In the Command list box, you can edit any of the listed commands. The command line for the cleanup task has four parameters:

- The name of the distribution database and the stored procedure sp_replcleanup.

- The name of the publication server, ZELDA.

- The name of the subscription server, ZENA.

- The retention period setting. The default setting is 0 hours, forcing the removal of all transactions which have been distributed to the subscription server whenever the cleanup task is run.

Click the cursor beside the 0 in the list box, delete the 0, and type **48** as the number of hours to retain transactions that have been distributed. If necessary, you can also change other settings, such as how often the cleanup task is run by changing options in the Schedule group.

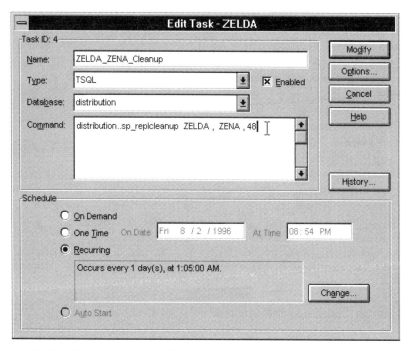

Figure 12.21: The new setting for the retention period is 48 hours.

5.   Click the Modify button to save your new retention setting.

6.   You will now see a dialog box asking if you want to clear the prior task history list since you have changed the task's definition. If you click the Yes button, all of the previous history about this task will be deleted. Clicking No will retain the earlier history. Be sure about your decision to delete the prior history before doing so.

7.   You should also change the retention settings for any other subscribing servers so that they are all the same. Once you have made all of the necessary changes, you can close the Manage Scheduled Tasks window.

Two-phase Commit

The two-phase commit transaction is a transaction that updates, inserts, or deletes data on more than one server, often in different locations. The transaction is one which can normally be broken down into at least two parts, but you do not want the first half of the transaction to be committed without being sure that the second half is also committed.

Earlier in this book, an example of a banking transaction was given. A customer goes to the bank to transfer money from savings to checking. While this seems to be a relatively straight-forward transaction, it can suffer from timing problems for committing the transaction on all servers, in the event of a failure to the bank's computer hardware, software, or communications.

SQL Server works with Microsoft Distributed Transaction Coordinator (MS DTC) to coordinate transactions such as the two-phase commit. MS DTC uses a *two-phase commit protocol* to ensure that all SQL Server's involved in the transaction are in agreement about what is happening. In other words, MS DTC ensures that all of the servers agree that each part of the transaction has been committed, and if they are not in agreement then the transaction is rolled back by all servers involved. This is the crucial part of a two-phase commit: Each part of the transaction must be committed by all stations or none of it can be committed.

In the two-phase commit transaction, SQL Server works as a resource manager to MS DTC's job as the transaction manager. With this first implementation of MS DTC, it works with one resource manager—SQL Server. Other resource managers are planned for future implementations.

Definitions

In order for a transaction to fit within the definition of a two-phase commit transaction, it must meet the **ACID** properties.

- *Atomicity*: The entire transaction must either be committed or aborted. When the transaction does commit, then it commits throughout the entire transaction. If it aborts, then it aborts through the entire system, changing nothing. At any point, either the server or the application can abort the transaction.

- *Consistency*: The transaction must ensure that consistency is maintained throughout the system.

- *Isolation*: One transaction is isolated from another incomplete transaction. This has often been called *serializability*, whereby transactions can not perform updates at the exact same point in time.

- *Durability*: When a transaction is committed, it will have been committed throughout the system and will remain even if there is a system failure in one part.

The transaction must be consistent within SQL Server's frame of reference. SQL Server acts as a resource manager for the transactions that are being processed on it. MS DTC manages transactions that are processed through multiple resource managers. MS DTC will create the transaction object that brackets the transaction, and monitors its progress as it moves from one resource manager (server) to another. As this movement is being accomplished, MS DTC carries out the two-phase commit protocol, ensuring the transactions remain atomic and durable.

How the Two-phase Commit Works

The two-phase commit requires a great deal of coordination between SQL Server, as the resource manager, and MS DTC as the transaction manager. MS DTC must ensure that all resource managers have received the necessary information to process the transaction, that they are ready to do so, and that each server does in fact, commit the transaction. If there is a failure at any point in the communication, then all resource managers must abort the transaction and roll it back.

When a resource manager comes online, it notifies the local MS DTC that it is available. When a transaction arrives from an application, the local resource manager enlists in the transaction and notifies MS DTC. MS DTC keeps track of all resource managers that have enlisted in the transaction.

When the application asks that the transaction be committed, MS DTC initiates the two-phase commit protocol. This begins with MS DTC asking each resource manager, in this case SQL Server's, if they are ready to prepare to commit the transaction. In figure 12.21, you can see how information flows from the application to transaction manager to the resource managers.

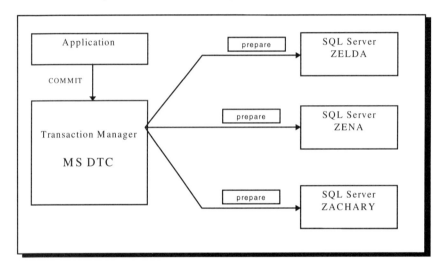

Figure 12.22: Each of the three SQL Servers that have enlisted in this transaction are asked if they are prepared to commit the transactions.

Once the request to prepare to commit the transaction has been sent to the various transaction managers, they must take the necessary steps to ensure that the transaction can be rolled back if it is aborted. If any one of the servers is not prepared to commit this transaction, it will send a message back to MS DTC that it is not prepared and the transaction will be aborted. If all of the servers do state that they are ready to commit the transaction, they wait for MS DTC's decision to commit or abort the transaction.

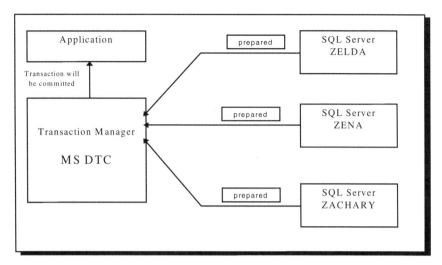

Figure 12:23: The transaction has been committed to the application and all servers have informed MS DTC that they are prepared to commit the transaction.

Once all servers have informed MS DTC that they are prepared to commit the transaction, MS DTC must decide whether to commit the transaction or to abort it.

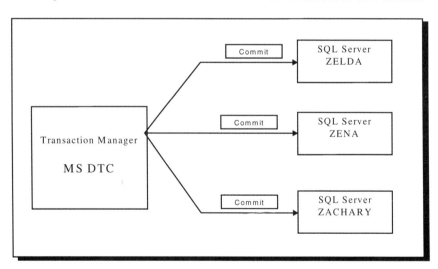

Figure 12.24: MS DTC makes the decision to commit the transaction and tells the resource managers to commit the transaction.

At this point, MS DTC does not know if all of the resource managers did indeed commit the transaction, and waits for a message from each server that the transaction was successfully committed or not. During this time period MS DTC is in doubt of the transaction's outcome: Have all of the resource managers committed the transaction? With a resource manager located in a different city, or even country, there can be occasional periods of communication delay. During this period when MS DTC is in doubt of the transaction's commitment state, a lock is maintained on the information that is to be modified by this transaction. This ensures that the transaction remains isolated from other transactions, which may try to update information in a doubtful state. Since MS DTC must track what happens with the transactions it is managing, even in the event of a failure by a resource manager, it maintains a log of all transactions it is managing. This log can be used to recover a failed commit attempt by one of the resource managers in the case of a failure. This ensures that a transaction that is committed by MS DTC can be committed by all resource managers, or will be rolled back by all.

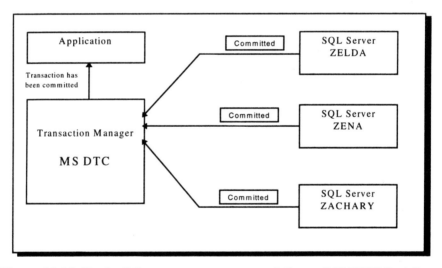

Figure 12.25: Each of the resource managers informs MS DTC that they have committed the transaction.

Once all of the resource managers has reported to MS DTC that they have successfully committed the transaction, the process is complete.

Configuring MS DTC

MS DTC is easy to install and set up. There are two versions of MS DTC that come with SQL Server 6.5:

- Full MS DTC service for a SQL Server database server.

- MS DTC client utility for use on the client side.

Install MS DTC on the client side only if the client application resides on the client's computer and the client application must call to a C or C++ BEGIN TRANSACTION statement. MS DTC will catch this statement and create the transaction object, sending the transaction onto the necessary resource managers. Otherwise, simply install the full MS DTC service on the server. When using MS DTC on the server, distributed transactions must use the T-SQL statement BEGIN DISTRIBUTED TRANSACTION. This tells everyone that this transaction will require resources other than only those residing on the local server.

MS DTC is automatically installed on any computer on which you install SQL Server 6.5. Configure MS DTC by following these steps:

1.   Open SQL Server Enterprise Manager and right-click on the Distributed Transaction Coordinator icon. Select Configure from the shortcut menu and open the MS DTC Configuration dialog box.

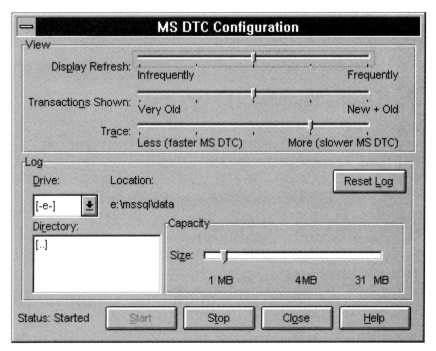

Figure 12.26: Use the MS DTC Configuration dialog box to change the available options.

2.   The primary options you can configure are views and logs.

The View box has three options that operate through slider bars. To change settings, simply drag the slider bar up or down with your mouse.

- Display Refresh: This setting controls how often transaction lists, trace messages, and statistical information is sent from MS DTC processes to the SQL Server graphical interface. The more frequent the updates, the more overhead accumulated while running the transactions. The slider allows you to adjust the refresh rate from a low of every 20 seconds to every second.

- Transactions Shown: This setting allows you choose how long a transaction must be active before it is displayed. The slider adjusts from five minutes to one second.

- Trace: This slider controls the level of trace information from MS DTC. The slider settings range from no traces to all traces.

The Log box has several settings, all of which concern MS DTC's transaction log. Before making any changes to the location and size of the transaction log, you must first stop the MS DTC process. After making the changes, restarting the processes will put your changes in effect.

- **D**rive: Allows you to choose the drive on which to place the transaction log files.

- Directory: Select the directory in which to place the log files. The default setting is the location of the master database. You should place the log files on a separate device.

- Size: Allows you to change the size of the transaction log.

- Reset **L**og: Selecting this button will reset or truncate MS DTC's transaction log. Do not do this when there are unresolved transactions pending.

3.   Close the MS DTC Configuration dialog box.

4.   Right-click on the MS DTC icon again. Select Statistics from the shortcut menu. This provides a graphical representation of transactions which are being currently processed. Here there is one transaction in process.

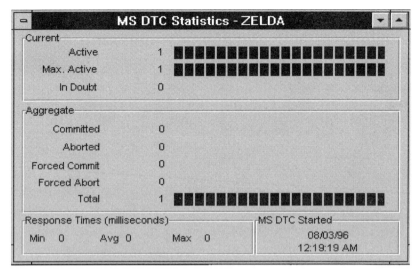

Figure 12.27: Use the MS DTC Statistics dialog box to monitor how many transactions are being processed.

5.   Again, right-click the MS DTC icon and select Transactions from the shortcut menu. The MS DTC Transactions dialog box displays a listing of all transactions and their current status.

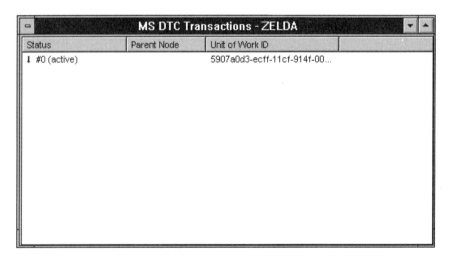

Figure 12.28: The MS DTC Transactions dialog box shows you the current status of all transactions.

You can also use the **Tr**ace option on the shortcut menu to display the MS DTC Trace window. Any trace messages from transaction will be displayed there.

Problem Areas

Transactions that remain in doubt for long periods of time can cause systems to become bogged down at many points, waiting for resolution. They also will cause MS DTC to lock data that other applications may need to have access to.

MS DTC provides the operator with the ability to force a resolution to these conflicts. The system administrator can force a transaction to either commit on the available resource managers or to abort. The resource manager/server that was the cause of the in doubt status will be brought up to date on the transactions status when it comes back online—either committing or rolling back the transaction.

You can break an in-doubt lock of system resources by following these steps:

1.   Right-click on the Distributed Transactions Coordinator (MS DTC) icon in the Server Manager window and select **T**ransactions from the shortcut menu. You will see the MS DTC Transactions window displayed.

2.   Select the transaction that is in doubt and right-click on it. You will see a shortcut menu with two options: View and Resolve. Select the Resolve option, displaying the next level of short-cut menu. This has three options: Commit, Abort, and Forget.

- Commit: will force the commitment of the transaction on the node.

- Abort: will force the transaction to be aborted.

- Forget: forces the node to forget the transaction.

These three options are used to complete a transaction that has become hung up for some reason. You may have a communications break between two nodes. Because of the way in which MS DTC handles communications between the various phases of the two-phase commit, manual resolves should be handled on the nodes which are immediately upstream and downstream of the communications break.

Nodes involved in the two-phase commit transaction are considered parent and child in the transaction. The node that passes the transaction to another node is considered the parent to the other. When a transaction is placed in an in-doubt status, look to the parent node to determine the outcome of the transaction.

- If the transaction is not displayed in the MS DTC window of the parent node, the transaction has been aborted. You can safely manually abort the transaction on each child node downstream from the parent.

- If the transaction is displayed in the MS DTC window of the parent node, but with Only Failed to Remain to Notify status, then the transaction has been committed by the child nodes. Manually commit the transaction on the parent node. All further upstream parent nodes will be notified and will then commit and forget the transaction.

- If the transaction has a status of In Doubt on the parent node, look at the MS DTC window in the parent immediately upstream from this node. Continue to examine each parent further upstream until you find a parent node where the transaction has been aborted—and so does not show in the MS DTC window—or is shown in the Only Failed Remain to Notify status—indicating that the transaction has committed. If the transaction is shown to have aborted, then manually abort the transaction on all child nodes downstream from that point. If the transaction was committed, then manually commit the transaction on all of the child nodes downstream.

When the transaction is in the Only Failed Remain to Notify status, it indicates that the transaction has been committed, but that one of the child nodes downstream has failed to notify the parent node that they have completed their task. The only way to determine which of the child nodes has not notified the parent is by examining each child node manually. You must look for an in-doubt transaction with the same global identifier as the Only Failed Remain to Notify transaction on the parent node. As you locate each child node with this transaction, force each to manually commit the transaction. When this has been completed through the entire stream of child nodes, go back to the first parent node and force it to forget the transaction.

> **Note**
>
> Be cautious with the use of the Forget option. Do not use it until you have completely resolved all of the child nodes downstream of the parent. Doing so may leave a transaction that has not been committed or aborted properly.

Summary

In this chapter, you have learned to use replication and distributed transactions. Specifically, you have learned:

- To create a distribution server to hold the articles that you want to publish.

- To create publishing and subscribing servers.

- How to select databases to use for publishing, and then to create an article for publication from the selected database.

- How to provide security for your articles.

- To use either a push or pull subscription.

- How the cleanup process works with the Task Scheduler and how to edit the task.

- How to use Microsoft DTC to coordinate two-phase commit transactions.

- To correct problems that may occur with a two-phase commit transaction.

- How to configure MS DTC and view the various statistics available on a distributed transaction.

Index

A

alias, 31, 238–41
allocating memory, 191–94
allocation unit, 84, 89
alter table command, 117
ANSI-SQL, 14,63, 72
architecture, 92
article, 296
 defined, 306
 filtering, 311

B

backup
 creating, 263–69
 database
  dropping defective, 270–74
 defined, 260
 full, 50, 260
 incremental, 50, 260
 offline, 261
 online, 261
 restoring, 269–70, 274–78
  date/time, 279
  for load, 271
  lost device, 285–86
  master database, 282–85
 restoring transaction logs, 279–81
 strategy, 261–63
 striped, 265
 table, 260
backup device, 44, 50
 creating, 266
backup devices, 93
 creating, 93

bcp, 34
BEGIN TRANsaction. *See* transactions
begin transactions, 39
 implied, 40
binary
 datatypes, 125

C

character
 datatypes, 124
checkpoint, 102, 258
client/server, 2–4
 business procedures, 7
 multiprocessing, 9
 multithreaded, 9
 PC/LAN, 2
 security, 216
 T-SQL, 22
 uses for, 5
clustered index, 65, 67–68, 207–8
 required space, 67
commit transactions, 39
 implied, 40
constraint
 check, 126–27
 foreign key
  creating, 130–33
 no check, 126–27
 primary key, 116
  creating, 130–33
 unique, 118–19
cursors, 63
 close, 63
 deallocate, 64
 declare, 63
 fetch, 63

insensitive, 63
open, 63

D

data cache, 185
Data Control Language (DCL), 22, 23
Data Definition Language (DDL), 22
data integrity, 3, 17
Data Manipulation Language (DML), 22, 23
database
  allocation unit, 84
  dropping, 212–13
    defective, 270–74
  extent, 84
  field, 19
  owner, 236–38
  page, 84, 88
  record, 19
  setting size, 163–65
  size planning, 162–63
  sizing, 84–87
  table, 19
  transaction log, 165
database design, 15
database device, 44
  creating, 45
database devices, 92
  dropping, 179–80
  expanding
    on different device, 175
    on same device, 168–74
  shrinking, 175–78
database object, 51
database owner
  using an alias, 238–41
datatypes, 120–26
  binary, 125
  character, 124
  date, 123
  logical, 123
  numeric, 121, 122
  text, 124
date

datatypes, 123
dbcc dbrepair, 270
dbcc memusage, 185
dbcc show _statistics, 206
dbcc show_statistics, 200
dbcc shrinkdb, 175, 176
deadlocks, 147
default device
  changing, 46
default statement, 70
default values, 70–72
delete statement, 38
denormalizing, 18. *See* normalizing
devices
  backup, 44, 50, 93
  creating, 45
  database, 44
  default device, 46
  master, 44
  MSDBData, 44
  MSDBLog, 44
dirty page, 103
dirty pages, 258
disk
  optimizing, 194–96
  segments, 196–97
  striping, 195
disk refit statement, 285
disk reinit statement, 285
disk subsystem, 194
distributed database, 294
Distribution Server, 295
  setup, 296–99
domain integrity, 119
  datatypes, 120
domain rules, 119–20
drop constraint command, 118
DTC. *See* Microsoft Distributed
  Transaction Coordinator (MS DTC)
dump device. *See* backup device

E

entity integrity, 116
exclusive lock, 143

extent, 84, 88

F

field, 19
for load, 271
foreign key, 20, 128
    creating, 130–33
from clause, 26

G

grant statement, 242
groups, 234–36
guest user, 233

H

Hypertext Markup Language (HTML),
    104–13

I

identifiers, 80
    object names, 82
    quoted, 83–84
    rules for, 81–82
index, 64–67
    clustered, 65
    nonclustered, 65, 68
indexes
    Manage Indexes, 65
insert statement, 34–37
integrated security, 220–26
integrity
    domain, 119
    entity, 116
    referential, 127–30
    user-defined, 134–37
intent lock, 147
Internet features, 104–13
isolation level, 149
ISQL/w, 21, 24

J

joining tables
    with SELECT query, 27

K

kill, 96

L

lock
    exclusive, 143
    granularity, 143–45
    intent, 147
    page, 146–47
    row, 145–46
    shared, 142
    table, 147
    update, 142–43
locks
    deadlocks, 147–48
log reader process, 317–18
logical
    datatypes, 123

M

master database, 98
    rebuilding, 282
memory
    allocating, 191–94
    data cache, 185
    procedure cache, 185, 194
    system, 184–91
Microsoft Distributed Transaction
    Coordinator (DTC), 294
Microsoft Distributed Transaction
    Coordinator (MS DTC), 322
    configuring, 327–31
    problem areas, 331–32
mixed security, 227
model database, 99

MS DTC. *See* Microsoft Distributed
   Transaction Coordinator (MS DTC)
msdb database, 100

N

names. *See* identifiers
nonclustered index, 65, 68, 208
normalized, 16, 17, 18
normalizing, 19
numeric
   datatypes, 121, 122

O

object names
   identifiers, 82
objects
   cursors, 63
   database, 51
     new, 52
   rules, 72
   stored procedures, 78–80
   triggers, 74
   views, 59
ODBC
   and replication, 296
optimizer, 64, 200
order by command, 61

P

page, 84, 88
page lock, 146
password, 241–42
pausing SQL Server, 156–57
PC/LAN, 2, 3
Performance Monitor, 188
permissions, 242–49
   by object, 245–47
   by user, 248–49
point-in-time recovery, 279
primary key, 21, 116–18, 128

creating, 130–33
relationships, 20
procedure cache, 185, 194
procedure statement, 79
process
   server, 95
   user, 95
publication
   creating, 306–16
   defined, 306
publications
   filtering, 311
Publishing Server, 295, 299–305
pull subscription, 307
push subscription, 306

Q

query
   clustered index, 207–8
   nonclustered index, 208
   optimizer, 199, 200
   range operators, 207
   statistics, 200–204
     update, 204–7
query optimizer, 64
quoted identifiers, 83–84

R

RAID, 290
record, 19
recover lost device, 285–86
recovery, 257
recovery interval, 102
Redundant Array of Inexpensive Disks
   (RAID). *See* RAID
referential integrity, 127–30
   cascading delete, 133
   cascading update, 133
   enforcing, 133
relational database management system,
   14

relational database-management system
(RDBM), 2
relationships, 19
  foreign key, 20, 21
  many-to-many, 129
  one-to-many, 129
  one-to-one, 129
  primary key, 20, 21
removable media, 291–92
renaming columns
  using an alias, 31
replication, 295, 306–16
  article, 306
  cleanup, 319–22
  defined, 306
  distribution database, 318
  log reader, 317–18
  publication, 306
  setting up servers, 299–305
  subscription
    pull, 307
    push, 306
  synchronization, 317
replication topology, 305
revoke statement, 244
ROLLBACK TRANsaction. *See*
  transactions
rollback transactions, 39
row lock, 145
rule statement, 72
rules, 72–74
  domain, 119
  for identifiers, 81–82

```
                    S
```

satistics
  update, 204–7
SAVE TRANsaction. *See* transactions
save transactions, 40
scheduling tasks, 319
security
  and Windows NT, 218
  audit, 217
  creating username, 230–33

database, 219
integrated, 220–26
mixed, 227
password, 217
quest user, 233
replication, 315
selecting, 220
setting, 228–30
SQL Server, 218
  creating new users, 230–33
  groups, 234–36
  password, 241–42
  permissions, 242–49
  Security Manager, 249–53
standard, 226–27
system administrator, 219
trusted, 227
username, 217
Windows NT
  new group, 222
  new user, 223
segment, 196–97
SELECT
  joining tables, 27
select statement, 24–27
set command, 83
shared lock, 142
SQL
  Data Control Language, 22
  Data Definition Language, 22
  Data Manipulation Language, 22
  statement, 140
  transactions, 140
SQL Performance Monitor, 188
SQL Server
  mirror, 287–90
  pausing, 156
  security
    standard, 226–27
  starting, 152–54
  stopping, 156, 157
  unmirror, 289
SQL Server Web Assistant, 104–13
starting SQL Server, 152–54
startup options, 154–56

stopping SQL Server, 156, 157–59
stored procedure
  extended, 78
  sp_bindrule, 74
stored procedures, 78–80
  creating, 78
  sp_addalias, 238
  sp_addtype, 134
  sp_addumpdevice, 94
  sp_bindefault, 72
  sp_bindrule, 119
  sp_certify_removable, 291
  sp_changedbowner, 237
  sp_configure, 143, 146, 164, 186, 198
  sp_create_removable, 291
  sp_dboption, 176
  sp_dbremove, 270
  sp_dropdevice, 179
  sp_droptype, 134
  sp_dropwebtask, 104
  sp_logdevice, 167
  sp_makewebtask, 104
  sp_password, 241
  sp_replcleanup, 321
  sp_runwebtask, 104
  sp_tableoption, 146
  sp_unbindrule, 120
  sp_who, 96, 229
stripe sets, 195
Structured Query Language. *See* SQL
Subscribing Server, 295, 299–305
subscription
  synchronization, 307
Symmetric Multi Processor (SMP), 197
sysalternates, 238, 240
sysconstraints, 133
sysdatabases, 270
sysdevices, 179, 270
syslogins, 227, 229, 238
syslogs, 101, 260
sysprocesses, 95
sysprotects, 242
sysreferences, 133
system catalog, 89
sysusages, 270

sysusers, 238, 239

T

table, 19
table lock, 147
tables, 55
  Advanced Features, 58
  index, 64–67
  Manage Tables, 56
  system, 55
    defined, 98
  user, 55
text
  datatypes, 124
thread affinity, 197
transaction
  two-phase commit, 322, 323–27
transaction log, 101–4
  sizing, 165–67
  truncate, 102
transactions, 39
  begin distributed statement, 327
  implicit begin, 40
  implicit commit, 40
  isolation level, 149–50
Transact-SQL, 22
triggers, 74–77
  deleted table, 76
  inserted table, 76
two-phase commit transaction, 322, 323–27
  defined, 323

U

unique constraint, 118–19
update lock, 142
update statement, 34, 37–38
user-defined integrity, 134–37
username
  creating, 230–33

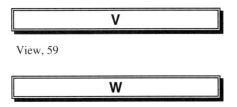

View, 59

W

web pages, 104–13

where clause, 26, 37
Windows NT
   mirror, 287
Windows NT service
   SQL Server, 152